earch
Research

Search
& Research

Joel C. Stevenson

Published by Deseret Book Co., Salt Lake City, Utah, 1977

© 1977 by Noel C. Stevenson
All rights reserved
Printed in the United States of America

Library of Congress Cataloging in Publication Data

Stevenson, Noel C
Search and research.

Includes bibliographies and index.
1. United States—Genealogy—Bibliography.
2. United States—History—Sources—Bibliography.
3. United States—History, Local—Sources—Bibliography. 4. Canada—Genealogy—Bibliography.
I. Title.
Z5313.U5S8 1977 [CS47] 016.929'373 77-21845
ISBN 0-87747-660-8 pbk.

ontents

Analyzing research problems

When a researcher studies the facts involved in any research problem, those facts should suggest to him certain definite steps he should take toward the solution of the problem. If the facts disclose that a person named Silas Swampspook was born, married, and died on certain dates, those facts should suggest certain things to do, such as obtaining birth, marriage, and death certificates, examination of the probate proceedings in his estate, ascertaining whether a Swampspook family history has been published and whether there are any town, county, or other place histories of the localities where the Swampspook family resided, and so on.

The following list of questions is offered as an aid in assisting you in analyzing your genealogical problems. It is not represented as being complete, for there are other questions that might be listed. As you study the facts written on your pedigree chart or other records, ask yourself these questions. As you study the names, dates, and places on your pedigree and answer these questions with respect to those facts, you will likely think of ways in which you can profitably continue your research.

1. Are any birth, marriage, or death certificates obtainable?

2. Are any wills or administrations of estates obtainable?

3. Is it possible to obtain proof of births, marriages, or deaths from church records?

4. Did any of these persons serve in the Revolutionary War or any of the colonial, Indian, or civil wars?

5. Did a widow draw a pension because of the war service of her husband?

6. Will records of colleges, schools, societies, firms, or corporations be helpful?

7. Would the federal or state census records be helpful?

8. Have I tried correspondence with persons of the same name? (Use *Handbook of American Genealogy,* telephone and city directories, and registers of voters.)

9. Is there a family association bearing the same name as any of my lines?

10. Is it possible that information might be obtained from land, civil, and criminal courts, probate, register of voters, tax rolls, or vital records?

11. Have I written to all relatives or friends of the family to obtain all known information?

12. Are there any family histories in print on any of the families in which I am interested?

13. Have I searched town, county, and state histories? (A good bibliography for this is *Catalogue of Genealogical and Historical Works* in the Library of the National Society of the Daughters of the American Revolution, 1940. See also Peterson's *Bibliography of County Histories.*)

14. Have I corresponded with archives, state libraries, and historical societies? (See *Historical Societies in the United States and Canada,* 1944. See also *The American Library Directory.*)

15. Are there any problems that might be solved through searching old newspaper files or advertising? (Try Hartford *Times,* and see Ayer's *Newspaper Guide* for a list of newspapers; also *Union List of Newspapers,* and Brigham's *Bibliography.*)

Study the following *Sources for Research* as a further aid in helping you to analyze your research problems.

Sources for research

There are many sources available to aid you in your genealogical research. The following outline is only a suggested list of possible sources, and no attempt has been made to include details of all sources of foreign countries or of the United States. These suggestions are made to help you begin thinking of places where you can go to get help. More specific information can also be found in the sections under the various states and territories of the United States and the provinces of Canada.

Sources for research

I. Official Records
- A. Federal records
  - 1. Land records
    - a. Patents and other land records (General Land Office and National Archives)
    - b. Bounty land warrants (National Archives)
      Bounty land affidavits (National Archives)
      Bounty land applications (National Archives)
  - 2. Military records
    - a. Service records for various wars (National Archives)

b. Pension files and applications for various wars (National Archives)

3. Census (National Archives)
   a. The 1790 census is printed and indexed and available in most libraries.
   b. Censuses for 1800 to 1880, in the National Archives
   c. Censuses subsequent to 1880, in the Census Bureau
4. Court records (civil and criminal)
   Files and court reports of:
   a. U.S. District Courts
   b. Circuit Courts of Appeal
   c. U.S. Supreme Court
5. Legislative records (journals, laws, etc.)
6. Miscellaneous records
   a. Shipping and passenger lists (National Archives)
   b. Immigration records
   c. Passport records and applications (1791-1879, National Archives)
   d. Naturalization records

B. State records
   1. Vital statistics; birth, death, and marriage certificates
   2. Files and reports of appellate courts
   3. State libraries and archives
   4. Censuses and records taken by state authority
   5. State land office records
   6. Records of Secretary of State (often this officer is also the custodian of miscellaneous collections of early official records from different parts of a state)
   7. Legislative journals
   8. Session laws
   9. Court reports
   10. Administrative records (e.g., inheritance tax files)
   11. Executive records

C. County records
   1. Court records (civil and criminal)
      (Custodian: generally the county clerk)
      a. Probate files and record volumes
         (1) Wills
         (2) Petitions for letters testamentary
         (3) Petitions for letters of administration
         (4) Decrees of distribution and orders
         (5) Inventories
         (6) Miscellaneous affidavits
         (7) Petitions to determine heirship
         (8) Guardianship matters

(9) Adoption proceedings
(10) Affidavits

b. Civil actions (other than probate), law and equity (consult files and record volumes)
   (1) Partition
   (2) Quiet title
   (3) Divorce
   (4) Foreclosures
   (5) Actions for possession of real and personal property
   (6) Other actions too numerous to mention

2. Vital records
   a. Birth certificates
   b. Marriage licenses and intentions to marry
   c. Marriage records
   d. Death certificates
3. Land records (Custodian: generally county recorder)
   a. Deeds
   b. Mortgages
   c. Leases
   d. Recorded wills
   e. Powers of attorney
   f. Miscellaneous affidavits
   g. Judgments and decrees affecting realty
   h. Contracts pertaining to real property
4. Miscellaneous records
   a. Assessment and tax rolls
   b. Register of voters
   c. Coroner's files
   d. Maps and plats
   e. In every records office, particularly in the land records, are many miscellaneous records that do not fit in any of the above sources; they are recorded in separate volumes. A good example is an agreement for support of children.
5. Town and Municipal records
   a. Vital records—birth, marriage, and death records
   b. Court records of various types
   c. Land records are kept in some towns and cities
   d. Miscellaneous records (Often the same types of records are in the custody of both the town clerk and the county recorder or the county clerk, depending on the state)

II. Records of Church Organizations, Schools, etc.
   A. Church records
      1. Baptisms

2. Banns
3. Marriages
4. Burial records
5. Membership rolls
6. Disciplinary proceedings
7. Churchwarden's accounts
8. Charity accounts
9. Glebe Terriers, tithe records, and others
10. Miscellaneous records
11. Cemetery records

B. Records of Business Organizations

C. School and college records
1. Roster and rolls
2. Biographical material

III. Family Records and Other Private Sources

A. Family records
1. Bibles and other books
2. Diaries and journals
3. Letters
4. Samplers and other fanciwork
5. Photographs and photograph albums
6. Jewelry, such as funeral rings
7. Silverware
8. Scrapbooks
9. Family associations
10. Documents such as—
   a. Marriage contracts
   b. Deeds
   c. Mortgages
   d. Leases
   e. Unprobated wills
   f. Birth and baptism certificates
   g. Marriage licenses and certificates
   h. Death records
   i. Tax bills and receipts
   j. Insurance papers
   k. Lodge and church records
   l. Military service documents

B. Corporation records and files
1. Records of land title companies
2. Employment records
3. Entries made in the course of business

C. Hospital records

D. Records of undertakers

E. Lodge records
1. Records of birth and death, etc.
2. Biographical data
3. Rosters

F. Newspapers (for advertising see Ayer's *Guide*)
1. Old files (see Union List and Brigham's *Bibliography*)

2. Genealogical columns for queries and answers
    a. Boston Transcript (discontinued—see old files)
    b. Hartford *Times* (discontinued—see old files)
    c. Genealogy and history (discontinued—see old files)
    d. Genealogical periodicals

IV. Miscellaneous Sources
- A. Directories (city, telephone, trade, and professional)
- B. State associations
- C. Family associations
- D. *Handbook of American Genealogy*
- E. Cemeteries

V. Libraries and Historical Societies
See Karl Brown, *The American Library Directory; Directory of Historical Societies and Agencies of Historical Societies and Agencies in the United States and Canada,* 1956.
- A. Printed and typescript family genealogies
- B. Genealogical dictionaries, compendiums, and lineage books
- C. Periodicals containing—
    1. Family genealogies
    2. Copies of official and other records
- D. County, town, and other place histories
- E. Printed copies of official and semi-official records
- F. Military rolls, rosters, and registers
- G. Reference books and indexes for locating genealogy in libraries
- H. Historical geographical material
- I. Examine latest microprint materials (see microfacsimiles)
- J. *American Genealogical and Biographical Index*
- K. Published cemetery records

Age and legal capacity

An understanding of age and legal capacity will aid you in the analysis of your research problems. Knowing the age when a man or woman may legally marry or perform certain other acts or duties is absolutely essential to successful research.

Age in the law is that period of life which is applied for the purpose of ascertaining those special times that enable persons of both sexes to do specific acts or discharge certain functions which for lack of years they were prohibited from doing or undertaking before.

Laws concerning legal age vary from country to country—and even from state to state in the United States—and may be different for particular periods in the past. It is thus advisable to check on the laws in existence for the area and time period in which you are planning to do research.

icro-
csimiles

If you have access to reading machines for microfilms or microcards, it is possible for you to undertake research in your own locality through the purchase or loan of microfilm or microcards. For a bibliography or "Union List" of photocopied records, see *Guide to Photocopied Historical Materials in the United States and Canada,* edited by Richard W. Hale, Jr., Cornell University Press, Ithaca, New York, 1961.

brary
Congress

Washington, D.C.
The photo duplication service of the Library of Congress makes it possible to purchase microfilms of printed source material if there is no restriction on reproduction. Inasmuch as many family genealogies and local histories are not copyrighted or the copyright for them has expired, it is possible to have these books and records microfilmed. However, before doing so it is wise to check with the Godfrey Memorial Library (see below) to see whether the family genealogy you are interested in has been reproduced in microcard form.

Microfilm copies of early state records consisting of legislative records and journals, session laws, and some court records are available through the photo duplication service of the Library of Congress. See "A Guide to the Microfilm Collection of Early State Records," prepared by the Library of Congress in association with the University of North Carolina and published by the Photoduplication Service of the Library of Congress, Washington, 1950.

ational
chives

Washington, D.C.
It is possible to obtain microfilm copies of United States Census Records from the National Archives and microfilms of other records in the custody of the National Archives, in Washington, D.C.

odfrey
emorial
brary

134 Newfield Avenue, Middletown, Connecticut
This organization is the pioneer in microcard reproduction. It has published in microcard form many rare family genealogies; the Catalog of American and English Genealogies in the Library of Congress; Boston Transcript Genealogical Column, 1904-1941; the 1790 Census for many of the original colonies and Vermont, and other printed sources.

e Genea-
gical So-
ety of The
urch of
sus Christ
Latter-
y Saints

50 East North Temple, Salt Lake City, Utah 84150
This organization has the largest collection of genealogical microfilms. These microfilm records are available for use at the society's headquarters. They are also available through branch genealogical libraries of the Church established in meetinghouses in the United States and parts of Canada. For information concerning the nearest

branch library, call the Latter-day Saint ward or branch in your own area.

The American Council of Learned Societies

This organization microfilmed a large volume of manuscripts in England and Wales between 1941 and 1945. A checklist of the microfilms has been published by the Library of Congress and is sold by the Photoduplication Service for $2.00. The title of the book is *British Manuscripts Project,* compiled by Lester K. Born, Washington, 1955. 179 pages.

Every major library provides a microfilm service. For information and details write to the library that has material in which you are interested.

Microxerobooks: University Microfilms, Ann Arbor, Michigan, has succeeded in producing copies of out-of-print books at a nominal sum. By combining the advantages of microfilm and xerography a copy of an out-of-print book can be produced for about three cents a page, plus a seventy-cent charge for a paper binding. Thus, a 200-page family genealogy or county history, so rare you cannot even buy it, could be copied for you at a cost of about $6.70.

Research through correspondence

Regardless of how much research a person does in libraries or in the archives of various political subdivisions, a very valuable source of obtaining genealogy is through correspondence. This method of research may be broken down as follows:

1. *Correspondence with persons of similar name.* If you are tracing a family with an unusual surname, it is often practical to write to every person bearing that name in the United States. The question is to decide whether it is practical or not. If the name is Smith, it isn't. If the name is Zeller, it is. To aid in deciding on the practical aspects, consult the surname frequency table in the *Journal of the American Name Society,* September 1955, volume 3, pp. 172-84. The next problem is to find names and addresses of persons to write to. This can be done through the following sources:

a. *The Handbook of American Genealogy* (1943). In this book are the names and addresses of numerous people who have information on families willing to exchange, give away, or charge for information. The information they furnish is not always accurate and must be used with care. Names and addresses of family associations are incompletely given in this book also.

b. *City directories and telephone directories.* These may be examined without charge in the directory department of a large library or the telephone office in the larger cities. (Early Directories, see "e" below.)

c. *Registers of voters.* This source gives the name and address of the voter; generally the state or country in which the voter was born; and, if a naturalized citizen, the place and date where he was naturalized by judicial decree. The fact that the place of birth is given is important, because it is possible to locate people from the same place your ancestors lived.

d. *Indexes to the real and personal property tax rolls of the tax collector.* This is another source that can be used for obtaining names and addresses, although not as good as the register of voters, and should be used only after the register of voters has been exhausted.

e. *Early directories: Bibliography of American Directories Through 1860,* by Dorothea N. Spear, 1961.

2. *Advertising in genealogical periodicals and newspapers.* It is possible to publish queries in some genealogical periodicals. In your local library, consult the periodicals listed in the chapter on research in libraries, under the heading "Genealogical periodicals." The advantage of advertising your problem is that people in all parts of the country read these queries, and many respond.

The Boston *Transcript* and the Hartford *Times* published genealogical queries and answers for many years, but this service has been discontinued. Some libraries have preserved back issues, and these old queries and answers are available for research. (Refer also to pages 41-44.)

Another method that has proved successful in some cases is to place an advertisement in a newspaper in the locality where your ancestors resided. With sufficient identifying information concerning the problem you are trying to solve, readers of the papers may respond with suggestions or the desired information. In order to find the names of newspapers in the localities where your ancestors lived, consult Ayer's *Newspaper Guide,* available in the reference departments of most libraries.

3. *Obtaining information from record sources by letter.* It may be possible to obtain certificates of birth, death, and marriage in some communities, states, and countries. Also, certified copies of wills, deeds, and other records may be procured by writing to the proper public officials. This method of procuring information requires special study and will be considered later.

4. *Correspondence with societies, public officials, and genealogists.* Some people have been successful in writing to the postmasters of towns in the United States, in England, and in other places, requesting the postmaster to forward the letter to a person of a similar name. The superintendents of libraries of towns in England might be helpful, or the librarians of towns in the United States. Sometimes your letter will be placed on a bulletin board. Last, but not least, a professional, competent genealogist who specializes in the territory where you are searching for your ancestors may prove helpful.

In writing your letter, give sufficient identifying information as to names, dates, and places. If the information sought is not likely to be known to the person to whom you write, suggest that it be handed or sent to someone who does know or ask for the name and address of that person. If many questions are asked, it is a good idea to put the communication in the form of a questionnaire, with enough space between the questions for the answers, and have the recipient send that part of the letter back to you. Enclose a stamped, self-addressed envelope, or use double postcards, with a reply card attached, which you should self-address. These are good to use for short matters. Offer to pay for the information if necessary. Continue writing every few weeks until you receive an answer. Make your letter specific and to the point. A letter that is indefinite or requires too much time to answer may be answered merely by a statement that a private researcher should be consulted, whereas one asking for specific information would probably get results. Any person who sends a long, rambling, ambiguous account of his research problem can expect it to be consigned to the nearest wastepaper basket.

Official records and original sources

The importance of using official records in research cannot be overemphasized. If you have never had experience in searching the official records of towns, counties, and other political subdivisions, the easiest way is to have someone who is experienced in this field do the work, since the only way to learn is by experience, and every locality has special features that are learned only by working in the records. There is also the problem of interpretation. Unless you are familiar with legal terms and customs, there is danger that serious mistakes can be made because of incorrect interpretation of the records if they are located. Familiarity with the law and experience in the field of title searching or abstracting are invaluable. If you reside a great distance from the record sources, employ a competent genealogist or record searcher to make the necessary search.

Official records are records kept as provided by law by public officials, such as county clerks, county recorders, and other officials. Common examples are wills, deeds, mortgages, leases, and court proceedings. A distinction should be made between the records of federal, state, and local governments.

The federal government, states, counties, towns, and cities all have their own court records. When we think of court records, we should divide them into criminal and civil records. Civil court records pertain to actions between private parties, and probate records would be included in civil court records.

Generally the records pertaining to a family are located in the record offices where the family lived. In some localities land records are kept in the Registry of Deeds or Recorder's Office at the county seat. However, in some places, such as Vermont and Connecticut, the land records are in the custody of the town clerk. Reference to the section of this book devoted to the custody of official records will familiarize you with the location and custody of official records of the various states.

Although the local land, vital, and probate records are probably the most valuable, look also to Washington, D.C., for help. The National Archives contain invaluable original records, such as censuses, pension files, military service records, and general land office records, and many other sources.

ital statistics

Vital records consist of birth, marriage, and death records. In recent years a uniform type of certificate for these records has been adopted throughout the United States; and the records are registered in one central location, as well as duplicate copies or originals retained in the county, town, or city where the birth, marriage, or death occurred. Prior to the time a state commenced registration, records of birth, marriage, and death were kept in the locality where the birth, marriage, or death occurred, although in most states vital records prior to central registration are scanty, and in many instances there were no vital records kept at all. In this book, to ascertain the custody of vital records, examine that subject under the state in which you are interested; instructions are given on where to communicate with the correct official.

If you visit a record office to examine its vital records, and you are not familiar with their procedure, ask the person in charge to show you how to use the name index.

A distinction should be made between marriage licenses and marriage records. In jurisdictions where licenses are issued, they are usually issued by the county clerk, and then after the marriage is performed the certificate of marriage is filed with the county recorder by the person performing the ceremony. The point to be stressed is that the searcher should examine both the marriage license and the certificate of marriage for obvious reasons. Often it will not be possible to find both or even one of them.

Court records

Criminal. If you should fail to find the information you are seeking in the civil court records or other sources, you might find the answers in this class of records.

Civil Court Records. This category includes the records and files of such courts as probate, equity, courts of common pleas, superior courts, and many other trial courts with titles provided by the law of the particular state. The records of civil and criminal courts are usually in the custody of the county clerk, register of probate, or other public officer, depending on the state.

The parties to civil actions (other than probate proceedings) are plaintiffs and defendants, and the custodians of civil court records index the records according to the names of these parties. There is an "Index to Plaintiffs" and an "Index to Defendants," and if a searcher visits a record office, his search should commence by using these indexes and examining them for the names of the parties he is seeking. The case or filing number is also given in the indexes.

Civil court records generally consist of the following types of records, and all of them should be examined, if possible:

1. Files. These consist of all documents filed by the plaintiff and the defendant. Examples: complaint, bill, petition or declaration, answer, demurrer, replication.

2. Dockets, registers of action. These volumes contain an outline of the case, the papers filed, when filed, disposition.

3. Minutes. A record of the proceedings during the trial of the action (in book form or record volume).

4. Reporter's transcript. Unfortunately, in many trials no reporter is engaged to take the testimony in shorthand, and if so, unless the matter is appealed, the shorthand notes are not transcribed.

5. Orders, decrees, and judgments of the court. A record of the formal disposition of the action (usually contained in a record volume in addition to a documentary copy in the file).

6. Exhibits. Original documents or various miscellaneous

articles filed with the clerk of the court as evidence; for example, promissory notes, family Bible records, and photographs.

To ascertain where to examine or write for civil court records, consult that subject in this book under the state in which you are interested.

Probate Records. Unfortunately, many people seem to think that wills are the only records involved in probate records. This is far from true. Probate records generally involve the following proceedings:

1. Probate of testate and intestate estates. This signifies the probate of wills and administration of estates. When the deceased left no will, it is said that he died intestate, and an administrator is appointed to handle the estate. Or if a person dies leaving a will, and no executor is appointed, or if one is appointed and he is unwilling or unable to act, "Letters of Administration cum testamento annexo" (with will annexed) or "Letters of Administration c.t.a." are issued to a relative of the deceased or some other eligible person.

2. Guardianship matters involving incompetent persons and minors are included in the jurisdiction of probate courts in some states.

As with civil and criminal court records, an index is needed to find the information sought. The index to probate records is usually called an index to "Administrations and Estates," and the index is arranged by surname and given name. The case of filing number is also given in the index.

Probate records consist generally of the following types of records and documents in addition to the original will:

1. Petition for probate of will (original or copy of will should be attached)
2. Petition for letters of administration, in the case of an intestate estate (a good source, as all heirs should be named)
3. Letters testamentary
4. Letters of administration (intestate estate)
5. Bond of executor or administrator
6. Inventory and appraisement
7. Notice to creditors
8. Miscellaneous affidavits
9. Decree of distribution and various other orders and decrees (the decree of distribution should set forth all heirs or devisees)
10. Numerous petitions that are sometimes filed, such as petitions for determination of heirship.

Record volumes contain copies of original wills.

As with other civil court records, there are docket books or registers of actions, minutes books, order and decree books, and the other sources previously mentioned in connection with civil court records.

To ascertain where to examine or write for probate records, consult that subject in this book under the state in which you are interested.

Land records. When land records are mentioned, people generally think only of deeds, but a deed is only one of the documents to be found in land records. The principal documents, in addition to deeds of various kinds, are mortgages, leases, liens, contracts, powers of attorney, releases, notices of action, judgments, decrees, and other documents that affect title to land.

The type of index used by the various land registry offices varies with the jurisdiction, but generally the principal indexes are "Grantors" and "Grantees." The index will disclose the book and page of the record volume in which a copy of the document appears.

In a few states land records are kept by the town clerk, but in most places they are in the custody of the county recorder, register of deeds, or other public official. In this book, in order to ascertain where to examine or write for land records, see that subject under the state in which you are interested.

Early deeds and other land records often contain considerable historical and genealogical data. This is particularly true of deeds prior to 1800. Modern deeds as a general rule do not contain much detail.

Miscellaneous Records. In every record office, and particularly in offices where land records are kept, are numerous documents, such as affidavits, contracts, marriage agreements. These documents are often recorded in separate volumes and have a special index. These valuable records should not be overlooked.

Records of Courts of Appeal. The records that prove to be of most help to the researcher in this category are the published court reports of appellate courts. These court reports are found in law libraries and are a valuable source for research.

Federal official records

For information concerning U.S. census, pension files, military service records, mortality schedules, land records, refer to the index. For a series of articles on record searching, see Noel C. Stevenson, "Record Searching Procedure and Technique," *Utah Genealogical and Historical Magazine,* volume 31 (1940), pp. 18, 75, 223.

esearch in ne National rchives

The information that follows regarding research in the National Archives is only a brief summary to familiarize researchers generally with the sources there. For a competent book on this subject see *Guide to Genealogical Records in the National Archives,* by Meredith B. Colket, Jr., and Frank E. Bridgers, published by the National Archives, Washington, D.C. 20408.

Regional branches of the National Archives are now established in Boston, New York City, Philadelphia, Atlanta, Chicago, Kansas City, Fort Worth, Denver, San Francisco, Los Angeles, and Seattle. Original records of the various regions and some microfilms from the National Archives are deposited, and there is provision for inter-archival and inter-library lending of microfilm records. Write to the National Archives, Washington, D.C. 20408 for ''Regional Branches of the National Archives,'' General Information Leaflet No. 22, for addresses of the regional branches.

ilitary ension ecords

By authority of various acts of Congress, pension provisions have been made for veterans of every war since the American Revolution. In order for a veteran of one of these wars to obtain a pension, he has to offer proof of service through documentary evidence, and a written application. Often the applications contain valuable data, including supporting affidavits made by his associates in the service that contain valuable information about the pensioner's family. Congress has provided that a widow of a veteran is entitled to a pension, and in order to qualify, she has to prove her marriage to the veteran. Due to the necessity of proving the marriage, many marriage certificates and family Bible records are found in the files. In 1855 Congress provided that certain veterans were entitled to a grant of land in consideration of their service, and Bounty Land Warrants (B.L.Wt.) were issued. When the veteran located the land he wished to settle on, he presented his Bounty Land Warrant to the nearest U.S. General Land Office, and eventually he received a patent or deed to the land.

Assume a person in whom you are interested was born when he would have been of age to participate in the American Revolutionary War. Say he was born in 1750, and you know he resided in Vermont during the war. In that case, and in similar cases, write to the National Archives, Washington, D.C., setting forth all pertinent facts regarding him and ask for an abstract of his pension file. For quicker service and broader scope of research coverage, it would be well to employ a professional searcher in Washington, D.C.

A name index of Revolutionary War pensions and Bounty Land Warrants was published by the National Genealogical

Society in 1966 in one volume of 1324 pages, entitled *Index of Revolutionary Pension Applications,* by various compilers and indexers, revised by Sadye Giller and William H. and Louise M. Dumont.

There are numerous rolls and registers of men who served in the American Revolution. See "Military Registers and Records—General Sources" and "Revolutionary War Rolls, etc.," in connection with most of the states in this book.

Likewise, if the person served in any other American wars, valuable information may be obtained from the pension files. The Civil War pension files contain valuable genealogical and historical information. This is especially true if a pensioner lived until 1900.

Military service records

These may be obtained through the National Archives, Washington, D.C. When you write, give as much information as possible about the service of the person about whom you are inquiring.

The United States census

The first federal census was taken in 1790. Some of the early census returns were lost, burned, or in some manner destroyed. This loss has been greatly compensated for by the publication of tax rolls.

The 1790 census listed only the head of the family, including the number of free white males over 16 years and under 16 years and the number of all other free persons. Other statistics were enumerated, but the above is the most important. From the information given, much valuable data can be ascertained. Information as to residence and size of an ancestor's family is extremely helpful in continuing the line further back.

A federal census is taken every ten years. In censuses after 1790 more detailed information was compiled, but it wasn't until the census of 1850 that all members of the household were enumerated. In this census, information as to the state or county of birth was given, as well as age, occupation, and other important information.

Censuses since 1850 go into additional detail, but the main information is names, ages, and places of birth of members of households.

Assume you know a person named Titus Tipple who was born in 1848 in Starke County, Ohio. If you had any reason to believe he was still living there in 1850, a search of the 1850 census should disclose circumstantial evidence of the names of his father, mother, brothers and sisters, if any, their ages, and state(s) where they were born. This same method can be employed for any census since 1850 open to the public. The censuses since 1900 are not available unless a person can show a relationship. Some of the more recent censuses have been indexed by name to facilitate queries regarding proof of birth. The 1890 census was destroyed by fire, except for some special schedules hereinafter mentioned.

All of the 1790 censuses have been printed and indexed and are found in most libraries. For information from 1790 to 1880, write to the National Archives, Washington, D.C. However, if you plan to have a search made of the census records, it will be necessary to employ a professional. It has been the custom of the National Archives to furnish a list of persons engaged in research in the National Archives. If you desire information from censuses 1900 to 1940, write to Director, Bureau of the Census, Washington, D.C., for instructions.

For a bibliography and finding aid to the U.S. Census between 1800 and 1870, see:

Special List Number 8 Population Schedules, 1800-1870. Volume Index to Counties and Major Cities, published by the National Archives, Washington, 1951 (reissued 1957).

Special Schedules of the Eleventh Census (1890) Enumerating Union Veterans and Widows of Union Veterans of the Civil War, microfilmed by the National Archives, 118 rolls. These special schedules include, among other things, the name of the veteran, or if he did not survive, the names of both the widow and her deceased husband, the veteran's rank, company, regiment or vessel, details concerning length of service and discharge, post office address. Practically all the schedules for the states of Alabama through Kansas and approximately one half of those for Kentucky were misplaced or destroyed before transfer of the records to the National Archives.

For a record of the records available on microfilm see *List of National Archives Microfilm Publications,* 1953, the National Archives, 1953, pp. 80-84. Some libraries have microfilm copies in their collections.

You may purchase microfilm copies of census records 1840-1880 from the National Archives. The National Archives have published a price list of microfilm copies of the original schedules. The list is entitled "Federal Population Censuses 1840-1880—A price list of microfilm copies of the original schedules."

ortality hedules

The enumerators of the 1850, 1860, 1870, and 1880 censuses were instructed to obtain, in addition to the usual data, information concerning all persons who died within the twelve-month period preceding the enumeration of the census. Generally the following information was obtained: person's full name, state of birth, date of death, age at time of death, and cause of death. The value of these mortality schedules is apparent, and a person should search the mortality schedules for this additional information. The custody of most of these records has been placed in the hands of state libraries and historical societies. To find the name and address of custodian of these records, see the section in this book on the state in which you are interested.

Church records

Although it should be possible to go to the clerk of the local church to obtain any records of a particular church, it doesn't always work that way. However, it is often worthwhile to make an effort to find the records of baptisms, marriages, and burials of the churches where the people you are seeking lived.

Much time can be saved in locating church records by using church directories, which practically every denomination publishes. Such a directory will give the addresses of the local churches throughout the United States and foreign countries.

A good idea when records of a specific church in a specific town are desired is to address the "Clerk of the Church." In some cases the minister *may* have the records, or they may be in a vault or deposited somewhere; but the clerk is often the custodian, and is usually the one who answers the inquiries. This is generally true of Baptist, Congregational, Methodist, and Presbyterian churches.

Often the state organization of the church has the records. In some cases the state library or a historical society has obtained custody. It is principally a matter of trying. The following notes are not to be considered complete.

1. *Surveys of Church Records:* The Historical Records Survey during its operation as a unit of the Works Progress Administration compiled many inventories of church records of many denominations in the various states. Some of these are listed in the reference work material in this book under the various states. Those listed and others should be examined in order to make a thorough search of church records pertaining to your particular problem.

For a survey of church record sources see E. Kay Kirkham, *A Survey of American Church Records,* Salt Lake City, Utah, 1958.

Carroll D. Wright, *Report of the Custody and Condition of the Public Records of Parishes, Towns, and Counties,* Boston, 1889 (pages 9 to 148 are devoted to church records of Massachusetts).

2. *Baptist Church Records:* Colgate University, Hamilton, N.Y., has a collection of Baptist Church Records relating to North America.

3. *Catholic Church:* Records are generally kept in the parish, and are very complete. A good source of information

is the Official Catholic Directory, 1822-1943, New York, 1943. Other sources include:

Librarian, Catholic University of America, Washington, D.C. (for information regarding Catholics).

Cora C. Curry, *Records of the Roman Catholic Church in the United States as a Source of Authentic Genealogical and Historical Material,* 1935, a pamphlet published by the National Genealogical Society.

4. *Episcopal Church Records:* Records are usually kept at church offices of the seat of the diocese, at the parish house, or at the bishop's residence.

5. *Jewish:* Jewish Central Library, Jewish Museum, Woburn House, Upper Woburn Place, London, W. C. 1. This library includes genealogical records of Anglo-Jewish families. The genealogical bureau gives advice to persons with Jewish ancestors who are writing family histories or compiling their pedigrees. Another source is Hermann Meyer, *Bibliographia Genealogica Judaica,* A Brief Introduction to the Pedigrees and Other Sources of Jewish Genealogy, Jerusalem, 1942.

6. *Methodist Church Records:* The Drew Theological Seminary, Madison, New Jersey, has a collection of Methodist church records.

7. *Mormon Church:* A fine collection of records of members is available at the Genealogical Society of The Church of Jesus Christ of Latter-day Saints, Salt Lake City, Utah 84150. This organization also has extensive microfilms of church records from various countries in Europe, manuscript genealogies, and printed books of interest to nonmembers as well as members.

8. *Quakers:* See the *Encyclopedia of Quaker Genealogy;* also, other notes in this book in the sections on Pennsylvania, New Jersey, New York. Other sources include:

Consuelo Furman and Robert Furman, *Quaker Bibliography for the Genealogist,* 1950(?), 44 pp. (manuscript, New York Public Library, typewritten, bound in with genealogy on several families).

Milton Rubincam, ''English Friends' Meeting Records,'' *National Genealogical Society Quarterly,* vol. 34 (September 1946), pp. 73-74.

Frederick B. Tolles, Librarian, Friends' Historical Library of Swarthmore College: *A New Tool for Genealogical Research—The William Wade Hinshaw Index to Quaker Meeting Records.* (See *National Genealogical Society Quarterly,* June 1950, vol. 38, p. 1.)

For a listing of church historical societies, see the index of this book and *Historical Societies—General List.*

Research in newspaper files

The answers to many research problems may be found in old newspaper files. This source would be used much more if genealogists were in a position to devote more time to the lengthy process of making a page by page search. Of course, if you know a specific date of birth, marriage, or death, it is quite simple to search a newspaper of that date before and after the event in hope that it appeared in print. This statement is made on the assumption that a newspaper is available.

Fortunately we are the beneficiaries of some excellent aids that previous generations did not have. Gregory's *Union List of American Newspapers,* 1821-1936, and Brigham's *History and Bibliography of American Newspapers,* 1690-1820, are reference works that make the researcher's pathway much less thorny. However, these fine bibliographies are not complete.

The American Antiquarian Society of Worcester, Massachusetts, is entitled to a genealogical medal of honor for pioneering in the early newspaper field. This organization has indexed many early newspapers. The society indexed (among other newspapers) a record of the marriages and deaths appearing in the *Columbian Centinel* of Boston, 1784-1840. That accomplishment doesn't seem to impress researchers generally until they learn that this newspaper printed notices of marriages and deaths *from all over the United States.* Also impressive is the fact that the index includes 80,000 names.

The American Antiquarian Society has deposited copies of its newspaper indexes in the Library of Congress, New York Public Library, and New England Historic Genealogical Society to make them available in places other than its own library. To realize the scope of this monumental undertaking, just consider *some* of the indexes (in addition to the *Columbian Centinel*):

Deaths published in the *Christian Intelligencer* of the Reformed Dutch Church from 1830 to 1871 (9 volumes)

Index of Marriages and Deaths in the New York *Weekly Museum,* 1788-1817 (2 volumes)

Index to Obituary Notices in the Boston *Transcript,* 1875-1899 (5 volumes)

Marriages Reported in the Boston *Recorder and Telegraph,* 1827-28

If you have a problem that might be solved by newspaper research, consider also the work undertaken by the Works Progress Administration. This organization did some good in the historical phases of newspapers as well as the Historical Records Surveys that you are more familiar with. The WPA compiled a *General Index to Contents of Savannah, Georgia,*

Newspapers. This index covers a period from 1763 to 1830 and adds up to the monumental total of twenty-seven volumes! Keep in mind that the Virginia *Gazette* has also been indexed from 1736 to 1780. These indexes are available in the Library of Congress.

Fortunately for genealogists, there has been considerable progress in recent years in microfilming, microprinting, and indexing of early newspapers.

The prime disadvantage of research in newspapers is the lack of an index; but to the ambitious researcher, who can take the time to make a page by page examination of old newspapers, the possibility of a valuable discovery is unlimited. Advertising in contemporary newspapers is also a valuable method of solving a research problem.

Another method of research through newspapers is placing a query and reading the answers and queries in genealogical sections of newspapers and in some genealogical periodicals.

For many years before it ceased publication, the Boston *Transcript* published a department for genealogical queries and answers. Most large genealogical libraries have mounted these queries and answers in scrapbooks or on cards. The Godfrey Memorial Library, Middletown, Connecticut, has now published the entire series on microcards. The Boston Public Library has indexed all of the names in the Boston *Transcript* genealogical section.

bliography

Brigham, Clarence S.: *History and Bibliography of American Newspapers,* 1690-1820, 2 vols., Worcester, 1947. Lists the newspapers and holdings in American libraries.

Greene, Evarts B.: *Guide to the Principal Sources for Early American History in the City of New York, 1600-1800,* 1929.

Gregory, Winifred, ed.: *American Newspapers,* 1821-1936. A union list of files available in the United States and Canada, New York, 1937. This compilation discloses the location of newspaper files between 1821 and 1936, giving name and location of repository.

Johnson, J. Percy H., ed.: N. W. Ayer & Sons *Directory Newspapers and Periodicals.* Published annually. An excellent source for placing advertisements. Contains names and locations of newspapers and periodicals in U.S. and possessions, Canada, and Bermuda.

United States: *Check List of Foreign Newspapers* in the Library of Congress, Government Printing Office, Washington, 1929.

United States: *Check List of American Eighteenth Century*

Newspapers in the Library of Congress. Government Printing Office, Washington, 1936.

United States: *Check List of American Newspapers* in the Library of Congress. Government Printing Office, Washington, 1900. This covers the American files through 1900.

Research in libraries

Every library has its own system of indexing and arrangement of material. But there are many similarities, and once a person has learned the system in one library, it is much easier to master the system of a strange library. A good rule to remember is that families are traced by their surname and the places where they resided or where they were born, married, or died through printed sources, official records, and original sources.

The key to successful library research is the use of the special indexes of the library and to standard reference books:

1. *Indexes:* The *General Index* contains all of the books contained in the library indexed and numbered according to author, title, and subject. By using this index it is possible to ascertain whether there is a family history, place history, or other publication in the library pertaining to a certain family or place.

Many libraries have a *Family History Index,* consisting of a card index of "buried" material concerning various families. This index is compiled by the librarians by indexing the names in genealogical magazines, county and other place histories, family genealogies, and other miscellaneous sources, and indexing the names of these families. The material is "buried" because if it weren't for this special type of index, it would be necessary for the searcher to make an examination of hundreds of volumes to find the same information.

The *Geographical Index* is a special type of index that discloses records and history of various localities, the parish records of a certain place, the vital records of a town, etc.

2. *Reference Books:* These are really indexes in book form. The main difference between this source and the card indexes described above is the fact that the books indexed in the card index are in the library, whereas the books referred to in the reference books are not necessarily in the library. These reference books are an index to "buried" genealogy.

These genealogies are termed "buried" because if it were not for these special reference books, the only way the material could be found would be by a search of all genealogical books from which these references are taken. For example, *Nathaniel Foote of Wethersfield, Conn., and His Descendants* is a well-known family genealogy. On pages 76 to 78 is considerable information on the Rockwell family. This information on the Rockwells is termed "buried" because the title of the Foote family genealogy does not indicate that there is anything in it on families other than Foote. The function of these reference books is to bring to light information on families included in books like the Foote genealogy, because every family genealogy contains information about other families that the title of the book does not disclose.

The one set of reference books that illustrates this point is the monumental *American Genealogical Index* and the new series the *American Genealogical and Biographical Index.* You should not fail to use these.

The most important reference books are listed in a section of this book under the title "Bibliographies of Family Histories and Place Histories."

The use of the card index and reference books is a simple process. Assume you were tracing the ancestry of Jeremiah Bowman, born 8 November 1740 in Woodbury, Litchfield County, Connecticut; died 1 September 1820 in Peru, Clinton County, New York. Also assume such a person married Charity Williams, 1 May 1775, in Rutland, Rutland County, Vermont. The following procedure is suggested for solving his ancestry:

1. Check the general index in the library to see if there is a Bowman genealogy in the library.

2. Search the reference books listed in this book under the following subheadings in this chapter: *"Bibliographies of Family Histories and Place Histories"; "Reference Books: Pre-American Ancestry"; "Genealogical Periodicals."*

3. If you have the maiden name of the wife, follow the same procedure to see if there is a family genealogy in print on her family. If so, examine the name index for his name, as there may be information about him because of his marriage into her family.

4. Check the general index and the geographical index to see if there are any vital records published in the places where he was born, married, or died, as the record of his birth, marriage, or death should disclose the names of his parents. Also check the general index to see whether there are any printed official records, such as wills or deeds of places where he resided.

5. Examine the library's general index or geographical index to see if there are any town, county, or state histories of places where he lived, and if so, examine the name index to see if there is any information on him or his family. Also check various reference books such as the place section of Jacobus's *Index to Genealogical Periodicals.*

6. Check other reference books, such as the name index in Jacobus's *Index to Genealogical Periodicals,* for leads in magazines and other sources.

7. After locating the title of the book in the card index, write down the title, author, and number of the book, which should be retained as a permanent record of source material searched in order to prevent duplication. When you get the books from the shelves, examine the name index in the book, and if the name of the person you are seeking is found, turn to the page it is on and analyze the information to see whether it is the same person whose ancestry you are searching for.

This same general procedure is followed in using any of the special indexes in a library. It may be used on any other family, whether the name is Bowman or some other surname. In addition to the library sources mentioned in this hypothetical Bowman case, important record sources should be considered. These include the following:

General reference books and sources

American Institute of Genealogy: *The Handbook of American Genealogy,* Chicago, first edition in 1932. (Use latest edition.) This source is useful for correspondence with persons working on the same lines.

Bardsley, Charles Wareing: *A Dictionary of English and Welsh Surnames.* London, 1901. A very good source for the origin of surnames.

Brown, Karl: *The American Library Directory.* New York, 1942. List of 11,764 libraries.

Curry, Cora C.: *Records of the Roman Catholic Church in the United States as a Source for Authentic Genealogical and Historical Material.* Washington, 1935.

Daughters of the American Revolution, Elizabeth Benton Chapter, Kansas City, Missouri: *Genealogical Guide—Master Index of Genealogy in the Daughters of the American Revolution Magazine.* 84 vols., 1892-1950. 137 pp.

Egle, William H., ed.: *Notes and Queries, Historical and Genealogical.* 1881-1900. 11 vols.

Historical Records Survey, WPA: *Guide to Depositories of Manuscript Collections in the United States.* Columbus, Ohio, 1938. 134 pp.

Hume, Major Edgar Erskine: "Institutions Awarding

Medical Degrees Prior to 1825." *The American Genealogist,* October 1934, p. 101.

Peterson, C. Stewart: *Bibliography of County Histories of the 3111 Counties in the 48 States.* Baltimore, 1946. See also *Supplements* published in 1950, 1955.

Robison, Jeannie F. J.: Genealogical Records: *Manuscript Entries of Births, Deaths and Marriages Taken from Family Bibles, 1581-1917.* 1917.

United States Department of the Interior: *Official Register of the United States.* Lists of officials in various departments of governmental service with the address and place of birth, etc., 1843 to date.

United States Department of Commerce, Bureau of the Census: *A Century of Population Growth from the First Census of the United States to the Twelfth 1790-1900.* Washington, 1909. In addition to valuable data on the historical geography of the colonies, pages 227 to 270 are devoted to "Nomenclature, dealing with the names represented by at least 100 white persons, by states and territories, at the first census: 1790." If a surname that is the subject of a search is uncommon, it is sometimes possible to narrow the search.

United States WPA: *Bibliography of Research Projects Report, Check List of Historical Records Survey Publication, Technical Series, Research and Records Bibliography,* No. 7, revised April 1943. See also "Unpublished Historical Records Survey Inventory," by Max E. Hoyt, *National Genealogical Society Quarterly,* 33:33-35.

erence ks: w England

Bodge, George Madison: *Soldiers in King Philip's War.* Boston, 3rd ed., 1906.

Bolton, Mrs. Ethel (Stanwood): *Immigrants to New England, 1700-1775.* Salem, 1931.

Bolton, Mrs. Ethel (Stanwood): *American Samplers.* Boston, 1921. Contains copies of genealogical samplers.

Drake, Samuel Gardner: *Result of Some Researches among the British Archives for Information Relative to the Founders of New England.* Boston, 1860.

Forbes, Harriette Merrifield: *New England Diaries 1602-1800.* A Descriptive Catalogue of Diaries, Orderly Books and Sea Journals. Topsfield, Massachusetts, 1923.

Holmes, Frank R.: *Directory of the Ancestral Heads of New England Families, 1620-1700.* New York, 1923.

Mather, Cotton: *Magnalia Christi Americana;* or, *The Ecclesiastical History of New England.* 2 vols. Hartford, 1853-1855. Best edition, contains an index.

McAuslan, William Alexander: *Mayflower Index.* 2 vols. 1932.

Pierce, Ebenezer Weaver: *Pierce's Colonial Lists: Civil, Military and Professional Lists of Plymouth and Rhode Island Colonies, 1621-1700.* Boston, 1881.

Rosenberry, Mrs. Lois (Kimball) Mathews: *The Expansion of New England; the Spread of New England Settlement and Institutions to the Mississippi River 1620-1865.* 1909.

Savage, James: *A Genealogical Dictionary of the First Settlers of New England, Showing Three Generations of Those Who Came before May, 1692.* 4 vols. Boston, 1860-1862. Also use O. P. Dexter's *A Genealogical Cross Index of Savage* and Mrs. C. W. Dall's *Genealogical Notes and Errata to Savage's Genealogical Dictionary.*

Military registers and records: Revolutionary War

Continental Congress: *Journals of the Continental Congress 1774-1789.* Edited from the original records in the Library of Congress. Volumes 1-34, 1904-1937.

Dandrige, Danske: *American Prisoners of the Revolution.* 1911.

Daughters of the American Revolution: *Lineage Books,* 1895. Contains lineages showing descent from Revolutionary ancestors. The DAR has published index volumes: Vol. 1, Index to vols. 1 to 40 of the lineage books; vol. 2, 41 to 80; vol. 3, 81 to 120; vol. 4, 121 to 160, etc.

Daughters of the American Revolution: *Revolutionary Pensioners 1827-1831.* 1827. This is a collection of Congressional documents bound in one volume in the library of the Daughters of the American Revolution, Washington, D.C.

Daughters of the American Revolution: *Some Veterans of the American Revolution Items from Various Newspapers.* 1923. Vol. 1, 1816-1842; vol. 2, 1820-1850; vol. 3, 1820-1853. Manuscript in custody of National Society, Daughters of the American Revolution, Washington, D.C.

Daughters of the American Revolution: *Revolutionary Records from Congressional Reports.* 5 vols. Indexed. These volumes contain a series of Congressional documents constituting claims for Revolutionary service, collected and bound into volumes in the Daughters of the American Revolution Library, Washington, D.C.

Duncan, Louis C.: *Medical Men in the American Revolution, 1775-1783.* 1931.

Gordon, Alex: *Anecdotes of the Revolutionary War in America.* Page 165 contains names of prisoners taken to Saint Augustine, Florida (then Spanish territory).

Headley, J. T.: *The Chaplains and Clergy of the Revolution.* New York, 1864.

Heitman, Francis B.: *Historical Register of Officers of the Continental Army during the War of the Revolution, April 1775 to December 1783.* 1914.

Heitman, Francis B.: *Historical Register and Dictionary of the United States Army from its Organization September 29, 1783 to March 2, 1903.* Washington, 1903. This is a record of officers for the most part.

New York Historical Society: *Muster and Pay Rolls of the War of the Revolution, 1775-1783.* 1916.

Sabine, Lorenzo: *Biographical Sketches of the American Revolution.* 1864. 2 vols.

Saffell, William Thomas Roberts: *Records of the Revolutionary War,* 1858.

Tower, J.M.: *The Medical Men of the Revolution:* Containing the Names of Nearly Twelve Hundred Physicians. Philadelphia, 1876.

United States Department of State: *Census of Pensioners for Revolutionary or Military Service with their Names, Ages* (etc.). Washington, 1841. Reprinted 1954, Southern Book Co.

United States: *Report from the Secretary of War in Relation to the Pension Establishment of the United States.* Washington, 1835. 3 vols. Vol. 1, Northeastern States. Vol. 2, Middle Atlantic States. Vol. 3, Southern and Western States.

United States: *List of Pensioners on the Roll January 1, 1883,* giving the name of each pensioner . . . address, etc. 5 vols. Washington, 1883.

United States War Department: "Register of the Certificates Issued by John Pierce, Esquire, Paymaster General and Commissioner of Army Accounts for the United States." To Officers and Soldiers of the Continental Army under Act of July 4, 1783. First edition 1786. Included in the 17th report of the National Society, Daughters of the American Revolution. Washington, 1915.

United States Congress: *List of the Names of Such Officers and Soldiers of the Revolutionary Army as Have Acquired a Right to Lands from the United States and Who Have Not Yet Applied Therefor.* Senate Document 42, 20th Congress, 1st Session, January 16, 1828. Washington, 1828.

United States Congress: *Report of the Secretary of the Interior with a Statement of Rejected or Suspended Applications for Pensions.* February 16, 1852. Senate Ex. Doc. 37. 32nd Congress, 1st Session.

United States Congress: *American State Papers, Documents, Legislative and Executive of the Congress of the United States, from the First Session of the First to the Second Session of the Seventeenth Congress, Inclusive.* Commencing March 4, 1789, and ending March 3, 1823. Washington, 1834. Claims volume contains index to Claims of Revolutionary War Soldiers and other claims.

United States Congress: *Digested Summary and Alphabetical List of Private Claims Which Have Been Presented to the House of Representatives from the First to the Thirty-first Congress Exhibiting the Action of Congress on Each Claim.* 3 vols. Washington, 1853.

United States Secretary of War: *Letter from the Secretary of War Communicating a Transcript of the Pension List of the United States Showing the Number of Pensioners in the Several Districts, June 1, 1813.* Washington, 1813. Reprinted 1958, Southern Book Co.

United States War Department: *Letter from the Secretary of War transmitting a report of the names, rank, and line of every person placed on the pension list, Jan. 20, 1820.* Washington, 1820. Reprinted 1955, Southern Book Co.

Loyalist Records

To obtain information regarding British soldiers who served in the American Revolutionary War, write to: Keeper of Public Records, Rolls House, Chancery Lane, London, England.

American Loyalist manuscript records

The New York Public Library has a collection of 35 volumes of claims filed in London of loyalists whose property was destroyed or damaged in the colonies during the Revolutionary War.

Civil War records

United States War Department: *Official Army Register of the Volunteer Force of the United States Army for the years 1861-1865.* In eight parts. Washington, 1865.

United States War Department: *The War of the Rebellion: A Compilation of the Official Records of the Union and Confederate Armies. . . . General Index and Additions and Corrections.* John S. Moodey, indexer. Government Printing Office, Washington, 1901.

United States War Department: *Bibliography of State Participation in the Civil War 1861-1866.* Washington, 1913. War Department Library, Subject Catalogue No. 6.

Special Schedules of the Eleventh Census (1890) Enumerating Union Veterans and Widows of Union Veterans of the Civil War. Microfilmed by the National Archives, 118 rolls. These special schedules include, among other things, the name of the veteran or, if he did not survive, the names of both the widow and her deceased husband, the veteran's rank, company, regiment, or vessel, details concerning length of service and discharge, post office address. Practically all of the schedules for the states of Alabama through Kansas and approximately one-half of those for Kentucky were misplaced or destroyed before transfer of the records to the National Archives. For a record of the records available on microfilm see *List of National Archives Microfilm Publications, 1953.* National Archives, 1953, pp. 80-84. Some libraries have microfilm copies in their collections. For an article explaining this source, see the *National Genealogical Society Quarterly,* 34:7-9.

nfederate :ords

The larger part of the records of the Confederate States of America that came into the possession of the United States Government is a part of the War Department record group in the National Archives. For a description of these records see pp. 213-14, Guide to the Records in the National Archives, Washington, 1948. Also see Civil War references listed for the various states.

mily tories d place tories

American Genealogical Index. (See Rider, Fremont, below.)

Bridger, Charles: *An Index to Printed Pedigrees Contained in County and Local Histories, the Herald's Visitations and in the More Important Genealogical Collections.* London, 1867.

Durrie, Daniel S.: *Bibliographia Genealogica Americana:* An Alphabetical Index to American Genealogies and Pedigrees Contained in State, County, and Town Histories, Printed Genealogies, and Kindred Works. Albany, 1868. 2d ed., revised and enlarged, Albany, 1878. 3d ed., revised and enlarged, Albany, 1886. Supplement, 1888.

Genealogies in the Library of Congress, A Bibliography. Edited by Marion J. Kaminkow. Baltimore, Magna Carta Book Co., 1972. Two vols. (Note: This bibliography is indispensable. Most libraries have bought it.)

Index to American Genealogies and to Genealogical Material Contained in All Works such as Town Histories, County Histories, Local Histories, Historical Society Publications, Biographies, Historical Periodicals, and Kindred Works. 4th ed., revised and enlarged, containing nearly 40,000 references. Albany, 1895. 5th ed., revised and enlarged, Albany, 1900. Supplement, 1900-1908, Albany, 1908.

Kaminkow, Marion J.: Refer to *Genealogies in the Library of Congress,* above.

Jacobus, Donald Lines: *Index to Genealogical Periodicals.* New Haven, 1932. Vol. 2, 1948. Vol. 3, 1953.

Long Island Historical Society, Brooklyn, New York: *Catalogue of American Genealogies in the Library of the Long Island Historical Society*. 1935.

Marshall, George W.: *The Genealogist's Guide.* 1903. English sources.

Munsell, Joel, Sons: *List of Titles of Genealogical Articles in American Periodicals and Kindred Works.* 1899. Gives the name, residence, and earliest date of the first settler of each family, with deficiencies in brackets.

Munsell's *Genealogical Index.* South Norwalk, Connecticut, 1933-.

National Society, Daughters of the American Revolution: ''Catalogue of Genealogical and Historical Works.'' Washington, 1940.

Newberry Library, Handbook of. Chicago, 1933.

Osborne, Georgia L.: *A List of the Genealogical Works in the Illinois State Historical Library.* 1914.

Peterson, C. Stewart: *Bibliography of County Histories of the 3111 Counties in the 48 States.* Baltimore, 1946.

Rider, Fremont, ed.: *The American Genealogical and Biographical Index.* Indexed according to both surnames and Christian names.

Stewart, Robert Armistead: *Index to Printed Virginia Genealogies.* 1930.

Stuart, Margaret: *Scottish Family History—A Guide to Works of Reference on the History and Genealogy of Scottish Families.* 1930.

Swem, Earl Gregg: *Virginia Historical Index.* 2 vols. 1934, 1936.

Thomson, T. R., comp.: *A Catalogue of British Family Histories.* London, 1928.

United States Library of Congress, Washington, D.C.: *American and English Genealogies in the Library of Congress.* 2d ed. Washington, 1919. This out-of-date bibliography has been superseded by *Genealogies in the Library of Congress,* edited by Marion J. Kaminkow.

Reference books: Pre-American ancestry

American Irish Historical Society Journal, ''How to Trace Your Irish Relatives and Ancestors,'' vol. 28, pp. 124-39.

Austin, John Osborne: *The Genealogical Dictionary of Rhode Island, Comprising Three Generations of Settlers Who Came Before 1690.* 1887.

Baird, Charles Washington: *History of the Huguenot Emigration to America.* 2 vols. New York, 1885.

Banks, Charles Edward: *Topographical Dictionary of 2885 English Emigrants to New England, 1620-1650.* Edited, indexed, and published by Elijah Ellsworth Brownell, Philadelphia, 1937. (Contains mistakes and wrong clues.) See *National Genealogical Society Quarterly* 33: 7-10, Rubincam: "The Banks Manuscripts in the Library of Congress."

Banks, Charles Edward: *The English Ancestry and Homes of the Pilgrim Fathers.* c. 1929.

Banks, Charles Edward: *The Planters of the Commonwealth: A Study of the Emigrants and Emigration in Colonial Times* (1620-1640). 1930. (Passenger lists.) Contains many mistakes.

Banks, Charles Edward: *The Withrop Fleet of 1630.*

Bardsley, Charles W. E.: *A Dictionary of English and Welsh Surnames, with Special American Instances.* 1901.

Bardsley, Charles W. E.: *Curiosities of Puritan Nomenclature.* 1880 and 1897.

Blegen, Theodore Christian: *Norwegian Migration to America.* 1931.

Bolton, Charles Knowles: *Scotch-Irish Pioneers in Ulster and America.* 1910.

Bolton, Ethel Stanwood: *Immigrants to New England, 1700-1775.* 1931.

Bowman, George Ernest: *The Mayflower Compact and Its Signers, and a List of the Mayflower Passengers.* 1920.

Bowman, William Dodgson: "Bristol and America, A Record of the First Settlers in the Colonies of North America, 1645-1685. . . ." London (n.d.).

Browning, Charles Henry: *The Welsh Settlements of Pennsylvania.* 1912.

Cameron, V. R.: *Emigrants from Scotland to America, 1774-1775.* 1930.

Chambers, Theodore Frelinghuysen: *The Early Germans of New Jersey; Their Early History, Churches, and Genealogies.* 1895.

Daughters of American Revolution: "Early American Use of Arms as a Clue to Family Origin." *National Historical Magazine,* 74 (July 1939), p. 73.

Drake, Samuel Gardner: *Result of Some Researches among the British Archives for Relatives to the Founders of New England.* Boston, 1860.

Farmer, John: *Genealogical Register of First Settlers of New England.* 1829.

Faust, Albert Bernhardt: *The German Element in the United States*. 1927.

Faust, Albert Bernhardt: *Lists of Swiss Emigrants in the Eighteenth Century to the American Colonies*. 2 vols. 1920, 1925. (Vol. 1, Zurich archives, 1734-44; vol. 2, Berne archives, 1734-1794.)

Flagg, Ernest: *Founding of New England*. 1927.

Ford, Henry Jones: *The Scotch-Irish in America*. 1915.

Fosdick, Lucian John: *The French Blood in America*. 1915.

Fothergill, Gerald: *A List of Emigrant Ministers to America, 1690-1811*. 1904.

Gibbs, Vicary, ed.: *The Complete Peerage*, London.

Hinman, Royal Ralph: *A Catalogue of the Names of the Early Puritan Settlers of the Colony of Connecticut*. 1852-1856.

Holmes, Frank R.: *Directory of the Ancestral Heads of New England Families, 1620-1700*. 1923.

Hotten, John Camden: *The Original Lists of Persons of Quality: Emigrants . . . Who Went from Great Britain to the American Plantations, 1600-1700*. 1880.

Journal of American History: "English Ancestry of American Families in Feudal Times." 6:329.

Lancour, A. Harold: *Passenger Lists of Ships Coming to North America, 1607-1825*. A bibliography, published in the *Bulletin of the New York Public Library*, May 1937, 41:389.

Lawrence, Ruth, ed.: *Colonial Families of America*. 15 vols. 1928.

MacLean, John Patterson: *An Historical Account of the Settlements of Scotch Highlanders in America Prior to the Peace of 1783*. 1900.

McGee, Thomas D'Arcy: *A History of the Irish Settlers in North America from the Earliest Period to the Census of 1850*. 5th ed., 1852.

Myers, Albert Cook: *Immigration of the Irish Quakers into Pennsylvania, 1682-1750.*

New England Historical and Genealogical Register: "Emigrants from England, 1773-1776." Boston, 1913. Reprint from vols. 62-65.

Rupp, Israel Daniel: *A Collection of Upwards of Thirty Thousand Names of German, Swiss, Dutch, French, and Other Immigrants in Pennsylvania from 1727 to 1776*. 1931.

Savage, James: *A Genealogical Dictionary of the First Settlers of New England, Showing Three Generations of Those Who Came before May, 1692*. 4 vols. Boston, 1860-

62. Use in conjunction with Savage, "A Genealogical Cross Index of Savage," by O. P. Dexter, and also "Genealogical Notes and Errata to Savage's Genealogical Dictionary," by C.W. Dall.

Sherwood, George F. T.: *American Colonists in English Records.* 1932.

Waters, Henry F.: *Genealogical Gleanings in England.* 2 vols. 1901.

Withington, Lothrop: *English Notes about Early Settlers in New England.* Published in Essex Institute Historical Collection, 52:50.

nealogical riodicals

American Genealogist, Box 3032, Westville Station, New Haven, Connecticut, Quarterly. 1923-.

Colorado Genealogist.

Daughters of the American Revolution. The monthly magazine of this organization commenced in 1892.

Detroit *Society for Genealogical Research Magazine.*

Essex Institute Historical Collections.

Filson Club History Quarterly, Kentucky

Genealogy and History, Washington, D.C. (Queries and answers.)

Genealogical Forum of Portland, Oregon.

Genealogical Helper, 526 N. Main Street, Logan, Utah.

Genealogical Magazine of New Jersey.

Genealogical Newsletter, 4724 5th St., N.W., Washington, D.C.

Genealogists Magazine, Society of Genealogists, London, England.

Kentucky State Historical Society, Register of.

Kentucky Genealogist, Box 4894, Washington, D.C.

Maryland Genealogical Bulletin.

Maryland Historical Magazine.

National Genealogical Society Quarterly, 1912-.

New England Historical and Genealogical Register, 1847-.

New Jersey Genesis, 49 Grosvenor Road, Short Hills, N.J.

New Jersey Historical Society, Proceedings of.

New York Genealogical and Biographical Record, 1870-.

New York Historical Society quarterly bulletins.

Niagara Frontier Genealogical Magazine.

North Carolinian, Box 531, Raleigh, N.C.

Norwegian-American Historical Association, publications of St. Olaf College, Northfield, Minn.

Pennsylvania Genealogical Magazine.

Seattle Genealogical Society, Bulletin of.

South Carolina Historical and Genealogical Magazine.

Tyler's *Quarterly,* formerly Tyler's *Quarterly Historical and Genealogical Magazine* (1919-), 1952-. 126 Third Avenue North, Nashville, Tennessee.

Virginia Genealogist, published by John F. Dorman, Box 4883, Washington, D.C.

Virginia Magazine of History and Biography.

William & Mary College Historical Magazine, 1893-.

Historical societies

American-Irish Historical Society, 991 Fifth Avenue, New York, N.Y.

American-Jewish Archives, Clifton Ave., Cincinnati, Ohio.

American-Jewish Historical Society, 150 Fifth Avenue, New York, N.Y.

American-Scandinavian Foundation, 127 East 73rd St., New York, N.Y.

American Society of Church History, 1100 S. Goodman St., Rochester, N.Y.

American-Swedish Institute, 2600 Park Ave., Minneapolis, Minn.

Disciples of Christ Historical Society, Joint University Libraries, Nashville, Tenn.

Episcopalian Church Historical Society, Divinity School of the Protestant Episcopal Church in Philadelphia, 4205 Spruce Street, Philadelphia, Pa.

Evangelical United Brethren Church Historical Society, Knott Building, Dayton, Ohio.

French Institute in the United States, 22 East 60th Street, New York, N.Y.

Friends Historical Association, Swarthmore College, Swarthmore, Pa.

Historical Society of the Evangelical Church, Albright College, Reading, Pa.

Historical Society of the Evangelical and Reformed Church in the United States, Fackenthal Library, Franklin and Marshall College, Lancaster, Pa.

Historical Society of the United Lutheran Church in America, Gettysburg, Pa.

Huguenot Society of America, 122 East 58th Street, New York, N.Y.

Italian Historical Society of America, 26 Court St., Brooklyn, N.Y.

Presbyterian Historical Society, 520 Witherspoon Building, Philadelphia, Pa.

Polish-American Historical Association, 984 Milwaukee Ave., Chicago, Ill.

Sons and Daughters of Pioneer River Men, Campus Martius Museum, Marietta, Ohio.

Southern Historical Association, History Department, University of Kentucky, Lexington, Ky.

Alabama

neral ormation

Capital: Montgomery. Organized as a territory: March 3, 1817. Entered Union: Dec. 14, 1819. Seceded from Union: Jan. 11, 1861. Reentered Union: July 13, 1868.

raries, torical ieties, d archives

For a complete list see: Brown, Karl: *The American Library Directory.* Also, *Directory of Historical Societies and Agencies in the United States and Canada.* 1956.

Alabama Conference Historical Society (Methodist), Montgomery.

Alabama Historical Association, 4212 Overlook Road, Birmingham.

State Department of Archives and History, Montgomery.

Birmingham Public Library, 2020 7th Ave. North, Birmingham.

Birmingham Historical Society, Public Library, Birmingham.

bama earch gestions

"Alabama Counties," *National Genealogical Society Quarterly,* March 1949, p. 3.

Brantley, W. H., Jr.: *Law and Courts in Pioneer Alabama.* October 1945, pp. 390-400.

Kelly, Maud McLure: "Alabama Records for Genealogical Research," *National Genealogical Society Quarterly,* March 1949, p. 3.

erence ks

Brant and Fuller Publishing Co.: *Memorial Record of Alabama.* 2 vols. Personal memoirs.

Brewer, Willis: *Alabama—Her History . . . Public Men,* etc. 1872.

Daughters of the American Revolution: *Complete Index of the Wills of . . . Alabama.* 1808-1870. 1956.

Garrett, William: *Reminiscences of Public Men in Alabama for Thirty Years.* 1872. 809 pp. Indexed.

Hamilton, Peter J.: *Colonial Mobile.* 1910.

Harllee, William Curry: *Kinfolks, A Genealogical and Biographical Record of Thomas and Elizabeth* (*Stuart*) *Harllee.* 1934.

Jones, Kathleen Paul, and Pauline Jones Candrud: *Records from Newspapers . . . 1823-1867.* Alabama Records, vol. 86. Typed, indexed.

McMorries, Edward: "History of the First Regt. Ala., Volunteer Infantry Civil War—C.S.A.—." *Alabama Department of Archives and History Bulletin.*

Mell, A. R. W.: *Revolutionary Soldiers Buried in Alabama.* 1904.

Northern Alabama Historical and Biographical History of Northern Alabama. 1888.

Owen, Thomas: *History of Alabama and Dictionary of Alabama Biography,* 1921.

Owen, Thomas: *Revolutionary Soldiers in Alabama.* 1911. List of names and some biographical data.

Owen, Thomas M.: *A Bibliography of Alabama.* (n.d.) 1248 pp.

Peterson, C. Stewart: *Bibliography of County Histories of the 3111 Counties in the 48 States.* Baltimore, 1946.

Saunders, James E.: *Early Settlers of Alabama.* 1896. Genealogies. Many came from Virginia.

Smith and DeLand: *Northern Alabama, Historical and Biographical.* 1888.

United States Department of State: *Territorial Papers of the United States.* Clarence E. Carter, ed. 1952. Vol. 18, Territory of Alabama, 1817-1819. (For a review of this source see *National Genealogical Society Quarterly,* 37:93.)

Military rosters, rolls, and records

The Alabama Department of Archives and History, Montgomery, has records of the Indian Wars, the war between Mexico and Texas, and many records of the War between the States, including many pension applications of Confederate veterans and widows of Confederate veterans. There is a charge for service.

The National Archives has compiled the *Consolidated Index to Compiled Records of Confederate Soldiers.* The index is on cards that give the name of the soldier, his rank, the unit in which he served, and often a statement concerning the origin of that unit. There are cross-reference cards for soldiers' names that appear in the records under more than one spelling. This index is available for personal search or by an agent. It is microfilmed.

ficial cords

Vital Records: Fee for birth records, $3.00; marriage records, $2.00; death certificates, $3.00.

State Custodian: State Registrar, Bureau of Vital Statistics, Montgomery, Alabama 36104.

Birth Records: Subsequent to 1908: Above-named State Custodian. Approximate date and name of county necessary to make a satisfactory search. Give full name of child at birth and the full name of father and mother. *Prior to 1908:* Clerk, Probate Court, at the county seat of the county in which the birth occurred. Also try city or county board of health. *Delayed Birth Certificates:* State Custodian will furnish information.

Marriage Licenses: Clerk, Probate Court of the county in which the license was issued.

Marriage Records: Subsequent to August 1936: Above-named State Custodian. Marriage records are filed according to counties and arranged by months and years. *Prior to August 1936:* Clerk, Probate Court, county in which the license was issued.

Death Records: Subsequent to 1908: Above-named State Custodian. Name of county and approximate date necessary to make a satisfactory search. *Prior to 1908:* Clerk, Probate Court, at the county seat of the county where the death occurred. Also try city or county board of health.

Divorce Records: See court records, below.

Court Records: Wills, administrations, and other probate matters: *Custodian:* Clerk, Probate Court, at the county seat where the estate was probated. Also try Circuit Court. *Other Civil Actions:* Clerk, County Court, County Seat.

Land Records: Deeds, mortgages, leases, and other matters affecting title to land: Probate Judge, county seat of each county.

deral nsus ords

1. See index for section on United States Census.

2. Custody of mortality schedules, 1850, 1860, 1870, 1880: Department of Archives and History, Montgomery, Alabama.

3. The original 1880 United States Census records for Alabama were transferred to the Department of Archives and History, Montgomery, in 1956.

bama e census ords

Censuses were taken by the authority of the State of Alabama in 1850, 1855, and 1866. These censuses were made by county, and at least the names of heads of families are disclosed in the records. *Custodian:* Department of Archives and History, Montgomery, Alabama 36104.

Alaska

General information

Capital: Juneau. Organized as a territory: 1912. Entered Union: January 3, 1959.

Official records

Vital Records: Fee for birth, marriage, and death certificate: $3.00

Custodian: Bureau of Vital Statistics, Pouch H, Juneau, Alaska 99801.

Birth Records: Subsequent to 1913: Above-named Custodian. *Prior to 1913:* Above-named Custodian, incomplete prior to 1913. *Delayed birth certificates:* Custodian will furnish information.

Marriage Records: Subsequent to 1913: Above-named Custodian. *Prior to 1913:* Above-named Custodian. Prior to 1913, the United States Commissioner received some marriage certificates.

Death Records: Custodian subsequent to 1913: Above-named Custodian. *Custodian prior to 1913:* Above-named Custodian.

Divorce Records: Since 1950: Custodian, Bureau of Vital Statistics, Alaska Department of Health, Pouch H, Juneau, Alaska 99801. Certified copy $3.00. *Prior to 1950:* Clerk of the United States District Court, Judicial Division where divorce was granted: Juneau (First Division), Nome (Second Division), Anchorage (Third Division), Fairbanks (Fourth Division). Cost of certified copy varies.

Court Records: Civil Actions: Clerk, United States District Court. Divisions: 1, Juneau; 2, Nome; 3, Anchorage; 4, Fairbanks.

Land Records: Deeds, mortgages, leases, and other matters affecting title to land: Register of various registration districts.

Arizona

General information

Capital: Phoenix. Organized as a territory: February 24, 1863. Entered Union: February 14, 1912.

Libraries, historical societies and archives

For a complete list see Brown, Karl: *The American Library Directory.* Also, *Directory of Historical Societies and Agencies in the United States and Canada.* 1956.

Arizona Pioneers' Historical Society, 949 E. Second St., Tucson.

Department of Library and Archives, State House, Phoenix.

Prescott Historical Society, Old Governor's Mansion, Prescott.

ference oks

Chapman Publishing Co.: *Portrait and Biographical Record of Arizona.* 1901. 1034 pp.

Farish, Thomas Edwin: *History of Arizona.* 8 vols. San Francisco: The Filmer Brothers Electrotype Company, 1915-1918. Index, 1920.

Historical Records Survey, WPA: *The 1864 Census of the Territory of Arizona.* 1938. 210 pp.

Peterson, C. Stewart: *Bibliography of County Histories of the 3111 Counties in the 48 States,* Baltimore, 1946.

ficial records

Vital Records: Fee for birth certificate, $2.00; death certificate, $2.00.

State Custodian: Division of Vital Records, Department of Health, P.O. Box 3887, Phoenix, Arizona 85030.

Birth Records: Subsequent to July 1, 1909: Above-named State Custodian. *Prior to July 1, 1909:* Above-named State Custodian. *Delayed birth certificates:* State Custodian will furnish information.

Marriage Licenses: Clerk of Superior Court, County Seat.

Marriage Records: Clerk of Superior Court, County Seat.

Death Records: Subsequent to July 1, 1909: Above-named State Custodian. *Prior to July 1, 1909:* Above-named State Custodian.

Divorce Records: See court records, below.

Court Records: Wills, administrations, and other probate matters; Custodian: Clerk of Superior Court, County Seat. *Other Civil Actions:* Clerk of Superior Court, County Seat. Cost of certified copy of divorce decree varies.

Land Records: Deeds, mortgages, leases, and other matters affecting title to land: County Recorder, County Seat.

deral census cords

1. See index for section on United States Census.

2. Custody of mortality schedules, 1870, 1880: DAR, Washington, D.C.

3. In 1956 the original 1880 United States census records for Arizona were transferred by the National Archives to: National Society, Daughters of the American Revolution, Administration Building, 1776 D Street, N.W., Washington, D.C.

rritorial nsus records

Historical Records Survey, WPA: *The 1864 Census of the Territory of Arizona.* Phoenix, 1938. vi, 210 pp. Mimeographed. This census was provided to aid in establishing the territory. Information included name, age, sex, marital status, place of birth, length of residence, citizenship status, family residence of married individuals, occupation, and value of estate.

Territorial Census of 1866: See: Farish, Thomas E.. *History of Arizona.* Phoenix, 1916. 163 pp. General results of this census are set forth in this book. The National Archives has custody of the original or copies of the following territorial censuses for Arizona: 1860, 1864, 1866, 1867, 1869, 1870, and 1880.

Arizona state census records

No census records taken by state authority have ever been located.

Arkansas

General information

Capital: Little Rock. Organized as a territory: March 2, 1819. Entered Union: June 15, 1836. Seceded from Union: May 6, 1861. Reentered Union: June 22, 1868.

Libraries, historical societies, and archives

For a complete list see Brown, Karl: *The American Library Directory.* Also, *Directory of Historical Societies and Agencies in the United States and Canada,* 1956.

Arkansas History Commission, State Capitol, Little Rock.

State Department of Archives and History, Little Rock.

Reference books

Goodspeed Publishing Co.: *Biographical and Historical Memoirs of Northeast Arkansas,* 1889. Contains a short history of the counties of the state.

Hallum, John: *Biographical and Pictorial History of Arkansas.* Albany, 1887. Vol. 1, 581 pp.

Historical Survey Project, WPA: *Guide to Vital Statistic Records in Arkansas.* Vol. 2, Church Archives (n.d.). 618 pp.

Historical Records Survey, WPA: *A Directory of Churches and Religious Organizations in the State of Arkansas.* Preliminary edition, May 1942. 176 pp.

Historical Records Survey, WPA: *Union List of Newspapers, 1819-1942.* June 1942. 240 pp. A partial inventory of Arkansas newspaper files available in offices of publishers, libraries, and private collections in Arkansas.

Peterson, C. Stewart: *Bibliography of County Histories of the 3111 Counties in the 48 States.* Baltimore, 1946.

Shinn, Josiah H.: *Pioneers and Makers of Arkansas.* 1908.

Thomas, David Y.: *Arkansas and Its People, a History, 1541-1930.* 4 vols. 1930. (Vols. 3 and 4, Biographical and Genealogical.)

United States, Department of State: *Territorial Papers of the United States.* Clarence E. Carter, ed. 1953, 1954. Vols. 19, 20, 21: The Territory of Arkansas, 1819-1836. For a summary of this source see *National Genealogical Society Quarterly* 37:93-.

United States, WPA: *Bibliography of Research Projects Reports—Check List of Historical Records Survey Publications.* April 1943.

itary rosters, ls, and cords

Civil War—State Roster: Arkansas Adjutant-General's Office (Union): Report of the Adjutant-General (A. W. Bishop) of Arkansas for the period of the Late Rebellion, and to November 1, 1866. Washington, 1867. 278 pp. (See also for material on various military organizations.)

Confederate Military Records: The National Archives has compiled the *Consolidated Index to Compiled Records of Confederate Soldiers.* The index is on cards that give the name of the soldier, his rank, the unit in which he served, and often a statement concerning the origin of that unit. There are cross-reference cards for soldiers' names that appear in the records under more than one spelling. This index is available for personal search or by an agent. It is microfilmed.

icial records

Vital Records: Fee for birth, $2.00; marriage, $2.00; and death certificate, $3.00.

State Custodian: Arkansas State Department of Health, Bureau of Vital Statistics, Little Rock, Arkansas 72201.

Birth Records: Subsequent to February 1, 1914: Above-named State Custodian. *Prior to February 1, 1914:* If the birth occurred in either Little Rock or Fort Smith, certificates may be obtained from above-named State Custodian. *Delayed birth certificates:* State Custodian will furnish information.

Marriage Licenses: County Clerk.

Marriage Records: Subsequent to April 1917: Above-named State Custodian. Marriage records filed alphabetically by counties. *Prior to April 1917:* County Clerk.

Death Records: Subsequent to February 1, 1914: Above-named State Custodian. *Prior to February 1, 1914:* If the death occurred in either Little Rock or Fort Smith, write to City Clerks of these two cities.

Divorce Records: Clerk of county or Chancery Court in county where divorce was granted. Cost of certified copy varies. *Since 1923:* Copy of partial record available from

Bureau of Vital Statistics, State Department of Health, Little Rock, Arkansas. Cost of certified copy is $2.00.

Court Records: Wills, administrations, and other probate matters: Clerk, Probate Court, County Seat.

Land Records: Deeds, mortgages, leases, and other matters affecting title to land: Clerk, Circuit Court, County Seat.

Federal census records

1. See index for section on United States Census.

2. Custody of mortality schedules, 1850, 1860, 1870, 1880: Hendrix College, Conway, Arkansas.

3. The Arkansas History Commission, Old State House, West Wing, Little Rock, Arkansas, has copies of the U.S. Census records for 1850, 1860, 1870, and 1880.

4. The original 1880 United States census records for Arkansas were transferred in 1956 by the National Archives to Arkansas History Commission, Little Rock, Arkansas.

Arkansas state census records

Census records taken by state authority: None.

California

General information

Capital: Sacramento. Entered the Union: September 9, 1850.

Libraries, historical societies, and archives

For a complete list see: Brown, Karl: *The American Library Directory.* Also, *Directory of Historical Societies and Agencies in the United States and Canada,* 1956.

California Genealogical Society, 926-8 de Young Building, San Francisco.

Los Angeles Public Library, Genealogy Division, 630 W. 5th St., Los Angeles.

Sons of the Revolution, 600 South Central Ave., Glendale, California.

State Library, California Section, Sacramento.

Sutro Branch of the California State Library, 2130 Fulton Street, San Francisco.

California Historical Society, 2090 Jackson Street, San Francisco.

San Diego Public Library, Genealogy Room, 820 E St., San Diego.

Society of California Pioneers, 456 McAllister St., San Francisco.

Southern California Genealogical Society, P.O. Box 7665, Bixby Station, Long Beach.

Santa Barbara Historical Society, 128 E. Cañon Perdido Street, Santa Barbara.

eference oks

Coy, Owen C.: *Guide to the County Archives of California.* 1919.

Bancroft, Hubert Howe: See his works for the California Pioneer Register.

Daughters of the American Revolution, California Society: *Records of the Families of California Pioneers Gathered by the Various Chapters from Original Sources in the Years 1925-1926.*

Hoover, Mildred Brook: *Historic Spots in California.* 1948.

Hunt, Rockwell D., ed.: *California and Californians.* 4 vols. 1932.

Society of California Pioneers: *Quarterly of the Society of California Pioneers,* San Francisco. 1924-.

Peterson, C. Stewart: *Bibliography of County Histories of the 3111 Counties in the 48 States.* Baltimore, 1946.

ilitary rosters, lls, and cords

Civil War—State Rosters:

California Adjutant-General's Office: Annual reports of the Adjutant-General for 1861-1867.

Biennial Report of the Adjutant-General (J. M. Allen), October 31, 1867-November 1, 1869. (Sacramento? 1869?) 183 pp. Contains a list of officers and enrolled men of the California Volunteers who died while in the service of the U.S., pp. 108-125.

Orton, Brig. Gen. R.H., Adjutant General: *Records of California Men in the War of the Rebellion, 1861-1867.* Sacramento, 1890. 887 pp.

ficial records

Vital Records: Fee for birth, marriage, and death certificates, $2.00.

State Custodian: State Department of Public Health, Bureau of Vital Statistics, 410 N St., Sacramento, California 95814.

Birth Records: Subsequent to July 1, 1905: Above-named State Custodian. *Prior to July 1, 1905:* County Recorder at the county seat of the county in which the birth occurred. Or, if the birth was in an incorporated city, write to the City Health Department of that city. *Delayed birth certificates:* State Custodian will furnish information.

Marriage Licenses: County Clerk.

Marriage Records: Subsequent to July 1, 1905: Above-named State Custodian. *Prior to July 1, 1905:* County Recorder.

Death Records: Subsequent to July 1, 1905: Above-named State Custodian. *Prior to July 1, 1905:* County Recorder, or if the death was in an incorporated city, write to the City Health Department of that city.

Divorce Records: Clerk of Superior Court in county where divorce was granted. Cost of certified copy varies.

Court Records: Wills, administrations, and other probate matters: County Clerk.

Land Records: Deeds, mortgages, leases, and other matters affecting title to land: County Recorder.

Federal census records

1. See index for section on United States Census.

2. Custody of mortality schedules, 1850, 1860, 1870, 1880: California State Library, Sacramento, California.

3. The original 1880 United States census records of California were transferred in 1956 by the National Archives to: Archives and Central Records Depository, State of California, 1108 R Street, Sacramento, California.

California state census records

Pre-Statehood Censuses: During the Spanish regime a census was taken in 1798. This census discloses the population of the area within the jurisdiction of what is now San Francisco, Santa Clara, San Jose, and Santa Cruz. *Custodian:* California Section, California State Library, Sacramento, has a photographic copy. The original manuscript is in the Secretary of State's office.

There was a census of the Los Angeles District in 1836. It is reproduced in the *Quarterly of the Historical Society of Southern California,* Vol. 18, No. 3. Sept.-Dec. 1936.

State Census of 1852: The census of 1852 (and the only state census taken by California) contains the names, ages, sex, race, occupation, state or country of birth and residence. *Custodian:* Original census records: Secretary of State. Typewritten copies, made by the California Society of the Daughters of the American Revolution, are in the custody of the California Section, California State Library, Sacramento, and in the Library of the NSDAR in Washington, D.C.

Colorado

General information

Capital: Denver. Organized as a territory: February 28, 1861. Entered Union: August 1, 1876.

Libraries, historical societies, and archives

For a complete list see: Brown, Karl: *The American Library Directory.* Also, *Directory of Historical Societies and Agencies in the United States and Canada,* 1956.

State Historical Society of Colorado, State Museum, 14th & Sherman Streets, Denver.

Denver Public Library, 1357 Broadway, Denver.

ference oks

Baker, James H., ed.: *History of Colorado.* 5 vols. 1927. Vols. 4 and 5, Biographical.

Byers, William N.: *Encyclopedia of Biography of Colorado.* 1901. Vol. II, 477 pp.

Chapman Publishing Co.: *Portrait and Biographical Record of the State of Colorado,* 1899. 1492 pp.

Colorado Genealogical Society: *The Colorado Genealogist.* Denver. Vols. 1-18, 1939-1957.

Historical Records Survey, WPA: *Guide to the Vital Statistics Records in Colorado.* Denver, 1942. Vol. 1, Public Archives, 145 pp. Vol. 2, Church Archives, 165 pp.

Peterson, C. Stewart: *Bibliography of County Histories of the 3111 Counties in the 48 States.* Baltimore, 1946.

itary rosters, s, and cords

Colorado Adjutant General's Office: First records begin in 1861 with the volunteers of the Civil War. See Nankevell, Major John H.: *History of the Military Organization of the State of Colorado, 1860-1935.*

icial records

Vital Records: Fee for birth and death certificates, $2.00.

State Custodian: Colorado Department of Public Health, Records and Statistics Section, 4210 East 11th Avenue, Denver, Colorado 80220.

Birth Records: Subsequent to January 1907: Above-named State Custodian. *Prior to January 1907:* County Clerk. *Delayed birth certificates:* State Custodian will furnish information.

Marriage Licenses: Write to above-named State Custodian.

Marriage Records: County Clerk. No state records were kept by State Custodian. Prior to 1881, there was no law requiring record of marriages.

Death Records: Subsequent to January 1900: Above-named State Custodian. *Prior to January 1900:* County Clerk.

Divorce Records: Clerk of District Court, or Clerk of County Court, in county where divorce was granted. Cost of certified copy varies.

Court Records: Wills, administrations, and other probate matters: County Clerk, County Seat. *Other Civil Actions:* County Clerk, County Seat.

Land Records: Deeds, mortgages, leases, and other matters affecting title to land: County Recorder, County Seat.

Federal census records

1. See index for section on United States Census.

2. Custody of mortality schedules, 1870, 1880: DAR, Washington, D.C.

3. The original 1880 United States census records for Colorado were transferred in 1956 by the National Archives to: Division of State Archives and Public Records, State of Colorado, Denver.

4. *Census of 1885:* The National Archives has custody of the 1885 census of Colorado, which was authorized by 20 Statutes at Large 473 in 1879. This census included a census of population and mortality. The name of each person is given, relationship to the head of the family, race, sex, age, marital status, and place of birth. The National Archives has microfilmed this census, and positive prints are available for a fee. The Colorado State Archives in Denver and the University of Colorado Library in Boulder also have microfilm copies of this census. For further information on the Colorado State Census, write to the Colorado State Archives, 306 State Museum, Denver, Colorado.

Connecticut

General information

Capital: Hartford. Entered the Union: January 9, 1788.

Libraries, historical societies, and archives

For a complete list see: Brown, Karl: *The American Library Directory*. Also, *Directory of Historical Societies and Agencies in the United States and Canada,* 1956.

Clinton Historical Society, William Stanton Andrews Memorial, Clinton.

Connecticut Historical Society, 1 Elizabeth Street, Hartford.

Connecticut State Library, Hartford 06115.

Fairfield Historical Society, 1335 Post Road, Fairfield.

Godfrey Memorial Library, 134 Newfield Street, Middletown.

New Canaan Historical Society, St. John Memorial Room, New Canaan Library, New Canaan.

New Haven Colony Historical Society, New Haven.

New London County Historical Society, 11 Blinman Street, New London.

Middlesex County Historical Society, Middletown.

nnecticut
earch
ggestions

Case, Marjorie E.: "Connecticut Resources for Genealogical Research." *National Genealogical Quarterly.* Vol. 36 (March 1948), pp. 1ff.

Mignone, A. Frederick: "A Colonial Court Today: Connecticut's Probate Court System." *American Bar Association Journal.* Vol. 37 (May 1951), pp. 337ff.

Prager, Herta, and William W. Price: "A Bibliography on the History of the Courts of the Thirteen Original States, Maine, Ohio, and Vermont." *The American Journal of Legal History.* Vol. 1, p. 341.

ference
oks

Bailey, Frederic William: *Early Connecticut Marriages as Found on Ancient Church Records Prior to 1800.* 7 vols. New Haven, 1896-1906.

Connecticut (Colony): *The Public Records of the Colony of Connecticut, 1636-1776,* 15 vols. Hartford, 1850-1890.

Connecticut: *The Public Records of the State of Connecticut,* 3 vols. Hartford, 1894-1922. (See also additional volumes published.)

Connecticut Historical Society, Hartford: Collections, Hartford, 1860-.

The Connecticut Magazine. 12 vols. Hartford, 1895-1908.

Flagg, Charles Allcott: *Reference List on Connecticut Local History.* Albany, 1900.

Hinman, Royal Ralph: *A Catalogue of the Names of Early Puritan Settlers of the Colony of Connecticut, 1852-1856.*

Jacobus, Donald Lines: *List of Officials, Civil, Military, and Ecclesiastical of Connecticut Colony, from March 1636 through 11 October, 1677, and of New Haven Colony throughout its Separate Existence;* also *Soldiers in the Pequot War Who Then or Subsequently Resided within the Present Bounds of Connecticut.* New Haven, 1935.

Manwaring, Charles William: *A Digest of the Early Connecticut Probate Records.* 3 vols. Hartford, 1904-1906.

Mather, Frederick Gregory: *The Refugees of 1776 from Long Island to Connecticut.* Albany, 1913.

New Haven Colony Historical Society: Papers, New Haven, 1865-.

Peterson, C. Stewart: *Bibliography of County Histories of the 3111 Counties in the 48 States.* Baltimore, 1946.

Scranton, Helen Love: *Cross-Index to New Haven Genealogical Magazine.* Vols. 1 to 8 incl. *Families of Ancient New Haven.* 1939.

Shepard, James: *Connecticut Soldiers in the Pequot War of 1637.* Meriden, 1913.

United States Bureau of the Census: *Heads of Families at*

the First Census of the United States Taken in the Year 1790: Connecticut. Washington, 1908.

United States, WPA: *Bibliography of Research Projects Reports*—Check List of Historical Records Survey Publications. 1943.

Military rosters, rolls, and records

Revolutionary War, etc.:

Baker, Mary Ellen:

Bibliography of Lists of New England Soldiers. New England Historic Genealogical Society, Boston, 1911. 56 pp.

Connecticut, Adjutant General: *Record of Service of Connecticut Men in the Part I, War of the Revolution.* (Name Index, pp. 669-777.) *Part II, War of 1812.* (Names arranged alphabetically, pp. 3-169, following Part I.) *Part III, Mexican War 1889.*

Connecticut Historical Society: *Rolls and Lists of Connecticut Men in the Revolution, 1775-1783.* Hartford, 1909. Collections of the Connecticut Historical Society, vol. 12.

Connecticut Historical Society: *Rolls and Lists of Connecticut Men in the Revolution, 1775-1873.* Hartford, 1901.

Middlebrook, Louis F.: *History of Maritime Connecticut during the American Revolution, 1775-1783.* 2 vols. 1925.

United States Pension Bureau: *Pension Records of the Revolutionary Soldiers from Connecticut,* in Daughters of the American Revolution, Twenty-first Report, 1917-1918, pp. 131-299. Washington, 1919.

War of 1812: See adjutant general's record, above.

Civil War: Connecticut Adjutant General: *Record of Service of Connecticut Men in the Army and Navy of the United States during the War of the Rebellion.* Hartford, 1889.

See also: *Connecticut Adjutant General's Records:* Complete pension records for Connecticut men in the Civil War 1861-1865 are on file in the Connecticut adjutant general's office in Hartford.

Official records

Vital Records: Fee for birth, marriage, and death certificates subsequent to July 1, 1897, from State Custodian. $2.00.

State Custodian: State Registrar of Vital Statistics, State Department of Health, 79 Elm Street, Hartford, Connecticut 06115.

Birth Records: Subsequent to July 1, 1897: Above-named State Custodian. *Between 1850 and July 1, 1897:* Town Clerk. *Prior to 1850:* State Librarian, Hartford, has compiled a central name index for the entire state, including the vital records for each town. Certified copies obtainable from the Town Clerk. *Delayed birth certificates:* State Custodian will furnish information.

Marriage Licenses: Subsequent to July 1, 1897: Above-named State Custodian. *Between 1850 and July 1, 1897:* Town Clerk. *Prior to 1850:* Town Clerk for certified copy, or write to State Librarian, Hartford, who has a central name index for the entire state.

Marriage Records: Subsequent to July 1, 1897: Above-named State Custodian. *Between 1850 and July 1, 1897:* Town Clerk. *Prior to 1850:* Town Clerk for certified copy, or write to State Librarian, Hartford, who has a central name index for the entire state.

Death Records: Subsequent to July 1, 1897: Above-named State Custodian. *Between 1850 and July 1, 1897:* Town Clerk. *Prior to 1850:* Town Clerk for certified copy, or write State Librarian, Hartford, who has compiled a central name index for the entire state.

Divorce Records: Clerk of Superior Court in county where divorce was granted. Cost of certified copy, $3.00.

Court Records: Wills, administrations, and other probate matters: Connecticut is divided into probate districts. See *Biennial Report of the Examiner of Public Records,* 1930, 1940. Most of the original probate records have been deposited with the State Librarian, Hartford. An excellent estate index has been compiled. Probate records in the State Library are confined for the most part to original wills and administrations. Original record volumes, containing copies of wills, etc., are still located in the probate districts. Write to the clerk of the probate district in which the town in which you are interested is located. See above-named report for information regarding probate districts. The Connecticut State Library has the files of some early court records from all the districts of the state.

Land Records: Deeds, mortgages, leases, and other matters affecting title to land: Town Clerks are the custodians of the land records for their respective towns. Indexed by grantors and grantees.

deral
nsus
ords

1. See index for section on United States Census. The state library has a copy of the 1850, 1860, and 1870 censuses.

2. Custody of mortality schedules, 1850, 1860, 1870, and 1880: Connecticut State Library, Hartford, Connecticut.

3. The original 1880 United States census records for Connecticut were transferred in 1956 by the National Archives to: National Society, Daughters of the American

Revolution, Administration Building, 1776 D Street, N.W., Washington, D.C.

State census records

None.

Delaware

General information

Capital: Dover. Entered Union: December 7, 1787. Delaware, Pennsylvania, New Jersey, and New York comprise what was once New Netherlands.

Libraries, historical societies, and archives

For a complete list see: Brown, Karl: *The American Library Directory*. Also, *Directory of Historical Societies and Agencies in the United States and Canada*. 1956.

Historical Society of Delaware, Old Town Hall, Wilmington.

Public Archives Commission, Hall of Records, Dover.

Delaware research suggestions

De Valinger, Leon, Jr.: "Delaware Records for Genealogical Research." *National Genealogical Society Quarterly*. Vol. 35 (March 1957), pp. 1ff.

Prager, Herta, and William W. Price. "A Bibliography on the History of the Courts of the Original Thirteen States, Maine, Ohio, and Vermont." *The American Journal of Legal History*. Vol. 1, p. 344.

The Public Archives Commission, Dover, Delaware, has custody of all extant original public records of this state and its component counties dated before 1873 except the major part of the recorded deeds, which are retained in the Recorders' Offices in the respective county seats. New Castle County Deed Books, Series "A" and "B" only, containing entries dated prior to 1804, are in its custody. It also maintains a large reference library of published and manuscript materials of private origin as a supplement to the official records that make up its principal holdings. Existing land grants date from 1646; deed books are dated from 1673 in New Castle County, 1680 in Kent County, and about 1690 in Sussex County. Court records begin in 1676 for New Castle County, and 1680 for Kent and Sussex.

There are no vital records of official origin dated before 1913 other than those in its custody. Birth and death records date from the decade of 1860. Marriage bonds are dated from 1744, but do not comprise an extensive series before 1790. As a supplement to the very incomplete official vital statistics, it has also assembled a substantial number of references showing evidence of birth, parentage, marriage, or death, from court records, family Bible entries, church records, and similar sources.

ɘference ɔoks

Daughters of the American Revolution of Newark, Delaware: *Old Bible Records Copied from Bibles owned by Delaware Families.* 6 vols.

Delaware Historical Society: *Papers of the Historical Society of Delaware, 1879—.*

Delaware Public Archives Commission: Delaware Archives. 1911—.

Historical Records Survey, WPA: *Directory of Churches and Religious Organizations in Delaware.* 1942. 154 pp.

Louhi, Evert Alexander: *The Delaware Finns.* New York, 1925.

National Society of the Colonial Dames of America, Delaware: *A Calendar of Delaware Wills.* New Castle County, 1911.

Original Land Titles in Delaware, commonly known as *The Duke of York Record, 1664-1679.* Wilmington.

Peterson, C. Stewart: *Bibliography of County Histories of the 3111 Counties in the 48 States.* Baltimore, 1946.

Scharf, John Thomas: *History of Delaware,* 1609-1888. 2 vols. 1888.

Turner, Charles Henry Black: *Rodney's Diary and Other Delaware Records.* 1911.

United States, WPA: *Bibliography of Research Projects Reports—Check List of Historical Records Survey Publications.* April 1943.

'itary records, ɟisters, rolls, ɗ rosters

Revolutionary War:

Bellas, Henry Hobart: *A History of the Delaware Society of the Cincinnati.* Wilmington, 1895. (Papers of the Historical Society of Delaware, No. 13.)

Delaware Public Archives Commission: Delaware Archives. Wilmington. 1911—.

Whiteley, William Gustavus: *The Revolutionary Soldiers of Delaware.* Wilmington, 1896.

War of 1812: Public Archives Commission: Delaware Archives, Volumes IV and V. 1916.

Civil War: Scharf, J. Thomas: *History of Delaware, 1609-1888.* Philadelphia, 1888. (Muster rolls of Delaware's Civil War units were included as an appendix in Volume 1, pages i-xxxiii.)

'cial ords

Vital Records: Fee for birth, marriage, and death certificates: $2.50.

State Custodian: Bureau of Vital Statistics, Division of Public Health, Jesse S. Cooper Memorial Building, Dover, Delaware 19901.

State Custodian: Bureau of Vital Statistics, State Board of Health, State House, Dover, Delaware.

Birth Records: Custodian subsequent to 1881: Above-named State Custodian. (There are some records prior to 1881. It is reported that there are no birth records prior to 1861.) *Delayed birth certificates:* State Custodian will furnish information.

Marriage Licenses: Custodian subsequent to 1847: Above-named State Custodian. *Custodian prior to 1847:* Try Clerk of Justice of the Peace.

Marriage Records: Custodian subsequent to 1847: Above-named State Custodian.

Death Records: Custodian subsequent to 1881: Above-named State Custodian. Some records prior to 1881, but it is reported that there are no death records prior to 1861.

Divorce Records: Prothonotary of county where divorce was granted. Cost of certified copy of divorce is $2.50.

Court Records: Wills, administrations, and other probate matters: Public Archives Commission, Dover. *Other Civil Actions:* Clerk of the following courts, County Seat: Chancery, Orphans Court, Superior Court, Court of Common Pleas for New Castle County.

Land Records: Deeds, mortgages, leases, and other matters affecting title to land: Public Archives Commission, Dover, and County Recorder, County Seat.

Federal census records

1. See index for section on United States Census.

2. Custody of mortality schedules, 1850, 1860, 1870, 1880: State Library, Dover, Delaware.

3. In 1956 the original 1880 United States census records for Delaware were transferred by the National Archives to: Public Archives Commission, State of Delaware, Dover, Delaware.

"Reconstructed 1790 Census of Delaware," by Leon DeValinger, Jr., State Archivist, Dover, Delaware. *National Genealogical Society Quarterly,* commencing in the September 1948 issue, p. 95.

Delaware state census records

No census of persons has ever been made by the state of Delaware within the period 1790-1957.

District of Columbia

neral ormation

Seat of government transferred to the District of Columbia: December 1, 1800.

raries, orical ieties, l archives

For a complete list see: Brown, Karl: *The American Library Directory.* Also, *Directory of Historical Societies and Agencies in the United States and Canada,* 1956.

Daughters of the American Revolution Library, 17th and D Streets, N. W., Washington.

Library of Congress, Washington.

National Archives, Washington.

erence oks

Columbia Historical Society, Records of 1897—.

Historical Records Survey, WPA: *Inventory of the Municipal Archives of the District of Columbia.* April 1940. 31 pp.

Historical Records Survey, WPA: *A Directory of Churches and Religious Organizations in the District of Columbia.* 1939. 188 pp.

cial records

Vital records: Fee for birth and death certificates, $1.00.

District Custodian: Bureau of Vital Statistics, Health Department, Washington, D.C. 20001.

Birth Records: Subsequent to 1872: Above-named District Custodian. *Delayed birth certificates:* No provision for delayed birth certificates.

Marriage Records and Licenses: Subsequent to December 23, 1811, Clerk, U. S. District Court, Washington, D. C.

Death Records: 1855 to August 1874, incomplete. *Subsequent to August 1874,* complete, address above-named district custodian.

Divorce Records: Clerk: United States District Court, Washington, D.C. 20001. Cost of certified copy of divorce decree varies.

Court Records: Wills, administrations, and other probate matters: Register of Wills, Courthouse, D Street, between 4th and 5th, N.W., Washington, D.C.

Land Records: Deeds, mortgages, leases, and other matters affecting title to land: Recorder of Deeds, 6th and D Streets, N.W., Washington, D.C.

Federal census records

1. See index for section on United States Census.

2. Custody of mortality schedules, 1850, 1860, 1870, 1880: DAR, Washington, D.C.

3. The original 1860 United States census records for the District of Columbia were transferred in 1956 by the National Archives to: Columbia Historical Society, 1135 21st Street, N.W., Washington, D.C.

Florida

General information

Capital: Tallahassee. Organized as a territory: March 30, 1822. Entered Union: March 3, 1845. Seceded from Union: January 10, 1861. Reentered Union: June 25, 1868.

Libraries, historical societies, and archives

For a complete list see: Brown, Karl: *The American Library Directory.* Also, *Directory of Historical Societies and Agencies in the United States and Canada,* 1956.

Florida State Library, Tallahassee.

Florida Historical Society, Box 3645, University Station, Gainesville.

Jacksonville Public Library, 101 E. Adams Street, Jacksonville.

Miami Public Library, 1 Biscayne Blvd., Miami.

Reference books

Florida Controller: *Report of the Controller of the State of Florida . . .* (1886, 1898, and 1904). List of persons receiving pensions from the state of Florida.

Historical Records Survey: *Guide to Depositories of Manuscript Collections in the United States: Florida.* April 1940. 27 pp.

Historical Records Survey, WPA: *A Preliminary List of Religious Bodies in Florida.* June 1939. 239 pp.

Historical Records Survey, WPA: *Inventory of the Church Archives of Florida.* In 11 parts. Nos. 12-18.

Historical Records Survey, WPA: *Guide to Public Vital Statistics Records in Florida.* 1941. 70 pp.

Historical Records Survey, WPA: *Spanish Land Grants in Florida.* 5 vols. 1940-41. Briefed translations.

Lewis Publishing Company: *History of Florida, Past and Present.* 1923. 3 vols. Historical and biographical.

Peterson, C. Stewart: *Bibliography of County Histories of the 3111 Counties in the 48 States.* Baltimore, 1946.

United States Department of State: *Territorial Papers of the United States.* Florida. Clarence E. Carter, ed. 1956. Vol.

22: *The Territory of Florida,* 1821-1824. Vol. 23, 1958. (For a summary of this source see *National Genealogical Society Quarterly,* 37:93ff.)

tary rosters, s, and ords

Civil War and Indian Wars:

Soldiers of Florida in the Seminole Indian, Civil, and Spanish American Wars. Prepared and published under the supervision of the Board of State Institutions. (Live Oak, 1909?) 368 pp. (*Florida in the War between the States:* pt. 2, pp. 33-338.)

Florida Adjutant General's Records: Records of this office pertaining to Seminole Indian Wars, 1830-1857, and the War Between the States, 1861-1865, comprise photostatic copies of salvaged muster rolls and are considered incomplete, somewhat inaccurate, and in many instances illegible. *Custodian:* Office of the Adjutant General, State Arsenal, St. Augustine, Florida.

Confederate Pension Records: Secretary, State Board of Pensions, Tallahassee, Florida.

Confederate Military Records: The National Archives has compiled the *Consolidated Index to Compiled Records of Confederate Soldiers.* The index is on cards which give the name of the soldier, his rank, the unit in which he served, and often a statement concerning the origin or background of that unit. There are cross-reference cards for soldiers' names that appeared in the records under more than one spelling. This index is available for personal search or by an agent. It is microfilmed.

cial records

Vital Records: Fee for birth, marriage, and death certificate: $2.00. Send for application form.

State Custodian: Florida State Division of Health, Bureau of Vital Statistics, P.O. Box 210, Jacksonville, Florida 32201.

Birth Records: Subsequent to 1865: Above-named State Custodian. *Delayed birth certificates:* State Custodian will furnish information.

Marriage Licenses: Subsequent to 1887: County Judge of the county in which the license is issued. *Prior to May 27, 1887:* Clerk, Circuit Court, County Seat.

Marriage Records: Subsequent to June 1927: Above-named State Custodian. *Prior to June 1927:* County Judge, County Seat, of the county where the license was issued.

Death Records: Subsequent to 1877: Above-named State Custodian.

Divorce Records: Since 1927: Bureau of Vital Statistics, State Board of Health, P.O. Box 210, Jacksonville, Florida. (If year is unknown, fee ranges from a minimum of $1.00 for each calendar year to be searched, to a maximum of

$25.00.) *Prior to 1927:* Clerk of Circuit Court in county where divorce was granted. Cost of certified copy of divorce decree varies.

Court Records: Wills, administrations, and other probate matters: Clerk, County Court, County Seat. *Other Civil Actions:* Clerk, Circuit Court, County Seat.

Land Records: Deeds, mortgages, leases, and other matters affecting title to land: Clerk, Circuit Court, County Seat.

Federal census records

1. See index for section on United States census.

2. Custody of mortality schedules, 1850, 1860, 1870, 1880: Department of Agriculture, Tallahassee, Florida.

3. The original 1880 United States census records for Florida were transferred in 1956 by the National Archives to: Florida State Library, Tallahassee, Florida.

4. *Census of 1885:* The National Archives has custody of the 1855 census of Florida, which was authorized by 20 Statutes at Large 473, in 1879. This census included a census of population of mortality. The name of each person is given, relationship to the head of the family, race, sex, age, marital status, occupation, and place of birth.

Florida state census records

The original schedules of the Florida State census prior to 1935 have been destroyed. The schedules for 1935 and 1945 are in the office of the Commissioner of Agriculture, Tallahassee, Florida. The state population census was discontinued after the latter date.

Georgia

General information

Capital: Atlanta. Entered Union: January 2, 1788. Seceded from Union: January 19, 1861. Reentered Union: July 15, 1870.

Libraries, historical societies, and archives

For a complete list see: Brown, Karl: *The American Library Directory*. Also, *Directory of Historical Societies and Agencies in the United States and Canada,* 1956.

Atlanta Historical Society, 1753 Peachtree Street, N.W., Atlanta.

Atlanta Public Library, 126 Carnegie Way, N.W., Atlanta.

Georgia Historical Society, Hodgson Hall, 501 Whitaker Street, Savannah.

Georgia Historical Commission, Secretary of State's Annex, 116 Mitchell Street, S. W., Atlanta.

State Department of Archives and History, Rhodes Memorial Hall, 1516 Peachtree Street, N. W., Atlanta.

De Renne Library, Savannah. (A large library containing rare and valuable records, but not open to the public at large.)

orgia earch ggestions

Bryan, Mary G.: "Land Grants in Georgia," *National Genealogical Society Quarterly.* Vol. 44 (March 1956), p. 1.

Bryan, Mary Givens.: "Genealogical Research in Georgia," *National Genealogical Society Quarterly.* Vol. 40 (June 1952), p. 1.

Prager, Herta, and William W. Price.: "The Bibliography on the History of the Courts of the Thirteen Original States, Maine, Georgia, Ohio and Vermont," *The American Journal of Legal History.* Vol. 1, p. 345.

ference oks

Candler, Allen D. and Clement A. Evans, eds.: *Cyclopedia of Georgia.* 3 vols. 1906. Contains sketches of counties, towns, events, institutions, and persons.

Colonial Records of the State of Georgia. 1904—.

Coulter, Ellis Merton, ed.: *A List of Early Settlers of Georgia.* 1949. 103 pp.

Coulter, E. Merton, and Albert B. Saye, eds.: *A List of the Early Settlers of Georgia.* 1949. 103 pp. Settlers from Europe prior to 1741.

Daughters of the American Revolution, Georgia: *Historical Collections of the Georgia Chapters.* Atlanta, 1926—. Index to vol. 1, published in 1931.

DAR, Georgia: *Historical Collections of the Joseph Habersham Chapter.* 3 vols. 1902-1910.

Davis, Harry Alexander: *Some Huguenot Families of South Carolina and Georgia.* 1927.

Gilmer, George Rockingham: *Sketches of Some of the First Settlers of Upper Georgia.* 1855.

Harllee, William Curry: *Kinfolks, A Genealogical and Bibliographical Record of Thomas and Elizabeth* (*Stuart*) *Harllee.* 1934. Volume 1 contains a chapter concerning states and county records and the derivation of the counties of a number of states, including Georgia.

Historical Records Survey, WPA: *Guide to Public Vital Statistics Records in Georgia.* June 1941. 72 pp.

Jones, Charles C., Jr.: *The Dead Towns of Georgia,* 1878. 263 pp.

National Society of the Colonial Dames of America, Georgia: *Some Early Epitaphs in Georgia.*

Peterson, C. Stewart: *Bibliography of County Histories of the 3111 Counties in the 48 States.* Baltimore, 1946.

Sherwood, Rev. Adiel: *A Gazetteer of the State of Georgia:* 1st ed. 1827. Reprint, 1939. 143 pp.

Strobel, Philip A.: *The Salzburgers and Their Descendants.* 1855.

United States, WPA: *Bibliography of Research Projects Reports—Check List of Historical Records Survey Publications.* 1940.

Military rosters, rolls, and records

Revolutionary War Rosters, Rolls, and Records:

Blair, Ruth: *Revolutionary Soldiers' Receipts for Georgia Bounty Lands.* 1928. 85 pp.

Houston, Martha Lou: *Six Hundred Revolutionary Soldiers Living in Georgia 1827-8.* Washington, 1932.

Knight, Lucian Lamar: *Georgia's Roster of the Revolution,* 1920. 658 pp. Also lists soldiers who settled in Georgia after the war.

McCall, Mrs. Howard H.: *Roster of Soldiers and Patriots of the American Revolution Buried in Georgia.* 1939.

McCall, Mrs. Howard H.: *Roster of Revolutionary Soldiers in Georgia.* 1941. 294 pp.

McGhee, Lucy Kate: *Georgia Pension List of All Wars from the Revolution down to 1883.* Washington, D.C., n.d. Typewritten.

War of 1812: The Adjutant General has no records of the War of 1812. These have been turned over to the Department of Archives and History, Atlanta. There are no published rosters or rolls; the existing records are in manuscript form and are available to persons who visit the archives in person. The archives cannot undertake research on staff time.

Confederate Military Records: The National Archives has compiled the *Consolidated Index to Compiled Records of Confederate Soldiers.* The index is on cards that give the name of the soldier, his rank, the unit in which he served, and often a statement concerning the origin or background of that unit. There are cross-reference cards for soldiers' names that appeared in the records under more than one spelling. This index is available for personal search or by an agent. It is microfilmed.

Confederate Pension Records: The National Archives does not have Confederate pension records. If a Confederate soldier or widow received a pension in Georgia after the war, this record will be on file with the Confederate Pension and Record Department, State Capitol, Atlanta. Confederate pensions commenced in 1879. The following information is needed to make a successful search:

1. The year the pension was applied for.

2. The county in which the pensioner made his application.

cial records

Vital Records: Fee for birth and death certificates: $3.00 each. Refer to marriage licenses and records, below.

State Custodian: Vital Records Unit, Georgia Department of Human Resources, 47 Trinity Ave., S.W., Atlanta, Ga. 30334.

Birth and Death Records: Subsequent to January 1, 1919: Above-named State Custodian. *Prior to January 1, 1919:* No records kept, except those voluntarily filed, except if birth occurred in either Atlanta or Savannah, write to Health Officer of that city. *Delayed birth certificate:* State Custodian will furnish information.

Marriage Licenses and Records: Clerk, Court of Ordinary, County Seat.

Divorce Records: Clerk of Superior Court in county where divorce was granted. Cost of certified copy of divorce decree varies.

Court Records: Wills, administrations, and other probate matters: Clerk, Court of Ordinary, County Seat. *Other Civil Actions:* Clerk, Superior Court, County Seat.

Land Records: Deeds, mortgages, leases, and other matters affecting title to land: Clerk, Superior Court, County Seat. Current records: Secretary of State (archives).

eral census
ords

1. See index for section on United States Census.

2. Custody of mortality schedules, 1850, 1860, 1870, 1880: DAR, Washington, D.C.

3. The original 1880 United States census records for Georgia were transferred in 1956 by the National Archives to: Department of Archives and History, State of Georgia, 1516 Peachtree Street, N.W., Atlanta.

rgia state
sus records

Georgia has no state census records. However, the Georgia Department of Archives and History, 1516 Peachtree Street, N.W., Atlanta, has available many yearly property tax digests by county between the years 1790 and 1820, which help supplement the lack of state censuses and any federal censuses that are missing. These records are unindexed. Records are available for personal search or by a professional; the staff does not furnish information on staff time.

Hawaii

General information

Territory of the United States since June 14, 1900. Admitted to the Union: 1959. Capital: Honolulu.

Official records

Vital Records: Fee for birth, marriage, and death certificates: $2.00. Request should state relationship and reason for which the certificate will be used in order to avoid delay.

State Custodian: State of Hawaii, Department of Health, Research and Statistics Office, P.O. Box 3378, Honolulu, Hawaii 96801.

Birth and Death Records: Write to above-named Territorial Custodian. Records commenced during the time of the Hawaiian monarchy. The records are incomplete. There has been no destruction of the records. The records are indexed.

Marriage Licenses: Marriages are required to be reported to the Circuit Court. Licenses are issued by agents appointed by the president of the Board of Health, who makes report to the Registrar of Births, Marriages, and Deaths.

Marriage Records: Records commenced as early as 1841 during the time of the monarchy. Write above custodian.

Court Records: Wills, administrations and other probate matters: Clerk, Circuit Court. *Other Civil Actions:* Clerk, United States District Court, and Circuit Court.

Land Records: (Deeds, mortgages, leases, etc.) Registrar of Conveyances, Honolulu.

Miscellaneous Records and Sources: Supreme Court Reports of the territory of Hawaii.

Idaho

General information

Capital: Boise. Organized as a Territory: March 3, 1863. Entered Union: July 3, 1890.

Libraries, historical societies, and archives

For a complete list see: Brown, Karl: *The American Library Directory.* Also, *Directory of Historical Societies and Agencies in the United States and Canada,* 1956.

Historical Society of the State of Idaho, State House, Boise.

Reference books

Daughters of the American Revolution: Idaho

Genealogical Records Committee: *Miscellaneous Records.* 1938—.

French, H.T.: *History of Idaho.* 1914. 3 vols.

Hawley, J.H.: *History of Idaho.* 1920. 3 vols.

Lewis Publishing Company: *Illustrated History of Idaho.* 1899.

Peterson, C. Stewart: *Bibliography of County Histories of the 3111 Counties in the 48 States.* Baltimore, 1946. (See also supplements for 1950 and 1955.)

Rees, J.E.: *Idaho Chronology, Nomenclature, Bibliography.* 1918.

tary rosters, s, and ords

Custodian: The Idaho Historical Society, 610 Parkway Dr., Boise, Idaho. The state militia was organized during the Nez Perce War in 1877. Discharge records of these troops are available. There is a roster of the Mount Idaho Volunteers.

cial records

Vital Records: Fee for birth, marriage, and death certificates: $2.00.

State Custodian: Bureau of Vital Statistics, Department of Environmental Protection and Health, State House, Boise, Idaho 83720.

Birth, Marriage (only a transcript sent to State Office), and Death Records: Custodian subsequent to July 1, 1911: Above-named State Custodian. *Custodian prior to July 1, 1911:* County Recorder of the County Seat in which the birth occurred. *Delayed birth certificates:* State Custodian will furnish information.

Divorce Records: County Recorder of county where divorce was granted. Cost of certified copy of divorce decree varies.

Marriage Licenses: County Recorder. No marriage licenses required prior to March 11, 1895.

Court Records: Wills, administrations, and other probate matters: Clerk, Probate Court, County Seat. *Other Civil Actions:* Clerk, District Court, County Seat.

Land Records: Deeds, mortgages, leases, and other matters affecting title to land: County Recorder, County Seat.

eral census ords

1. See index for section on United States Census.

2. Custody of mortality schedules: 1870 and 1880, Idaho Historical Society, 610 Parkway Drive, Boise, Idaho.

3. The original 1880 United States census records for Idaho were transferred in 1956 by the National Archives to: National Society, Daughters of the American Revolution, Administration Building, 1776 D Street, N.W., Washington, D.C.

o state sus records

No record of a census taken by authority of the state government has ever been found.

Illinois

General information

Capital: Springfield. Organized as a territory: February 3, 1809. Entered Union: December 3, 1818.

Libraries, historical societies, and archives

For a complete list see: Brown, Karl: *The American Library Directory.* Also, *Directory of Historical Societies and Agencies in the United States and Canada,* 1956.

Archives Division, Illinois State Library, State Archives Building, Illinois State Library, Springfield.

Bureau County Historical Society, Courthouse, Princeton.

Chicago Historical Society, Clark Street and North Avenue, Chicago.

Chicago Public Library, 78 E. Washington Street, Chicago.

Illinois State Historical Society, Illinois State Historical Library, Springfield.

Illinois State Library, Springfield.

McCormick Historical Assn., 679 Rush St., Chicago.

Newberry Library, 60 West Walton Street, Chicago.

Reference books

Bateman, Newton, and Paul Selby, eds.: *Historical Encyclopedia of Illinois.* 1900.

Galaxy Publishing Co.: *The Biographical Encyclopedia of Illinois of the 19th Century.* 1875.

Historical Records Survey, WPA: *Guide to Public Vital Statistics Records in Illinois,* 1941. 138 pp.

Historical Records Survey, WPA: *Guide to Depositories of Manuscript Collections in Illinois* (preliminary edition). 1940. 55 pp.

Illinois State Historical Society: *Journal of the Illinois State Historical Society.* Springfield.

Osborne, Georgia L.: *List of the Genealogical Works in the Illinois State Library.*

Peck, J. M.: *A Gazetteer of Illinois.* 2nd ed., 1837. 328 pp.

Peterson, C. Stewart: *Bibliography of County Histories of the 3111 Counties in the 48 States.* Baltimore, 1946.

Scott, Franklin William: *Newspapers and Periodicals of Illinois, 1814-1879.* Revised and enlarged, 1910.

United States, Department of State: *Territorial Papers of the United States.* Clarence E. Carter, ed. 1934. Vols. 2 and 3: *Territory Northwest of the Ohio River,* 1787-1803. 1948, 1950. Vols. 16, 17: *Territory of Illinois.* 1809-1818. For a summary of this source see *National Genealogical Society Quarterly, 37:93—.*

itary rosters, 's, and :ords

Revolutionary War:

Walker, Harriett J.: *Revolutionary Soldiers Buried in Illinois.* 1917.

War of 1812, Black Hawk War, 1831-32 and Mexican War, 1846-48: Illinois Adjutant General: *Record of Services of Illinois Soldiers in the Black Hawk War, 1831-32, and in the Mexican War, 1846-48,* with an appendix of the Illinois Militia, Rangers, and Riflemen in Protecting the Frontier from the Ravages of the Indians from 1810-13. By Isaac H. Elliott, Adjutant General. Springfield, 1882. This is reprinted in volume 9 of the reference immediately following.

Civil War: Report of the Adjutant General of the State of Illinois, 1861-1866. 9 vols. Phillips Bros., Springfield, 1900-1902. Previous editions of volumes 1 to 8, published in 1867 and 1886.

All Wars—Burials: Roll of Honor. Record of the Burial Places of Soldiers, Sailors, Marines, and Army Nurses of All Wars of the U.S. Buried in Illinois. 2 vols. Springfield, 1929.

Illinois Adjutant General's Records: The Illinois Adjutant General's original records for the Civil War (Illinois regiments only) have been transferred to the Illinois State Archives, Springfield. These records disclose military rank and service, age at enlistment, residence, marital status, occupation, and a physical description. Card indexes to these records are available at the State Archives.

The Graves Registration Section of the Illinois Veterans' Administration, Springfield, has such records as are available on soldiers' graves in Illinois. Also a card index to the rolls (War of 1812, Black Hawk, and Mexican wars) is printed in Elliot, *op. cit.,* and vol. 9, Illinois Adjutant General Report.

Illinois State Historical Library, Springfield (which is a separate entity) has a card index for the Black Hawk War only. In addition to indexing for military service, an effort has been made to identify the soldier.

icial records

Pease, Theodore Calvin: *The County Archives of the State of Illinois,* Springfield, 1915. Collections of the Illinois State Historical Library, Vol. XII; Bibliographical Series, Vol. III.

Vital Records: Fee for birth, marriage, and death certificates, $3.00.

State Custodian: Bureau of Statistics, Department of Public Health, Springfield, Illinois 62761.

Birth and Death Records: Subsequent to January 1, 1916: Above-named State Custodian. *Prior to January 1, 1916:* Chicago only: write Department of Health. If birth or death in an incorporated city: write City Clerk. If birth or death in an unincorporated area: write County Clerk of the County Seat. *Delayed birth certificates:* There is provision for delayed birth certificates.

Divorce Records: Clerk of the court in which divorce was granted. Courts having jurisdiction are the Circuit Court of each county, the Superior Court of Cook County, and certain city courts. Cost of certified copy varies.

Marriage Licenses: County Clerk of the County Seat.

Marriage Records: County Clerk of the County Seat. $2.00.

Court Records: Wills, administrations, and other probate matters: County Clerk, County Seat. (Counties over 70,000 have probate courts.) *Other Civil Actions:* County Clerk, County Seat; Circuit Court, County Seat.

Land Records: Deeds, mortgages, leases, and other matters affecting title to land: Recorder of Deeds, County Seat.

Federal census records

1. See index for section on United States Census.

2. The Illinois State Archives, Springfield, have microfilm copies of the United States Census records for Illinois counties for 1820-1880, except 1870. All names in the 1820 census, about 90 percent of the 1830 census, 30 percent of the 1840 census, and 25 percent of the 1850 census had been indexed as of March 3, 1958.

3. Custody of mortality schedules, 1850, 1860, 1870, 1880: Illinois State Library, Springfield, Illinois.

4. The original 1880 United States census records for Illinois were transferred in 1956 by the National Archives to: Illinois State Library, Springfield, Illinois.

Illinois state census records

1810 and 1818 Illinois State Census: See: Norton, Margaret C., ed.: *Illinois Census Returns 1810, 1818;* with introduction and notes. The trustees of the Illinois State Historical Library, Springfield, 1935. 329 pp. (Collections of the Illinois State Historical Library, v. XXIV.) Indexed.

The Illinois State Archives, Springfield, have custody of the original schedules of the censuses of the territory and state of Illinois taken in 1810, 1818, 1820, 1835, 1840, 1845, 1855, 1865. State census records have been indexed through 1845.

Availability of State and Federal Census Records—Correspondence. The Illinois State Archives will search for not more than two names in counties not indexed up to and including the 1850 census. For a search in the 1860 or 1880 census, the name of the city, village, or township must be specified. For a search in Chicago, the street and number must be given. No charge is made for this service.

Indiana

eneral formation

Capital: Indianapolis. Organized as a territory: May 7, 1800. Entered Union: December 11, 1816.

braries, storical cieties, d archives

For a complete list see: Brown, Karl: *The American Library Directory*. Also, *Directory of Historical Societies and Agencies in the United States and Canada,* 1956.

Citizens Historical Association, Chamber of Commerce Building, Indianapolis.

Henry County Historical Society, 614 South Fourteenth Street, New Castle.

Indiana Division, Indiana State Library, 140 North Senate Avenue, Indianapolis.

Indiana Historical Society, 408 State Library and Historical Building, 140 North Senate Avenue, Indianapolis.

Indiana Public Library, 40 E. St. Clair Street, Indianapolis.

Northern Indiana Historical Society, Old Courthouse, 112 South Lafayette Blvd., South Bend.

Old Settlers and Historical Association of Lake County, Crown Point.

Society of Indiana Pioneers, Indianapolis.

Spencer County Historical Society, 122 South Fourth Street, Rockport.

Tippecanoe County Historical Association, Historical Museum, 909 South Street, Lafayette.

diana search ggestions

Butz, Margaret (Ness): *Aids to Genealogical Research in the Genealogical Division of the Indiana State Library.* 19 pp. Mimeographed.

Dunn, Caroline: "Sources for Indiana Genealogical Research," *Indiana Magazine of History.* December 1943, pp. 413-21.

Genealogical Sources Available at the Indiana State Library of All Indiana Counties. 1946. 37 pp. Mimeographed.

Historical Records Survey, WPA: *A Directory of Churches and Religious Organizations in Indiana.* 3 vols. 1941.

Johnson, William Perry: "The Quaker Records of Indiana." *National Genealogical Society Quarterly.* Vol. 43 (March 1955), p. 5.

ference oks

Chamberlain, E.: *The Indiana Gazetteer,* or Topographical Dictionary of the State of Indiana. 3rd ed. 1849.

Daughters of the American Revolution (Indiana chapters): *Genealogical Records.* 5 vols. 1950-1954. Typewritten.

Peterson, C. Stewart: *Bibliography of County Histories of the 3111 Counties in the 48 States.* Baltimore, 1946. See also supplements published in 1950 and 1955.

United States Department of State: *Territorial Papers of the United States.* Clarence E. Carter, ed. 1934. Vols. 2 and 3: *Territory Northwest of the Ohio River,* 1787-1803. Vols. 7 and 8: *Indiana Territory,* 1800-1816. 1939. (For a summary of this source see *National Genealogical Society Quarterly,* 37:93ff.)

Waters, Margaret R.: *Indiana Land Entries* (1801-1877). 2 vols. 1948, 1949.

Woollen, William Wesley: *Biographical and Historical Sketches of Early Indiana.* 1883. 568 pp.

Military rosters, rolls, and records

Revolutionary War:

O'Byrne, Mrs. Roscoe C.: *Roster of Soldiers and Patriots of the American Revolution Buried in Indiana.* Indiana DAR, 1838.

Waters, Margaret R.: *Revolutionary Soldiers Buried in Indiana Not Listed in the Roster of Soldiers and Patriots of the American Revolution Buried in Indiana.* 1949. 42 pp. Mimeographed.

Waters, Margaret R.: *Revolutionary Soldiers Buried In Indiana.* A Supplement. (485 names not listed elsewhere.) 1954. 165 pp. Mimeographed.

Custodian: Indiana State Library, 140 North Senate Ave., Indianapolis.

War of 1812: The Indiana State Library has a four-volume set of photostatic copies of Muster Pay and Receipt Rolls of Indiana Territory Volunteers or Militia of the War of 1812, obtained from the Office of the War Department of the United States Adjutant General's Office. This library also has Pay Rolls of Militia in the Battle of Tippecanoe, consisting of photostats from the National Archives. The library has compiled an index to 1818 and 1835 list of pensioners and to the 1840 census of pensioners.

Mexican War: Incomplete war lists are indexed (see below).

Civil War: The Archives Division of the Indiana State Library has card files of Indiana Civil War soldiers. This index also includes some service records of the Indiana Militiamen 1860-1865 and incomplete lists of the Mexican War.

Civil War State Rosters:

Indiana Adjutant-General's Office: Report of the Adjutant-

General (Laz. Noble) of the State of Indiana, April 15, 1861-January 1, 1863. Indianapolis, 1863.

Indiana Adjutant-General's Office: Report of the Adjutant-General (Laz. Noble) January 1, 1863-November 12, 1864. Indianapolis, 1865. 33 pp.

Indiana Adjutant-General's Office: Report of the Adjutant-General (W.H.H. Terrell). Indianapolis, 1865-1869. 8 vols.

'cial records

Vital Records: Cost of birth and death certificates: $3.00.

State Custodian: Director, Division of Vital Records, State Health Department, 1330 W. Michigan St., Indianapolis, Indiana 46206.

Birth Records: Subsequent to October 1, 1907: Above-named State Custodian.

Custodian prior to October 1, 1907: County Health Officer, County Seat of the County where birth occurred. If birth occurred in a city, then write to City Health Officer of that city.

Delayed Birth Certificates: State Custodian will furnish information.

Marriage Records: Clerk, County Clerk at County Seat.

Death Records; Subsequent to October 1, 1899: Above-named State Custodian. *Prior to October 1, 1899:* Try County Health Officer, County Seat, if death in county territory; City Health Officer, City, if death occurred in a city.

Divorce Records: County clerk of county where divorce was granted. Cost of certified copy of divorce varies.

Court Records: Wills, administrations, and other probate matters: Clerk, Circuit Court, County Seat. *Other Civil Actions:* Clerk, Circuit Court, County Seat.

Land Records: Deeds, mortgages, leases, and other matters affecting title to land: County Recorder, County Seat.

deral census ords

1. See index for section on United States Census.

2. Custody of mortality schedules: 1850, 1860, 1870, 1880: Indiana State Library, Indianapolis, Indiana.

3. The original 1880 United States census records for Indiana were transferred in 1956 by the National Archives to: Library, University of Pittsburgh, Pittsburgh, Pennsylvania.

iana state nsus records

Custodian: County Auditor, County Seat. There is an incomplete preservation of state census records. Some of the counties have preserved them. Any particular record *might* be found in the custody of the County Auditor. Censuses of 1853, 1865, and 1877: Information includes names and ages.

Iowa

General information

Capital: Des Moines. Organized as a territory: June 12, 1838. Entered Union: December 28, 1846.

Libraries, historical societies, and archives

For a complete list, see: Brown, Karl: *The American Library Directory.* Also, *Directory of Historical Societies and Agencies in the United States and Canada,* 1956.

State Department of History and Archives, Des Moines.

State Historical Society of Iowa, 304 Schaeffer Hall, Iowa City.

Iowa research suggestions

McCracken, George E.: "Genealogical Resources in the Iowa Archives," *National Genealogical Society Quarterly,* vol. 41 (June 1953), p. 1.

Geographical data

Dubuque and Des Moines counties were originally a part of the territory of Wisconsin.

Reference books

Andreas, A. T.: *Historical Atlas of Iowa.* 1875.

Annals of Iowa. *A Historical Quarterly published by the Historical Department of Iowa.* 1893—.

Charts and Genealogies of Pioneer Families of Iowa. 55 pp. (N.d., no author.)

Gue, Benjamin F.: *History of Iowa.* 4 vols. 1903. Vol. 4, biographical.

Hair, James T.: *Iowa State Gazetteer . . .* 1865. 616 pp.

Historical Records Survey, WPA: *Guide to the Public Vital Statistics in Iowa.* 1941. 113 pp.

Historical Records Survey, WPA: *Guide to Depositories of Manuscript Collections in the United States.* Iowa, 1940. 47 pp.

Washington *Democrat—Independent.* Genealogical Department, Washington, Iowa.

Peterson, C. Stewart: *Bibliography of County Histories of the 3111 Counties in the 48 States.* Baltimore, 1946.

Military rosters, rolls, and records

Civil War:

Iowa State Rosters: Iowa Adjutant-General's Office: *Roster and Record of Iowa Soldiers in the War of the Rebellion, together with Historical Sketches of Volunteer Organizations, 1861-66.* 6 vols. Des Moines, 1908-11. Vol. 6 contains data on miscellaneous organizations of the Mexican War and Indian campaigns.

Iowa Adjutant-General's Office: *List of Ex-Soldiers, Sailors, and Marines Living in Iowa,* prepared by William L. Alexander, Adjutant-General. Des Moines, 1886. 772 pp.

Graves Registration: The Armed Forces Graves Registration, Adjutant-General's Office, Des Moines, has custody of a card index of veterans of all wars buried in Iowa, with records of over 86,000 soldiers. Several thousand records of veterans buried in other states and countries and lost at sea are also on file in a separate index.

icial records

Vital Records: Fee for birth, marriage, and death certificate: $2.00.

State Custodian: State Registrar, Records and Statistics Division, State Department of Health, Des Moines, Iowa 50319.

Birth, Marriage, and Death Records: Subsequent to July 1880: Above-named State Custodian. *Prior to 1880:* County Clerk, at the County Seat where birth, marriage, or death occurred. *Delayed birth certificates:* No statutory procedure for delayed birth certificate. Division of Vital Statistics issues a certificate if presented with an affidavit made by one having personal knowledge of date and place of birth.

Marriage Licenses: Clerk, District Court, County Seat.

Divorce Records: Clerk of County where divorce was granted. Cost of certified copy varies. Since 1907: Copy of partial record available. Division of Vital Statistics, State Department of Health, Des Moines, Iowa 50319.

Court Records: Wills, administrations, and other probate matters: County Clerk, County Seat.

Land Records: Deeds, mortgages, leases, and other matters affecting title to land: Recorder of Deeds, County Seat.

deral census
cords

1. See index for section on United States Census.

2. Custody of mortality schedules, 1850, 1860, 1870, 1880: State Historical Society, Iowa City.

3. The original 1880 United States census records for Iowa were transferred by the National Archives in 1956 to: National Society, Daughters of the American Revolution, Administration Building, 1776 D Street, N.W., Washington, D.C.

rritorial
nsus records

1836 Territorial Census: Des Moines and Dubuque counties only. See: *The First Census of the Original Counties of Dubuque and Des Moines.* Taken in July 1836. Benjamin F. Shambaugh, ed. Des Moines, Historical Department of Iowa, 1897-1898. 93 pp. Information included: Heads of families.

1844 Territorial Census: For Keokuk County only. Names head of family.

Iowa state census records

1847, 1849, 1854, 1856, 1885, 1895, 1905, 1915, and 1925: Information included: Head of family. (1905 Census records not available for search.) *Custodian:* Census Division, Iowa State Department of History, Historical Building, Des Moines, has custody of all territorial and state census records. Application forms are furnished.

Kansas

General information

Capital: Topeka. Organized as a territory: May 30, 1854. Entered Union: January 29, 1861.

Libraries, historical societies, and archives

For a complete list see: Brown, Karl: *The American Library Directory.* Also, *Directory of Historical Societies and Agencies in the United States and Canada,* 1956.

Augusta Historical Society, 305 State Street, Augusta.

Kansas State Historical Society, Memorial Building, Topeka.

Lyon County Historical Society, Civic Auditorium, 6th Avenue and Mechanic Street, Emporia.

Reference books

Andreas, A. T.: *History of the State of Kansas.* 1883. 1616 pp. (Some biographical sketches.)

Historical Records Survey, WPA: *Guide to the Public Vital Statistics Records in Kansas.* March 1942. 261 pp.

Kansas State Historical Society: Collections (or Transactions.) 1875—.

Lewis Publishing Company: *Genealogical and Biographical Record of Northeastern Kansas.* Illustrated. 1900.

Tuttle, Charles R.: *A New Centennial History (& Biographical Sketches) of the State of Kansas.* 1876.

Peterson, C. Stewart: *Bibliography of County Histories of the 3111 Counties in the 48 States.* Baltimore, 1946.

Military rosters, rolls, and records

Civil War—State Rosters; Kansas Adjutant-General's Office:

Report of the Adjutant General (C. K. Holliday), December 31, 1864. Leavenworth, 1865. 119, 714 pp.

Report of the Adjutant General (T. J. Anderson) of the State of Kansas in 1861-1865 (Vol. 1); 1867-1870 (Vol. 2).

Official records

Vital Records: Fee for birth, death, and marriage certificates: $2.00.

State Custodian: Division of Registration & Health Statistics, 6700 So. Topeka Ave., Topeka, Kansas 66620.

Birth and Death Records: Subsequent to July 1, 1911: Above-named State Custodian. *Prior to July 1, 1911:* Write to City Clerk, if in incorporated city or town; if in county or unincorporated area, write to County Clerk, County Seat. *Delayed birth certificates:* State Custodian will furnish information.

Marriage Licenses: Probate Judge, County Seat.

Marriage Records: Subsequent to May 1, 1913: Above-named State Custodian. *Prior to May 1, 1913:* Probate Judge, County Seat.

Divorce Records: Since July 1951: Above-named State Custodian. Cost of certified copy of divorce decree is $2.00. Prior to July 1951: Clerk of the District Court in which divorce was granted. Cost of certified copy of divorce decree varies.

Court Records: Wills, administrations, and other probate matters: Clerk, Probate Court, County Seat. *Other Civil Actions:* Clerk, District Court, County Seat.

Land Records: Deeds, mortgages, leases, and other matters affecting title to land: Recorder of Deeds, County Seat.

deral census cords

1. See index for section on United States Census.

2. Custody of mortality schedules, 1860, 1870, 1880: Kansas State Historical Society, Topeka. This society also has copies of the 1860, 1870, and 1880 Federal censuses.

3. The original 1880 United States census records for Kansas were transferred by the National Archives in 1956 to: National Society, Daughters of the American Revolution, Administration Building, 1776 D Street, N.W., Washington, D.C.

ate census cords

The Kansas State Historical Society, Newspaper, and Census Division, Topeka, Kansas, has custody of census records taken by the State of Kansas.

1855 Census: This was a territorial census. It contains the following information: head of house, age, sex, occupation, place of residence, emigrated from (state or nation), if a native of the U.S.

1865 Census: Head of house, members of household, age, sex, color, occupation, place of birth, value of estate, place of residence.

1875 Census: Same data as in 1865; added information: where from before moving to Kansas, if applicable.

1885 Census: Same data as in 1875 census, except value of estate not disclosed. Added information: military record.

1895, 1905, 1915, and 1925 state census records contain the same information as the 1885 state census.

These records are available for personal research. Minimum charge for search by the society: $1.00. If the Kansas State Historical Society is asked to make an extended search, an hourly rate is charged. An application form with instructions is furnished on request.

Kentucky

General information

Capital: Frankfort. Entered the Union: June 1, 1792.

Libraries, historical societies, and archives

For a complete list, see Brown, Karl: *The American Library Directory*. Also, *Directory of Historical Societies and Agencies in the United States and Canada,* 1956.

Filson Club, 118 W. Breckinridge Street, Louisville.

Henderson County Historical Society, Henderson Public Library, Henderson.

Kentucky Dept. of Library and Archives, Frankfort.

Kentucky Historical Society, Old State House, Frankfort.

Louisville Free Public Library, 301-333 Library Park, Louisville.

Southern Historical Association, History Department, University of Kentucky, Lexington.

Kentucky research suggestions

Burns, Annie Walker: "Aids to Genealogical Research in Kentucky," *National Genealogical Society Quarterly.* Vol. 38 (September 1950), pp. 74-76.)

Coleman, J. Winston, Jr.: *A Bibliography of Kentucky History.* 1949. 516 pp.

Dorman, John Frederick: "Some Sources for Kentucky Genealogical Research," *National Genealogical Society Quarterly.* Vol. 42 (March 1954), p. 1.

Hardin, Bayless E.: "Genealogical Research in Kentucky," *National Genealogical Society Quarterly,* Vol. 37 (September 1949), p. 1.

Place Names: For place name problems write the Department of Geography, University of Kentucky, Lexington. This institution is compiling a large-scale gazetteer of the state's 40,000 place names.

Reference books

Ardery, Mrs. William Breckinridge: *Kentucky Records, Early Wills and Marriages . . . Old Bible Records and*

Tombstone Inscriptions. Lexington, DAR, 1926. 206 pp. Vol. 2, 1932.

Armstrong, O.J. Co.: *Biographical Encyclopedia of Kentucky of the Dead and Living Men of the 19th Century.* 1878.

Burns, Annie W.: *County Marriages* (many volumes, military records from counties). Also *Kentucky Genealogical and Historical Recorder,* vols. 1-10. Mistakes found in spelling and copying—verify.

Collins, Richard H.: *History of Kentucky,* 1924.

Connelley, William E.: *Eastern Kentucky Papers—the Founding of Harman's Station.* 1910.

Ely, William: *Big Sandy Valley*—A History of the People and Country from the Earliest Settlement to the Present Time. 1887. Contains valuable genealogy.

Filson Club Publications, Louisville: *Historical Quarterly.* Contains valuable family history.

Green, Thomas Marshall: *Historic Families of Kentucky.* 1889.

Gresham, John M. Co.: *Biographical Cyclopedia of the Commonwealth of Kentucky.* 1896.

Hardin, Bayless E.: *Scott's Papers, Kentucky Court and Other Records.* Hattie Marshall Scott, comp. Kentucky Historical Society, 1953. 251 pp.

Heineman, Charles Brunk and Gaius Marcus Brumbaugh: *First Census of Kentucky.* 1940. Based on tax rolls of counties of Kentucky.

Historical Records Survey, WPA: *Guide and Check List of County Governmental Organization and County Record System, Past and Present of Kentucky Counties.* 1937. 77 pp.

Historical Records Survey, WPA: *Guide to Public Vital Statistics Records in Kentucky.* 1942. 255 pp.

Jillson, Willard Rouse: *Old Kentucky Entries and Deeds, Wills.* 1926. Valuable.

Jillson, Willard Rouse: *The Kentucky Land Grants, A Systematic Index to All Land Grants in the Land Office at Frankfort, 1782-1924.* 1925.

King, J. Estelle Stewart: *Abstract of Early Kentucky Wills and Inventories.* 1933. 281 pp. Mimeographed.

McAdams, Ednah Wilson: *Kentucky Pioneers and Court Records.* 1929. Contains abstracts of early wills, deeds, and marriages.

Peterson, C. Stewart: *Bibliography of County Histories of the 3111 Counties in the 48 States.* Baltimore, 1946.

Smith, W. T.: *A Complete Index of Names Mentioned in Littell's Laws of Kentucky.* 1931.

United States Department of State: *Territorial Papers of the United States.* Clarence E. Carter, ed. Vol. 4: Territory South of the River Ohio. For a summary of this source see *National Genealogical Society Quarterly,* 37:93ff.

Military rosters, rolls, and records

Revolutionary War Rolls, etc.:

Bell, Annie W. B.: *Revolutionary War Soldiers Who Settled and Lived in Kentucky Counties.* 1935. 63 pp. Typewritten.

Quisenberry, Anderson Chenault: "Revolutionary Soldiers in Kentucky." (See *S.A.R. Yearbook,* Kentucky Society, pp. 49-278, Louisville, 1896.)

War of 1812: Kentucky Adjutant General Sam E. Hill: *Report of the Adjutant General of Kentucky—Soldiers of the War of 1812.* Frankfort, 1891. 370 pp.

Peterson, Clarence Stewart: *Known Dead During the War of 1812.* April 1955. 75 pp. Pamphlet.

Civil War:

Kentucky Adjutant General: (Union) *Report of the Adjutant General* (D.W. Lindsey), 1861-1866. Frankfort, 1866; 1867. 2 vols.

Confederate Records: Report of Adjutant General of Kentucky. Abner Harris, comp. Vol. 1, c. 1915.

Report of the Office of Commissioner of Pensions. Vol. 2, 1918.

Official records

Vital Records: Fee for birth, marriage, and death certificates: $2.00

State Custodian: Office of Vital Statistics, State Department of Health, 275 East Main St., Frankfort 40601.

Birth and Death Records: Subsequent to January 1, 1911: Above-named State Custodian. *Prior to January 1, 1911:* No complete records. The cities of Louisville and Covington kept birth and death records from 1898 to 1911; address Health Department of these cities. *Delayed birth certificates:* There is no statutory provision for delayed birth certificates. If court proceedings instituted to prove birth, the rules of evidence apply.

Marriage Licenses: Clerk, County Court, county in which license is issued.

Marriage Records: County Clerk, County Seat.

Divorce Records: Clerk of District Court, or Clerk of Circuit Court, in county where divorce was granted. Since July 1, 1958, Office of Vital Statistics, State Department of Health, Louisville, Kentucky 40601. Cost of copy varies.

Court Records: Wills, administrations, and other probate matters: Clerk, County Court, County Seat. *Other Civil Actions:* Clerk, County Court, County Seat.

Land Records: Deeds, mortgages, leases, and other matters affecting title to land: County Clerk, County Seat.

deral census ords

1. See index for section on United States Census.

2. Custody of mortality schedules, 1850, 1860, 1870, 1880: DAR, Washington, D.C.

3. The original 1880 United States census records for Kentucky were transferred in 1956 by the National Archives to: Library, University of Pittsburgh, Pittsburgh, Pennsylvania.

ntucky state nsus records

State census records were taken from 1803 until 1890, but heads of families were not listed by name.

Louisiana

neral ormation

Capital: Baton Rouge. Organized as a territory: March 26, 1804. Entered Union: April 30, 1812. Seceded from Union: January 26, 1861. Reentered Union: May 26, 1865.

raries, orical ieties, d archives

For a complete list, see: Brown, Karl: *The American Library Directory.* Also, *Directory of Historical Societies and Agencies in the United States and Canada,* 1956.

Louisiana Genealogical & Historical Society, P.O. Box 335, Baton Rouge.

Louisiana Historical Society, Cabildo, 521 Carondelet Building, New Orleans.

Louisiana State Museum Library, New Orleans.

Louisiana State University Department of Archives and Manuscripts, Louisiana State University, Baton Rouge.

New Orleans Public Library, 1031 St. Charles Avenue, New Orleans.

Secretary, Howard Memorial Library, New Orleans.

erence ks

Arthur, Stanley C.: *Old Families of Louisiana* (Genealogical). 1931.

Davis, Edwin A.: *Plantation Life in the Florida Parishes of Louisiana.* 1836-46. Most of the parish records are of Catholics.

Grant, O. V.: Typed copy, *Cemetery Records of Louisiana.* 1935. 7 Parishes. Vol. 1: Morgan City, etc.

Historical Records Survey: *Inventory of the State Archives of Louisiana.* 1941-1942.

Historical Records Survey: *Guide to the Manuscript Collections in Louisiana.* William Ransom Hogan, ed. Department of Archives, Louisiana State University. Vol. 1., 1940. 55 pp.

Historical Records Survey, WPA: *County-Parish Boundaries in Louisiana.* October 1939. 139 pp.

Historical Records Survey, WPA: *Guide to the Public Vital Statistics Records in Louisiana.* 1942. 77 pp.

Historical Records Survey, WPA: *Guide to Vital Statistics Records of Church Archives in Louisiana.* 2 vols. 1942.

Kendall, John S.: *History of New Orleans, Louisiana.* 3 volumes and good index in vol. 1, 1922.

O'Pry, Maude Hearn: *Chronicles of Shreveport, Louisiana.* 1927.

Perrin, William: *Southwest Louisiana, Biographical and Historical.* 1891.

Peterson, C. Stewart: *Bibliography of County Histories of the 3111 Counties in the 48 States.* Baltimore, 1946.

Portre-Bobinski, Germaine: *"Natchitoches," The Oldest Town in Louisiana.* 1936.

Seabold, Herman B.: *Old Plantation Louisiana* (life, homes, family trees). 2 vols. 1941. Many illustrations and coat-of-arms.

Tanquay, Cyprien: *Dictionnaire genealogique des familles Canadiennes, etc.* 7 volumes written in French. Records of the first French inhabitants of Louisiana and the settlement between Louisiana and Canada. Vol. 4, mostly devoted to the families that were "taken" to La.P. Vol. 4, published 1887.

United States, Department of State: *Territorial Papers of the United States.* Clarence E. Carter, ed. 1940. Vol. 9, *Orleans Territory.* 1803-1812. For a summary of this source, see *National Genealogical Society Quarterly,* 37:93ff.

United States, WPA: *Bibliography of Research Projects Reports—Check List of Historical Records Survey Publications.* 1943.

Military rosters, rolls, and records

War of 1812:

There are two sets of records pertaining to the service of Louisianians in the War of 1812: *The Compiled Service Records of Louisianians* and the *Index* to the same. Both of these are held by the National Archives.

Louisiana State Military Records: Custodian: Office of the Adjutant General, Jackson Barracks, New Orleans.

War of 1812: The Louisiana Adjutant General has custody of a microfilm copy of the index to *The Compiled Service Records of Louisianians in the War of 1812,* the original of which is in the National Archives mentioned above. Some militia records of the period of 1812-1815 are also retained.

Civil War:

Confederate Military Records: The National Archives have compiled the *Consolidated Index to Compiled Records of Confederate Soldiers.* The index is on cards, which give the name of the soldier, his rank, the unit in which he served, and often a statement concerning the origin or background of that unit. There are cross-reference cards for soldiers' names that appeared in the records under more than one spelling. This index is available for personal search or by an agent. It is microfilmed.

Records of Louisiana Confederate Soldiers and Louisiana Confederate Commands. Andrew B. Booth, comp. 3 vols. 1920. These volumes comprise an "Alphabetical Roll of Such Official Records of the Individual Confederate Soldiers as Are to Be Found in the United States Records and State Official Rolls."

Louisiana Militia: Miscellaneous *Historical Military Data* (about 396 volumes), collected and compiled by the Historical Records Survey, WPA.

Louisiana Pension Records: Old pension records are maintained by the Office of Supervisor of Confederate Pensions, Louisiana State Department of Public Welfare, Baton Rouge, Louisiana.

Availability of Records: The Adjutant General will furnish statements of military service whenever identification can be made from the records. No other research is undertaken. The Louisiana Adjutant General's library and records are open to the public.

cial records

Vital Records: Fee for birth, marriage, and death certificate: $2.00.

State Custodian: Except New Orleans: Division of Public Health Statistics, Louisiana State Department of Health, P.O. Box 60630, New Orleans, Louisiana 70160. New Orleans only: Bureau of Vital Records, Room 1W03, City Hall, New Orleans, Louisiana 70112.

Birth and Death Records: Subsequent to July 1, 1914: Address above State Custodian, except for birth and death records of the parish and city of New Orleans. For birth and death records there, write to City Health Department, New Orleans. Fee: $1.00. *Prior to July 1, 1914:* Parish Clerk of the Parish Seat, except for birth and death records of the parish and city of New Orleans. For birth and death records there, write to City Health Department, New Orleans.

Local Custodian 1811-1845: Parish Judge.

Local Custodian 1845-1879: Parish Recorder of births and deaths.

Local Custodian 1879: Parish Recorder abolished. Clerk of District Court is recorder of many instruments, but no reference is made to birth and death records.

Local Custodian 1882-1914: Local boards of health in incorporated towns provided for the power to pass ordinances for registration of birth and death records.

Delayed Birth Certificates: State Custodian will furnish information.

Marriage Licenses: Clerks of the Court in the various parishes, parish seat. Except in the Parish of New Orleans and City of New Orleans, licenses are issued by the City Board of Health and the Judge of the City Court.

Marriage Records: Clerk of Court, Parish Seat of the parish has custody of marriage records, except in the parish and city of New Orleans; the City Bureau of Vital Records, City Health Department, New Orleans, has custody there. $2.00.

Divorce Records: Clerk of parish where divorce was granted. Cost of certified copy of divorce decree varies.

Court Records: Wills, administrations, and other probate matters: Clerk, District Court of the various parishes. *Other Civil Actions:* Clerk, District Court of the various parishes.

Land Records: Deeds, mortgages, leases, and other matters affecting title to land: Register of Conveyances of the various parishes.

Federal census records

1. See index for section on United States Census.

2. Custody of mortality schedules, 1850, 1860, 1870, 1880: DAR, Washington, D.C.

3. The original 1880 United States census records for Louisiana were transferred in 1956 by the National Archives to: Louisiana State University, Baton Rouge, Louisiana.

State census records

No census has ever been taken by Louisiana of genealogical value. However, some manuscript (unpublished) censuses may be in local courthouses in Louisiana together with such related records as lists of land owners and tax assessment rolls.

Pre-statehood census records

Spanish: Some censuses for Spanish colonial Louisiana are in the Spanish Archives in Seville, Spain. Some of the Spanish archives have been microfilmed, and the films are in the Library of Congress.

French: Some censuses for French colonial Louisiana are in the French National Archives in Paris. Copies of some were made and are published in the *Publications of the Louisiana Historical Society* and in the *Louisiana Historical Quarterly.*

v Orleans sus of 1805

New Orleans City Council: *New Orleans in 1805, A Directory and a Census.* The Pelican Gallery, Inc., 1936.

Maine

neral rmation

Capital: Augusta. Entered the Union: March 15, 1820.

aries, orical ieties, archives

For a complete list see: Brown, Karl: *The American Library Directory.* Also, *Directory of Historical Societies and Agencies in the United States and Canada,* 1956.

Aroostook County Historical Museum of Houlton, Main Street, Houlton.

Bangor Historical Society, Bangor Public Library, Bangor.

Camden Historical Society, 10 Main Street, Camden.

Kennebec Historical Society Library, Augusta.

Librarian, Dyer Library, Saco.

Lincoln Historical Society, 7 Main Street, Lincoln.

Maine Historical Society, 485 Congress Street, Portland.

Penobscot Historical Society, School Street, Brunswick.

Maine State Library, Augusta.

ne research gestions

The Seattle Genealogical Society reports the following caption errors affecting three towns in the printed 1790 Census for Maine. The correct captions are as follows: Waldoboro should be Bristol, Bristol should be Nobleboro, and Nobleboro should have been captioned Waldoboro.

erence oks

Daughters of the American Revolution: Genealogical Records (Vital, Cemetery and Church Records, etc.). Compiled and typed by various chapters of the DAR, arranged by the Genealogical Society, Salt Lake City, Utah. 1950. 239 pp.

Historical Records Survey, WPA: *Directory of Churches and Religious Organizations in Maine.* 1940. 166 pp.

Libby, Charles Thornton, Sybil Noyes, and Walter Goodwin Davis: *Genealogical Dictionary of Maine and New Hampshire.* 5 parts. 1928-1938.

Little, George Thomas: *Genealogical and Family History of the State of Maine.* 4 vols. 1909.

"Maine Genealogists and Biographer," *A Quarterly Journal.* 3 vols. 1875-1878.

Maine Historical and Genealogical Recorder. 9 vols. 1884-1898.

Maine Historical Society: Collections, 1st, 2nd, and 3d series. 1831—.

Maine Historical Society: *Documentary History of the State of Maine.* 24 vols. 1869-1916.

Peterson, C. Stewart: *Bibliography of County Histories of the 3111 Counties in the 48 States.* Baltimore, 1946.

Pope, Charles Henry: *The Pioneers of Maine and New Hampshire.* 1623 to 1660. 1908.

Province and Court Records of Maine. Portland. Vol. 1, 1928; vol. 2, 1931; vol. 3, 1947; vol. 4, 1957.

Prager, Herta, and William W. Price: "A Bibliography on the History of the Courts of the Thirteen Original States, Maine, Ohio and Vermont," *American Journal of Legal History.* Vol. 1, p. 348.

Sargent, William Mitchell: *Maine Wills.* 1640-1760. 1887.

Spencer, Wilbur Daniel: *Pioneers on Maine Rivers.* With lists to 1651. 1930.

Sprague's *Journal of Maine History.* 14 vols. 1913-1926.

United States Bureau of the Census: *Heads of Families at the First Census, 1790.* Maine, 1908. (Originally taken as part of Massachusetts.)

United States, WPA: *Bibliography of Research, Projects Reports—Check List of Historical Records Survey Publications.* 1943.

Varney, Geo. J.: *A Gazetteer of Maine.* 1881.

Military rosters, rolls, and records

Baker, Mary Ellen: "Autobiography of Lists of New England Soldiers." Boston. *New England Historic Genealogical Society,* 1911. 56 pp.

Revolutionary War: Flagg, Charles Allcott: "An Alphabetical Index of Revolutionary Pensioners Living in Maine, Dover, 1920." Reprint of Sprague's *Journal of Maine History.*

House, Charles J.: *Names of Soldiers of the American Revolution Who Applied for State Bounty, Augusta, 1893.* Maine was a part of Massachusetts at the time of the Revolution, and therefore the Massachusetts rolls should be examined.

War of 1812: Massachusetts Adjutant General's Office:

Records of Massachusetts Volunteer Militia called out by the governor of Massachusetts to suppress a threatened invasion during the War of 1812-14. John Baker, comp. Published by Brigadier General Gardner W. Pearson, the Adjutant General of Massachusetts. 1913. 448 pp.

Civil War: Maine Adjutant General's Office, Reports of the Adjutant General for 1861-1866. Supplement: "Index of Maine Volunteers—War of 1861." 1867.

cial records

Vital Records: Fee for birth, marriage, and death certificate: $2.00.

State Custodian: Office of Vital Statistics, Department of Health and Welfare, State House, Augusta, Maine 04333.

Birth, Marriage, and Death Records: Subsequent to 1892: Address above State Custodian. *Prior to 1892:* Address Town Clerk or City Clerk of the town or city in which the birth, marriage, or death occurred. *Delayed birth certificate:* Town or City Clerk will furnish information.

Marriage Licenses: Town Clerk or City Clerk. The above-named State Custodian states that copies of the local records in the custody of the Town or City Clerks are filed with the State Custodian, and the original records remain with the local custodian. Therefore, the local clerks are custodians of all their original vital records, and the state files have central registration dating from 1892.

Divorce Records: Clerk of Superior Court in county where divorce was granted. Letter verifying place and date available from Division of Vital Statistics, State Department of Health and Welfare, Augusta, Maine. Cost of certified copy of divorce decree is $2.00.

Court Records: Wills, administrations, and other probate matters: Register of Probate, County Seat. *Other Civil Actions:* Clerk, Superior Court, County Seat.

Land Records: Deeds, mortgages, leases, and other matters affecting title to land: Registry of Deeds, County Seat.

leral census ords

1. See index for section on United States Census.

2. Custody of mortality schedules, 1850, 1860, 1870, and 1880: Maine Historical Society, Portland.

3. The original 1880 United States census records for Maine were transferred in 1956 by the National Archives to: Division of Vital Statistics, Department of Health and Welfare of the State of Maine, Augusta.

e census ords

No record of a state census taken by state authority has ever been found.

Maryland

General information

Capital: Annapolis. Entered the Union: April 28, 1788

Libraries, historical societies, and archives

For a complete list, see: Brown, Karl: *The American Library Directory.* Also, *Directory of Historical Societies and Agencies in the United States and Canada,* 1956.

Enoch Pratt Free Library, 400 Cathedral Street, Baltimore.

Hall of Records of Maryland, Annapolis.

Historical Society of Frederick County, Frederick.

Historical Society of Harford County, Bel Air.

Maryland Historical Society, 201 W. Monument Street, Baltimore.

Maryland State Library, Annapolis.

Maryland research suggestions

Bulletin No. 10, Index Holdings, 1956. Maryland Hall of Records. Lists records available.

"Family Notes and Miscellaneous Index of Family Data in the Hall of Records at Annapolis, Maryland." *National Genealogical Society Quarterly.* 33:67-69; 34:11-12; 34:80-83.

Passano, Eleanor Phillips: *An Index of the Source Records of Maryland; Genealogical, Biographical, Historical.* 1940. 478 pp.

Prager, Herta, and William W. Price: "A Bibliography on the History of the Courts of the Thirteen Original States, Maine, Ohio and Vermont." *American Journal of Legal History.* Vol. 1, p. 349.

Reference books

Bell, Annie Walker Burns: *Maryland Wills 1686-1772.* (n.d.)

Bromwell, Henrietta Elizabeth: *Old Maryland Families:* A Collection of Charts Compiled from Public Records, Wills, Family Bibles, Tomb Inscriptions, and Other Original Sources. 1916.

Brumbaugh, Gaius Marcus: *Maryland Records,* Colonial Revolutionary, County and Church, from Original Sources. 1915, 1928.

Cotton, Jane (Baldwin): *The Maryland Calendar of Wills.* 1635-1743. 8 vols. 1904-1928.

Magruder, James Mosby: *Index of Maryland Colonial Wills,* 1634-1777, at Land Office, Annapolis, Md. 3 vols. c. 1933.

Magruder, James Mosby: *Magruder's Maryland Colonial Abstracts: Wills, Accounts and Inventories, c.* 1772-1777. 4 vols. 1934-35.

Maryland Genealogical Bulletin, January 1930—.

Maryland Historical Magazine, March 1906.

Maryland Publications of the Hall of Records Commission:

Catalogue of Archives Material, 1942.

Land Office and Prerogative Court Records of Colonial Maryland. 1946.

Calendar of Maryland State Papers: No. 1: *The Black Books,* 1943. No. 2: *The Bank Stock Papers,* 1947. No. 3: *The Brown Books,* 1948. No. 4, Pt. 1: *The Red Books,* 1950. No. 4, Pt. 2: *The Red Books,* 1953. No. 4, Part 3: *The Red Books,* 1955. No. 5: *Executive Miscellanea,* 1958.

Neil, Edward Duffield: *The Founders of Maryland as Portrayed in Manuscripts, Provincial Records and Early Documents.* 1876.

Peterson, C. Stewart: *Bibliography of County Histories of the 3111 Counties in the 48 States. Baltimore, 1946.*

Richardson, Mrs. Hester (Dorsey): *Sidelights on Maryland History, with Sketches of Early Maryland Families.* 2 vols. 1913.

Ridgely, Helen West: *A Calendar of Memorial Inscriptions Collected in the State of Maryland.* 1906.

Ridgely, Helen West: *Historic Graves of Maryland and the District of Columbia.* 1908.

Scharf, John Thomas: *History of Maryland from the Earliest Period to the Present Day,* 3 vols. 1879.

Scharf, John Thomas: *History of Western Maryland,* 2 vols. 1882.

Skirven, Percy Granger: *The First Parishes of the Province of Maryland.* c. 1923.

United States Bureau of the Census: *Heads of Families at the First Census of the United States Taken in the Year 1790. Maryland,* 1907.

United States WPA: *Bibliography of Research Projects Reports*—Check List of Historical Records Survey Publications. 1940.

tary rosters, ;, and ords

Pension Records: The Hall of Records, Annapolis, has custody of a photostatic copy of an index of the Laws of Maryland between 1800 and 1920, containing much material on military pensions.

Revolutionary War:

Brumbaugh, Gaius Marcus: *Revolutionary Records of Maryland,* 1924.

Maryland Historical Society: *Muster Rolls and Other Records of Service of Maryland Troops in the American*

Revolution, 1775-1783. Baltimore, 1900. (See Vol. 18, Archives of Maryland.)

War of 1812:

Marine, William N.: *British Invasion of Maryland, 1812-1815.* Baltimore, 1913. In this book is a list, prepared by Louis H. Dielman, of Marylanders who served in the War of 1812. It is not an official roster but may be used as a substitute.

Militia Appointments: This is a manuscript volume in the possession of the Hall of Records, Annapolis, Maryland, which discloses terms of service of those of rank before, during, and after 1812.

Civil War—State Roster:

History and Roster of Maryland Volunteers, War of 1861-65. Prepared under authority of the General Assembly of Maryland. 2 vols. Baltimore, 1898-1899.

Maryland Publications of the Hall of Records Commission No. 3: *Index to the Maryland Line in the Confederate Army.* 1945.

Official records

Centralization of Records: The Hall of Records, Annapolis, Maryland 21404, has custody of records from the beginning of Maryland to various periods in the nineteenth century, depending on the type of records. Among other records it has the following:

1. "All extant will records of all counties on microfim or volume form from the beginning to 1950," as well as many other probate records.

2. Land records from most counties up to 1850, either in original form or on microfilm.

3. A photostatic copy of an index of the Laws of Maryland between 1800 and 1920, with much material about pension records.

Vital Records: Fee for birth, marriage, and death certificate: $2.00.

State Custodian: Division of Vital Records, Maryland State Department of Health, 201 West Preston Street, Baltimore, Maryland 21203.

Birth and Death Records: Subsequent to 1898: Above-named State Custodian, except for City of Baltimore, for which custodian is Commissioner of Health, City Bureau of Vital Statistics, Baltimore. *Prior to 1898:* Records practically nonexistent except for city of Baltimore, for which address as above. *Delayed birth certificates:* State Custodian will furnish information.

Marriage Licenses: Clerk of Circuit Court in the county in which marriage was performed. In the city of Baltimore, Clerk of the Court of Common Pleas.

Marriage Records: Subsequent to April 13, 1914: Above-named State Custodian or same as marriage licenses. *Prior to April 13, 1914:* Same as marriage licenses.

Divorce Records: Except Baltimore: Clerk of the Circuit Court where divorce was granted. Cost of certified copy of divorce decree, $1.50. Baltimore city: Clerk of the Circuit Court of Baltimore city, or clerk of the Circuit Court Number 2, Baltimore. Cost of certified copy of divorce decree varies.

Court Records: Wills, administrations, and other probate matters: See Centralization of Records above. *Other Civil Actions:* Clerk, Circuit Court, County Seat. Supreme Bench for Baltimore city.

Land Records: Deeds, mortgages, leases, and other matters affecting title to land: Clerk, Circuit Court, County Seat, or for Baltimore, City Clerk, Superior Court, Court House, Baltimore, Maryland. (See Centralization of Records above.)

eral census rds

1. See index for section on United States Census.

2. Custody of mortality schedules, 1850, 1860, 1870, 1880: State Library, Annapolis, Maryland.

3. The original 1880 United States census records for Maryland were transferred in 1956 by the National Archives to: Maryland Hall of Records, State of Maryland, Annapolis, Maryland.

land state us records

Pre-Statehood Census:

Custodian: Hall of Records, Annapolis, Maryland.

1776, Colonial census: Nine counties.

1777, Colonial census: Statewide, though somewhat imperfect in coverage.

Information included in censuses: Heads of families, names of persons in the family, ages and sex. Availability of records: Card index of the name of every man is available for personal search or by agent.

Massachusetts

eral nation

Capital: Boston. Entered the Union: February 6, 1788.

ries, rical ties, archives

For a complete list, see: Brown, Karl: *The American Library Directory.* Also, *Directory of Historical Societies and Agencies in the United States and Canada,* 1956.

Adams Memorial Society, Adams Mansion, 135 Adams Street, Quincy.

Andover Historical Society, Amos Blanchard house, 97 Main Street, Andover.

American Antiquarian Society, Salisbury St. & Park Ave., Worcester.

Boston Public Library, Copley Square, Boston.

Beverly Historical Society, Andrew Cabot Mansion House, 117 Cabot Street, Beverly.

Billerica Historical Society, Billerica.

Brookline Historical Society, 347 Harvard Street, Brookline.

Connecticut Valley Historical Society, State & Chestnut Streets, Springfield.

Dedham Historical Society, 612 High Street, Dedham.

Dorchester Historical Society, Courthouse, Dorchester.

Essex Institute, 132 Essex Street, Salem.

Historical Society of Old Newbury, High and Winter Streets, Newburyport.

Hyde Park Historical Society, Weld Hall, Public Library Building, Hyde Park.

Lowell Historical Society, Memorial Building, 722 East Merrimack, Lowell.

Lynn Historical Society, 125 Green, Lynn.

Marblehead Historical Society, Lee Mansion, Washington Street, Marblehead.

Massachusetts Historical Society, 1154 Boylston Street, Boston.

Massachusetts State Library, Boston. (Newspaper collection.)

Nantucket Historical Association, Nantucket.

New England Historic and Genealogical Society, 101 Newbury, Boston 02116.

Northampton Historical Society, 58 Bridge Street, Northampton.

Old Bridgewater Historical Society, Howard Street, West Bridgewater.

Old Colony Historical Society, 66 Church Green, Taunton.

Pilgrim Society, Pilgrim Hall, Court Street, Plymouth.

Pocumtuck Valley Memorial Association, Memorial Hall, Deerfield.

Sandwich Historical Society, Main Street, Sandwich.

Somerville Historical Society, corner of Central Street and Westwood Road, Somerville.

South Natick Historical, Natural History and Library Society, Bacon Free Library Building, Elliot Street, South Natick.

Wenham Historical Association, Wenham.

Weymouth Historical Society, Library Building, Columbia Square, South Weymouth.

Winchester Historical Society, Public Library, Winchester.

Worcester Free Public Library, 12 Elm Street, Worcester.

Worcester Historical Society, 39 Salisbury Street, Worcester.

Berkshire Atheneum, Berkshire.

Springfield Public Library, Springfield.

Sudbury Public Library, Sudbury.

Westfield Public Library, Westfield.

sachusetts arch gestions

For a list of sources in which Massachusetts vital records have been published see: *National Genealogical Society Quarterly,* vol. 31, p. 83, and vol. 32, p. 17.

For a list of unpublished records of Massachusetts cities and towns incorporated after 1850, see an article by Winifred Lovering Holman, F.A.S.G., in *National Genealogical Society Quarterly, December* 1957, pp. 199ff.

Prager, Herta, and William W. Price: "A Bibliography on the History of the Courts of the Thirteen Original States, Maine, Ohio, and Vermont." *The American Journal of Legal History,* vol. 1, p. 351.

sachusetts graphical a

Cook, Frederic W.: *Historical Data Relating to Counties, Cities and Towns in Massachusetts.* 1948. This work of 92 pages discloses dates of formation of towns and counties. It also contains a valuable list of "Extinct Places," towns, and other places that no longer exist.

erence ks

Andrews, Henry Franklin: *List of Freemen, Massachusetts Bay Colony from 1630 to 1691.* 1906.

Bailey, Frederick William: *Early Massachusetts Marriages prior to 1800.* 3 vols. 1897—.

Banks, Charles Edward: *The English Ancestry and Homes of the Pilgrim Fathers.* c. 1929.

Banks, Charles Edward: *The Planters of the Commonwealth: A Study of the Emigrants and Emigration in Colonial Times, 1620-1640.* 1930.

Banks, Charles Edward: *The Winthrop Fleet of 1630.* 1930.

Bowditch, Nathaniel Ingersoll: *Suffolk Surnames.* 3d ed., 1861.

Bowen, Richard LeBaron: *Massachusetts Records.* 1957.

Bowman, George Ernest: *The Mayflower Compact and Its Signers.* 1920.

Colonial Society of Massachusetts: Publications, 1892. Index to vols. 1-25, published 1932.

Dedham Historical Register. 14 vols. 1890-1903.

Essex Antiquarian, 13 vols. 1897-1909.

Essex Institute: Historical Collections. 1859.

Flagg, Charles Allcott: *An Index of Pioneers from Massachusetts to the West.* 1915.

Flagg, Charles Allcott: *A Guide to Massachusetts Local History.* 1907.

Historical and Genealogical Researches and Recorder of Passing Events of Merrimack Valley. 1 vol. 1857-1858.

Hurd, Charles Edwin: *Genealogy and History of Representative Citizens of the Commonwealth of Massachusetts.* 1902.

Massachusetts (Colony and Province): *Records of the Governor and Company of Massachusetts Bay in New England.* 1853-1854. 5 vols. in 6.

Massachusetts (Colony): *The Probate Records of Essex Co., Massachusetts.* 3 vols. 1916-1920.

Massachusetts Historical Society: *Collections.* 1792.

Massachusetts Historical Society: *Proceedings.* 1859.

Massachusetts Magazine. 11 vols. in 10. 1908-1918.

Mayflower Descendant. 34 vols. January 1899.

McAuslan, William Alexander: *Mayflower Index,* 2 vols. 1932.

Peterson, C. Stewart: *Bibliography of County Histories of the 3111 Counties in the 48 States.* Baltimore, 1946.

Pope, Charles Henry: *The Pioneers of Massachusetts.* 1900. (Known as Pope's *Pioneers.*)

Pope, Charles Henry: *The Plymouth Scrapbook.* 1918.

Sewall, Samuel: *The Diary of Samuel Sewall, 1674-1729.* In Massachusetts Historical Society: *Collections.* Series 5, vols. 5-7, 1878-1882.

Shurtleff, N.B. et al., eds.: *Records of the Colony of New Plymouth in New England.* 1620-1692. 12 vols. Boston, 1855-1861.

Suffolk County: *Suffolk Deeds.* 14 vols. 1880-1906.

United States Bureau of the Census: *Heads of Families at the First Census of the United States Taken in the Year 1790.* Massachusetts, 1908.

United States, WPA: *Bibliography of Research Projects Reports*—Check list of Historical Records Survey Publications. 1943.

Whitmore, William Henry: *The Massachusetts Civil List for the Colonial and Provincial Periods, 1630-1774.* 1870.

Wright, Carroll D.: *Report on the Custody and Condition of the Public Records of Parishes, Towns, and Counties.* Boston. 1889. Valuable guide to official and church records.

Court Records, etc. (printed):

Records of the Court of Assistants. 1630-1692. 3 vols. Boston, 1901-1928.

Records and Files of Quarterly Courts of Essex County, Mass. 1638-1683. 8 vols. Salem, 1911-1921.

Records of the Court of General Sessions of the Peace of Worcester County. 1731-1737. Worcester, 1882.

Records of the Colony of New Plymouth in New England. 1620-1692. N. B. Shurtleff, et al., eds. 12 vols. Boston, 1855-1861.

Quincy, Josiah, Jr.: Reports of cases argued and adjudged in the Superior Court of Judicature of the Province of Massachusetts Bay, between 1761 and 1772. Boston, 1865.

tary rosters, s, and ords

Baker, Mary Ellen: "Bibliography of Lists of New England Soldiers." Boston. New England Historic Genealogical Society, 1911. 56 pp.

Revolutionary War:

Draper, Belle (Merrill): *Honor Roll of Massachusetts Patriots Heretofore Unknown, Being a List of Men and Women Who Loaned Money to the Federal Government During the Years 1777-1779.* Boston, 1899.

Massachusetts Secretary of the Commonwealth: *Massachusetts Soldiers and Sailors of the Revolutionary War.* 17 vols. Boston, 1896-1908.

Colonial Wars: The Secretary of State's office, Boston, has a card index of soldiers of the earlier wars, giving similar information to that published in the 17 volumes mentioned above on Revolutionary soldiers. This consists of a card index to muster rolls, 1710-1774.

War of 1812: Baker, John, comp.: Massachusetts Adjutant General's Office: *Records of Massachusetts Volunteer Militia Called Out by the Governor of Massachusetts to Suppress a Threatened Invasion During the War of 1812-14.* Published by Brigadier General Gardner W. Pearson, Adjutant General of Massachusetts. 1913. 448 pp.

Civil War: Massachusetts Adjutant General's Office: *Record of Massachusetts Volunteers,* 1861-65. Published by the Adjutant General, under a resolve of the General Court. Boston. 2 vols. 1868-1870.

Bureau of Labor Statistics: *A List of Soldiers, Sailors, and Marines of the War of the Rebellion in the Commonwealth of Massachusetts on May 1, 1905;* arranged alphabetically by cities and towns. Boston, 1907. 201 pp.

Official records

Vital Records (commence in early 17th century): Fee for birth, marriage, and death certificate: $2.00.

State Custodian: State Bureau of Vital Statistics, 1 Ashburton Pl., Boston, 02108.

Birth, Marriage, and Death Records: Subsequent to 1850: Above-named State Custodian. *Prior to 1850:* Town Clerk. For city of Boston, City Registrar of Vital Statistics. *Delayed birth certificates:* Town or city clerk will furnish information.

Marriage Licenses: Town Clerk or City Clerk.

Divorce Records: Massachusetts, except Boston: Clerk of Superior Court or Register of Probate in county where divorce was granted. Cost of certified copy varies. Boston: Clerk of Superior Court or Register of Probate, Boston, Massachusetts. Cost of certified copy varies.

Court Records: Wills, administrations, and other probate matters: Register of Probate, County Seat. *Other Civil Actions:* Clerk, Superior Court, County Seat.

Land Records: Deeds, mortgages, leases, and other matters affecting title to land: Register of Deeds, County Seat.

Federal census records

1. See index for section on United States census.

2. Custody of mortality schedules, 1850, 1860, 1870, 1880: Massachusetts State Library, Boston.

3. The original 1880 United States census records for Massachusetts were transferred in 1956 by the National Archives to: Office of the Secretary, Commonwealth of Massachusetts, State House, Boston.

Archives Division, Office of the Secretary of the Commonwealth, Room 438, State House, Boston, also has United States census records for 1850, 1860, 1870, and 1880.

Massachusetts state census

Archives Division, Office of the Secretary of the Commonwealth, Room 438, State House, Boston, has custody of the state census records.

1885 State Census: Contains the following data: Name of every person in the family on June 1, 1855, age, sex, color, occupation, place of birth (state, territory, or country), and miscellaneous data.

1865 State Census: Name of every person in the family on May 1, 1865, age, sex, color, place of birth (state, territory, or country), whether married, single, or widowed, occupation, and miscellaneous data.

The archives staff does not make searches for correspondents.

Michigan

eral rmation

Capital: Lansing. Organized as a territory: January 11, 1805. Entered Union: January 26, 1837.

aries, orical eties, and ives

For a complete list, see: Brown, Karl: *The American Library Directory.* Also, *Directory of Historical Societies and Agencies in the United States and Canada,* 1956.

Burton Historical Collection, a department of the Detroit Public Library, Woodward and Kirby Streets, Detroit.

Detroit Public Library, 5201 Woodward Avenue, Detroit.

Detroit Historical Society, Detroit Historical Museum, Detroit.

Detroit Society for Genealogical Research, Detroit Public Library, Detroit.

Michigan Historical Commission, 505 State Office Building, Lansing.

Michigan State Library, Lansing.

University of Michigan Library, Ann Arbor. (Data on some families can be found here.)

igan arch estions

The Burton Historical Collection, Detroit Public Library, is one of the two major family and local history collections in Michigan. It is rich in material on early Michigan and records of French families. It also has a large manuscript collection. Available for personal research or through a professional researcher.

Michigana, published by the Western Michigan Genealogical Society, 713 Bridge Street, N.W., Grand Rapids, is a six-page genealogical bulletin published quarterly.

rence ks

Historical Records Survey, WPA: *Guide to Manuscripts Depositories in the United States.* Michigan, 1940, 74 pp.

Historical Records Survey, WPA: *Inventory of Church Archives.* Inventories of various denominations in Michigan were published between 1939 and 1941 and are available in most large libraries.

Lanman, Charles: *The Red Book of Michigan; a Civil, Military, and Biographical History.* 1871. 549 pp.

Mohneke, Edward Harvey: *Cemetery Inscriptions, Michigan.* 3 vols. 1938-1944. Typewritten.

Massachusetts Magazine. 1-73. Contains information concerning Massachusetts pioneers to Michigan.

Peterson, C. Stewart: *Bibliography of County Histories of the 3111 Counties in the 48 States.* Baltimore, 1946.

Pioneer Society of Michigan (Lansing), Collections of 1877—.

Silliman, Sue Imogene: *Michigan Military Records.* 1920. A record of Revolutionary soldiers buried in Michigan and of pensioners.

United States, Department of State: *Territorial Papers of the United States.* Clarence E. Carter, ed. 1934. Vols. 2 and 3: *Territory Northwest of the Ohio River, 1787-1803.* 1942, 1945. Vols. 10, 11, 12. *Territory of Michigan, 1805-1837.* (For a summary of this source see *National Genealogical Society Quarterly,* 37:93ff.)

Military rosters, rolls, and records

State Rosters—Civil War: Turner, George H., comp.: Michigan Adjutant General's Office: *Record of Service of Michigan Volunteers in the Civil War, 1861-1865.* Published by authority of the Senate and House of Representatives of the Michigan Legislature under the direction of Brig. Gen. Geo. H. Brown, Adjutant General. Kalamazoo. 46 vols.

Official records

Vital Records: Fee for birth, marriage, and death certificate: $2.00.

State Custodian: Michigan Department of Public Health, 3500 North Logan St., Lansing, 48914.

Birth, Marriage, and Death Records: Subsequent to 1867: Above-named State Custodian. Also: For city of Detroit, Department of Health. Clerk, Circuit Court, has some records for Detroit and Wayne County, outside of city limits. Address, Clerk, Circuit Court, 212 County Building, Detroit, Michigan. *Prior to 1867:* Clerk, Circuit Court, county seat of the county where birth, marriage, or death occurred. *Delayed birth certificates:* State Custodian will furnish information.

Marriage Licenses: County Clerk of the county in which either party resides. No license required prior to September 28, 1887.

Marriage Records: County Clerk, County Seat.

Divorce Records: Since 1897: Above-named State Custodian, or County Clerk of county where divorce was granted. Cost of certified copy of divorce decree varies.

Court Records: Wills, administrations, and other probate matters: Clerk, Probate Court, County Seat. *Other Civil Actions:* County Clerk, County Seat.

Land Records: Deeds, mortgages, leases, and other matters affecting title to land: Register of Deeds, County Seat.

eral census rds

1. See index for section on United States Census.

2. Custody of mortality schedules, 1850, 1860, 1870, 1880: Michigan State Library, Lansing.

3. The original 1880 United States census records for Michigan were transferred in 1956 by the National Archives to: Library, University of Pittsburgh, Pittsburgh, Pennsylvania.

igan orial and census rds

For information about census records of Michigan Territory and censuses taken by state authority, write to Michigan Local and Family History Section, Michigan State Library, Lansing.

Minnesota

eral mation

Capital: St. Paul. Organized as a territory: March 3, 1849. Entered Union: May 11, 1858.

aries, rical eties, archives

For a complete list, see Brown, Karl: *The American Library Directory.* Also, *Directory of Historical Societies and Agencies in the United States and Canada,* 1956.

American Swedish Institute, 2600 Park Avenue, Minneapolis.

Minnesota Historical Society, Cedar and Central Avenues, St. Paul.

Minneapolis Public Library, 1001 Hennepin Avenue, Minneapolis.

rence ks

Daughters of the American Revolution, State of Minnesota: *Genealogical Collections of the Daughters of the American Revolution for the State of Minnesota: Early Minnesota Wills,* etc. 1945.

Daughters of the American Revolution, State of Minnesota: *Bible, Genealogical, Vital Records and Pioneer Stories of Minnesota.* 2 vols. 1946-47. Typewritten.

Historical Records Survey, WPA: *Guide to the Public Vital Statistics Records in Minnesota.* 1941. 142 pp.

Historical Records Survey, WPA: *Guide to Depositories of Manuscript Collections in the United States: Minnesota.* 1941. 84 pp.

Historical Records Survey, WPA: *Guide to Church Vital Statistics Records in Minnesota—Baptisms, Marriages, Funerals.* 1942. 253 pp.

Historical Records Survey, WPA: *Directory of Churches and Religious Organizations in Minnesota.* 1942. 583 pp.

Peterson, C. Stewart: *Bibliography of County Histories of the 3111 Counties in the 48 States.* Baltimore, 1946.

Military rosters, rolls, and records

State Rosters—Civil War:

Minnesota Adjutant General's Office: Annual reports of the Adjutant General. 1861-1865.

Minnesota Adjutant General: *Annual report of the Adjutant* (H.P. Van Cleve) for the Year Ending December 1, 1866, and of the Military Forces of the State from 1861-1866. Saint Paul, 1866. 805 pp.

Civil War Pensions: The Department of Veterans' Affairs of the State of Minnesota, St. Paul, Minnesota, has a pension record of those veterans who applied for Civil War pensions in Minnesota.

Official records

Vital Records: Fee for birth and death certificates: $2.00, payable to the "Treasurer, State of Minnesota."

State Custodian: Minnesota Department of Health, Section of Vital Statistics, 717 Delaware St., S.E. Minneapolis, 55440.

Birth and Death Records: Subsequent to 1900: Division of Birth and Death Records, Minnesota Department of Health, 469 State Office Bldg., St. Paul. *Prior to 1900:* Clerk of District Court, County Seat of the county where the birth or death occurred. *Delayed birth certificates:* Provision for delayed birth certificates by court proceedings only.

Divorce Records: Clerk of District Court in county where divorce was granted. Cost of certified copy of divorce decree varies.

Marriage Licenses and Marriage Records: Clerk of District Court of the county in which application was made for marriage license.

Court Records: Wills, administrations, and other probate matters: Clerk, Probate Court, County Seat.

Land Records: Deeds, mortgages, leases, and other

matters affecting title to land: Register of Deeds, County Seat.

eral census ords

1. See index for section on United States census.

2. Custody of mortality schedules, 1850, 1860, 1870, 1880: Minnesota State Library, St. Paul, Minnesota.

3. The original 1880 United States census records for Minnesota were transferred in 1956 by the National Archives to: Minnesota State Archives Commission, Minnesota Historical Society Building, St. Paul.

4. Minnesota Historical Society, St. Paul, has a duplicate original of the 1860 and 1870 federal censuses.

itorial and e census ords

Custodian of Territorial and State Census Records: Minnesota State Archives, Saint Paul.

Territorial Census of 1849: Head of the family, names of persons in the household, age, place of birth, and sex are disclosed. No value of real estate is given.

Territorial Census of 1857: Contains same information as the territorial census above mentioned plus value of real estate. The State Archives has a photocopy. National Archives has the original 1857 territorial census.

nesota state sus records

State Census of 1865: Original population census taken by the state. The listing of individuals is by township or municipality. The information is limited to name, sex, dumb or blind, and soldier. No age or head of family is given.

State Census of 1875: Original population census taken by the state. The record gives the name, age, sex, color, nativity (state or country), and parents' nativity. It is possible to determine the head of the family.

State Census of 1885: Original state population census. Name of person, age, sex, color, place of birth (state or territory), parentage, (father and/or mother of foreign birth), and if served in the Civil War.

State Census of 1895: Original state population census. Name and address, age, sex, color, place of birth (state or country), how long a resident of state and census district (males over 21), occupation, Civil War service, parentage (father and/or mother of foreign birth).

State Census of 1905: Original state population census. Name, address, sex, age, color, nativity (place of birth of person, the father and the mother), residence (how long a resident of the state and census district), occupation, military service.

Mississippi

General information

Capital: Jackson. Organized as a Territory: April 7, 1798. Entered Union: December 10, 1817. Seceded from Union: January 9, 1861. Reentered Union: February 23, 1870.

Libraries, historical societies, and archives

For a complete list, see: Brown, Karl: *The American Library Directory.* Also, *Directory of Historical Societies and Agencies in the United States and Canada,* 1956.

Mississippi Genealogical Society, Jackson.

Mississippi State Library, Jackson.

State Department of Archives and History, War Memorial Building, Box 571, 120 North State Street, Jackson.

Mississippi research suggestions

The Department of Archives and History, War Memorial Building, Jackson, publishes a ten-page booklet entitled *Research in the Mississippi Department of Archives and History.* It summarizes the department's sources and is available on request.

The Mississippi Genealogical Exchange, a quarterly devoted to the early families and records of Mississippi, is published and edited by Katie-Price Ward Esker, 214 Massachusetts Avenue, N.E., Washington, D.C.

Mississippi Blue Book.

Church Records: The Department of Archives and History has custody of some manuscript church records. *The Guide to Vital Statistics Records in Mississippi,* Vol. II, Church Archives, is a guide to custodians of church records.

Newspapers: The Department of Archives and History has a collection of Mississippi newspapers commencing in 1805.

Other Unofficial Records: The Department of Archives and History also has custody of a voluminous collection of private manuscripts, such as letters, business records, diaries, journals.

Reference books

Brown, A.J.: *History of Newton County, Mississippi, 1834-1894.* 1894.

Hendrix, Mary Louise Flowers: *Mississippi Court Records from the High Court of Errors and Appeals. 1799-1859.* 1950. 372 pp.

Historical Records Survey, WPA: *A Preliminary Union List of Newspaper Files . . . in Mississippi 1805-1940.* July 1942. 321 pp.

King, J. Estelle: *Mississippi Court Records 1799-1835.* 1936. Contains mostly wills.

Lipscomb, Dr. W. L.: *History of Columbus, Mississippi, 19th century.* 1909.

Marshall, Theadora Britton and Gladys Crail Evans: *They Found It in Natchez.* 1940.

Peterson, C. Stewart: *Bibliography of County Histories in the Forty-Eight States.* Baltimore, 1946. (Supplements 1950 and 1955.)

Rowland, Mrs. Duncan: *History of Hinds County, Mississippi, 1821-1922.* 1922.

United States Commissioner of the General Land Office: *A List of Purchasers of Public Lands at Columbus and Chocchuma, Mississippi.* October 1, 1833-January 1, 1834. 1834. 121 pp.

United States Department of State: *Territorial Papers of the United States.* Clarence E. Carter, ed. Vol. 4: *Territory South of the River Ohio.* 1937. Volumes 7 and 8: *Territory of Mississippi.* 1938. (For a summary of the scope of this source see *National Genealogical Society Quarterly* 37:93ff).

Welch, Alice Tracy: *Family Records—Mississippi.* Mississippi Society, DAR, 1953-56. 457 pp.

Winston, E. T.: *Story of Pontotoc County, Mississippi.* 1931.

'ary rosters, ;, and ords

Military Records: Department of Archives and History, P.O. Box 571, Jackson.

Revolutionary War: During the Revolutionary War Mississippi and Alabama were for the most part included within what was then Georgia. For information on soldiers in the Revolutionary War serving in those areas, write to Secretary, Georgia Historical Society, Savannah, Georgia.

War of 1812:

The Department of Archives and History, Jackson, has a roster of Mississippi men who served in the War of 1812.

Mississippi Historical Society Publications, *Centenary Series,* vol. 4, pp. 157-233, contains a roster of men who served in the War of 1812 from Mississippi Territory.

Mexican War: A roster of Mississippi men who served in this war is included in the military archives of the Department of Archives and History.

Civil War—Confederate Military Records: The National Archives has compiled the *Consolidated Index to Compiled Records of Confederate Soldiers.* The index is on cards that give the name of the soldier, his rank, the unit in which he served, and often a statement concerning the origin or background of that unit. There are cross-reference cards for soldiers' names that appeared in the records under more than one spelling. This index is available for personal search or by an agent. It is microfilmed.

The Department of Archives and History's official

Confederate military records includes more than 80,000 cards containing the name, rank, and organization of Mississippi soldiers in the C.S.A. This department also has custody of some original muster rolls and pension applications of Confederate veterans or their widows.

Official records

Vital Records: Fee for birth, marriage, and death certificates: $2.00

State Custodian: Division of Public Health Statistics, State Board of Health, P.O. Box 1700, Jackson, 39205.

Birth and Death Records: Subsequent to November 1, 1912: Above-named state custodian. *Prior to November 1, 1912:* There are some earlier records available for Jackson, Gulfport, and McComb, but no complete records elsewhere. (See also: *Church Records* and *Mortality Schedules.*)

Divorce Records: Chancery Clerk of county where divorce was granted. (Since 1926, the name of county may be obtained from Division of Vital Statistics, State Board of Health, P.O. Box 1700, Jackson.) Cost of a certified copy of divorce decree is $1.00.

Marriage Licenses: Clerk, Circuit Court, County Seat.

Marriage Records: Prior to 1926: Clerk, Circuit Court, County Seat. Marriage records available in the county court houses in 1926 were filmed by the State Board of Health, Bureau of Vital Statistics. The Department of Archives and History has a microfilm copy of the marriage records. (See also *Church Records.*)

Court Records: Wills, administrations, and other probate matters: Clerk, Court of Chancery, County Seat. *Other Civil Actions:* Clerk, Circuit Court, County Seat.

Land Records: Deeds, mortgages, leases, and other matters affecting title to land: Clerk, Court of Chancery, County Seat. The Land Commissioner, Jackson, has custody of early land records for southern and southwestern Mississippi.

Federal census records

1. See index for section on United States census.

2. The Department of Archives and History, Jackson, has microfilm copies of the U.S. census from 1830 to 1880.

3. Custody of mortality schedules, 1850, 1860, 1870, 1880: Department of Archives and History, 120 North State Street, Jackson.

4. The original 1880 United States census records for Mississippi were transferred in 1956 by the National Archives to: National Society, Daughters of the American Revolution, Administration Building, 1776 D Street, N.W., Washington, D.C.

sissippi state
sus records

The Department of Archives and History has custody of the Mississippi *territorial* and *state* (as distinguished from *federal*) census records for scattered years for scattered counties from 1805 through 1845. All of these records disclose the heads of families.

Missouri

neral
rmation

Capital: Jefferson City. Organized as a territory: June 4, 1812. Entered Union: August 10, 1821.

raries,
orical
ieties,
l archives

For a complete list, see: Brown, Karl: *The American Library Directory.* Also, *Directory of Historical Societies and Agencies in the United States and Canada.* 1956.

Clay County Historical Society, Liberty.

Kansas City Public Library, 9th at Locust Street, Kansas City. Valuable for Middle West records.

Missouri Baptist Historical Society, William Jewell College, Liberty.

Missouri Historical Society, Jefferson Memorial, St. Louis.

Phelps County Historical Society, 210 East Eighth Street, Rolla.

Public Library and Historical Association, Lexington.

St. Louis Public Library, Olive, 13th and 14th Streets, St. Louis.

State Historical Society of Missouri, Hitt and Lowry Streets, Columbia.

erence
oks

Bryan, William S.: *History of the Pioneer Families of Missouri.* 1876.

Campbell, R.A.: *Campbell's Gazetteer of Missouri.* 1875.

Conard, Howard L., ed.: *Encyclopedia of the History of Missouri.* A compendium of history and biography for ready reference. 1901. 6 volumes.

Daughters of the American Revolution: *Genealogical Records.* Compiled and typed by various DAR Chapters. Arranged by the Genealogical Society, Salt Lake City, Utah. Vol. 1, 1950; vol. 2, 1953. 234 pp. Family and cemetery records, newspaper extracts, etc.

Douglass, Robert Sidney: *History of Southeast Missouri.* 1912. 2 vols. Biography.

Historical Records Survey, WPA: *Guide to Depositories of Manuscript Collections in the United States: Missouri.* Preliminary edition. 1940. 17 pp.

Historical Records Survey, WPA: *Guide to Public Vital Statistics Records in Missouri.* July 1941. 114 pp.

Houck, Louis: *Memorial Sketches of Pioneers and Early Residents of Southeast Missouri.* 1915.

Hyde, William, and Howard L. Conard: *Encyclopedia of the History of St. Louis.* 4 vols. 1899.

Peterson, C. Stewart: *Bibliography of County Histories of the 3111 Counties in the 48 States.* Baltimore, 1946.

United States Department of State: *Territorial Papers of the United States.* Clarence E. Carter, ed. 1948-1951. Vols. 13, 14, 15, *Territory of Louisiana-Missouri,* 1803-1821. (For a summary of this source see *National Genealogical Society Quarterly,* 37:93ff.)

Military rosters, rolls, and records

State Rosters—Civil War: Missouri Adjutant General's Office: (Union) *Alphabetical Register of Officers Missouri Volunteers and Missouri State Militia Accompanying Adjutant General's Report for 1865.* (In Adjutant General's Office. *Annual Report of the Adjutant General,* December 31, 1865. Jefferson City, 1865. Pp. 705-781.)

Missouri Adjutant General's Office: (Union) Annual Reports, 1862-1865.

Official records

Vital Records: Fee for birth and death certificates: $1.00

State Custodian: Vital Records, Missouri Division of Health, Jefferson City, Missouri 65101.

Birth and Death Records: Subsequent to January 1910: Above-named State Custodian. *Prior to January 1910:* Recorder of Deeds, County Seat of the county in which the birth or death occurred; or if in the City of St. Louis, write to St. Louis Department of Health, Bureau of Vital Statistics, St. Louis. Kansas City also has records prior to 1910. *Delayed birth certificates:* State Custodian will furnish information.

Divorce Records: (Missouri, except St. Louis city) Clerk of the Circuit Court in county where divorce was granted. (Since 1947, name of county may be obtained without charge from Bureau of Vital Statistics, State Department of Public Health and Welfare, Jefferson City.) Cost of certified copy of divorce decree varies. St. Louis (city) since 1821: Clerk of the Circuit Court, Civil Courts Building, St. Louis. Cost of certified copy of divorce decree varies.

Marriage Licenses: Recorder of Deeds, County seat of the county where license was issued; or if in St. Louis, write to City Recorder.

Marriage Records: County Recorder, County Seat, of the county where the marriage was performed.

Court Records: Wills, administrations, and other probate matters: Clerk, probate court, County Seat. *Other Civil Actions:* Circuit Clerk, County Seat.

Land Records: Deeds, mortgages, leases, and other matters affecting title to land: Register of Deeds, County Seat.

deral census ords

1. See index for section on United States census.

2. Custody of mortality schedules, 1850, 1860, 1870, 1880: Missouri Historical Society, St. Louis.

3. The original 1880 United States census records for Missouri were transferred in 1956 by the National Archives to: National Society, Daughters of the American Revolution, Administration Building, 1776 D Street, N.W., Washington, D.C.

souri state nsus records

All state census records were destroyed in the burning of the state capitol in 1911.

Montana

neral ormation

Capital: Helena. Organized as a Territory: May 26, 1854. Entered Union: March 1, 1867.

raries, torical cieties, d archives

For a complete list, see: Brown, Karl: *The American Library Directory.* Also, *Directory of Historical Societies and Agencies in the United States and Canada,* 1956.

Historical Society of Montana, Room 106, Capitol Building, Helena.

ference oks

Bowen, A. W. & Co.: *Progressive Men of the State of Montana.* (n.d.?)

Historical Records Survey, WPA: *Inventory of the County Archives of Montana.* 1940. 658 pp.

Historical Records Survey, WPA: *Inventory of the Vital Statistics Records of Churches and Religious Organizations in Montana.* 1942. 117 pp.

Historical Records Survey, WPA: *A Directory of Churches and Religious Organizations in Montana.* 1941. 126 pp.

Peterson, C. Stewart: *Bibliography of County Histories of the 3111 Counties in the 48 States.* Baltimore, 1946.

Sanders, James U., ed.: *Society of Montana Pioneers,* Constitution Members and Officers, Register. 1899. Vol. 1, 262 pp.

Official records

Vital Records: Fee for birth and death certificate: $2.00

State Custodian: Registrar of Vital Statistics, State Board of Health, Helena, 59601.

Birth and Death Records: Subsequent to June 1907: Above-named State Custodian. *Prior to June 1907:* If the birth or death occurred in Great Falls, Helena, or Bozeman, write to the County Clerk there. No other complete records prior to 1907. Butte and Missoula: City Health Department. *Delayed birth certificates:* State Custodian will furnish information.

Marriage Licenses and Marriage Records: Clerk, District Court of the County.

Court Records: Wills, administrations, and other probate matters: Clerk, District Court, County Seat. *Other Civil Actions:* County Clerk, County Seat.

Divorce Records: Clerk of District Court in county where divorce was granted. (Since 1943, name of county may be obtained from Bureau of Vital Statistics, State Board of Health, Helena, Montana.) Cost of certified copy of divorce decree varies.

Land Records: Deeds, mortgages, leases, and other matters affecting title to land: County Clerk and Recorder, County Seat.

Federal census records

1. See index for section on United States census.

2. Custody of mortality schedules, 1870: State Historical Library, Helena, Montana.

3. The original 1880 United States census records for Montana were transferred in 1956 by the National Archives to: Historical Society of Montana, Helena, Montana.

Montana state census records (or substitute)

Custodian: Historical Society of Montana, Roberts Street between 5th and 6th Avenue, Helena, Montana.

"Inhabitants of Montana During the Winter of 1862-63." (In *Contributions,* vol. 1 (1876), pp. 305-8.)

Montana poll list, October 24, 1864, by county precincts: Beaverhead, Choteau, Deer Lodge, Jefferson, Madison, Missoula, and Yellowstone.

Nebraska

eral
rmation

Capital: Lincoln. Organized as a Territory: May 30, 1854. Entered Union: March 1, 1867.

aries,
rical
eties,
archives

For a complete list, see: Brown, Karl: *The American Library Directory.* Also, *Directory of Historical Societies and Agencies in the United States and Canada,* 1956.

Lincoln City Library, Lincoln.

Madison County Historical Society, Public Library, Madison.

Mississippi Valley Historical Association, 1500 R Street, Lincoln.

Native Sons and Daughters of Nebraska, Room 1020, State Capitol, Lincoln.

Nebraska State Historical Society, 1500 R Street, Lincoln.

erence
ks

Alden Publishing Co.: *Compendium of History, Reminiscences, and Biography of Western Nebraska,* Containing Biographical Sketches of Hundreds of Prominent Old Settlers. 1909. 1135 pp.

Historical Records Survey: *Guide to Public Vital Statistics Records in Nebraska,* 1941. 96 pp.

Historical Records Survey, WPA: *Preliminary Edition of Guide to Depositories of Manuscript Collections in the United States* (Nebraska). 1940. 43 pp.

Lewis Publishing Co.: *A Biographical and Genealogical History of Southeastern Nebraska.* 1904. 2 vols.

Peterson, C. Stewart: *Bibliography of County Histories of the 3111 Counties in the 48 States.* Baltimore, 1946.

ary rosters,
, and
ords

State Roster: Civil War.

Nebraska Adjutant-General's Office: *Roster of Nebraska Volunteers from 1861-1869.* Compiled from Books, Records, and Documents on File in Office of Adjutant General of State. Hastings, 1888. 236 pp.

cial records

Vital Records: Fee for birth, marriage, and death certificate: $3.00.

State Custodian: Bureau of Vital Statistics, State Dept. of Health, 1003 "O" Street, Lincoln, Nebraska 68508.

Birth and Death Records: Subsequent to January 1, 1905: Above-named State Custodian. *Prior to January 1, 1905:* County Clerk, County Seat of the county in which birth or death occurred. *Delayed birth certificates:* By court proceedings only.

Divorce Records: Since 1909: Bureau of Vital Statistics, State Department of Health, Lincoln, Nebraska 68508. Cost of certified copy of divorce decree is $3.00. Prior to 1909 in some counties: Clerk of District Court where divorce was granted. Cost of certified copy of divorce decree varies.

Marriage Licenses: Clerk, County Court, County Seat.

Marriage Records: Subsequent to January 1909: Above-named State Custodian. *Prior to January 1909:* Clerk, County Court, County Seat.

Court Records: Wills, administrations, and probate matters: Clerk, County Court, County Seat. *Other Civil Actions:* Clerk, County Court, County Seat.

Land Records: Deeds, mortgages, leases, and other matters affecting title to land: Register of Deeds, County Seat.

Federal census records

1. See index for section on United States census.

2. Custody of mortality schedules, 1860, 1870, 1880: Nebraska State Historical Society, Lincoln, Nebraska.

3. The original 1880 United States census records for Nebraska were transferred in 1956 by the National Archives to: Administration Building, 1776 D Street, N.W., Washington, D.C.

State census records

The Nebraska State Historical Society, 1500 R Street, Lincoln, has custody of the territorial and state census records listed below:

Nebraska territorial census records for 1854, 1855, and 1856 states the head of the family, age, place of birth, and sex.

1865 territorial census covers the following counties: Otoe, Cuming, and Lancaster.

There are also state census records for the following counties and years: Lancaster: 1870, 1874, 1875, 1878, 1879, and 1880. Butler: 1869. Stanton: 1869. Frontier: 1874 and 1876.

Census records 1865-1876 disclose the head of the family, names of persons in the household, age, place of birth, and sex.

The Lancaster County records are typed, bound, and indexed as the *Historical Records of Lancaster County.* Compiled by the Deborah Avery Chapter of the DAR, Lincoln. Published as a report of the Works Progress Administration. Some of the original records are in the Lancaster County Courthouse. The above-listed census records with the exception of those for Lancaster and Frontier counties were published intermittently in the

Nebraska and Midwest Genealogical Record, Lincoln, Nebraska, beginning with volume 13, no. 1, January 1935.

Census of 1885: The National Archives has custody of the 1885 census of Nebraska, which was authorized by 20 Statutes at Large 473 in 1879. This census included a census of population and mortality. The name of each person is given, relationship to the head of the family, race, sex, age, marital status, occupation, and place of birth.

Nevada

ıeral ırmation

Capital: Carson City. Organized as a Territory: March 3, 1861. Entered Union: October 31, 1864.

raries, orical ieties, l archives

For a complete list, see: Brown, Karl: *The American Library Directory.* Also, *Directory of Historical Societies and Agencies in the United States and Canada,* 1956.

Las Vegas Public Library, Las Vegas Genealogical Society, Las Vegas.

Nevada State Historical Society, 1650 N. Virginia St., Reno, 89503.

erence oks

Daughters of the American Revolution: *Genealogical Records.* Compiled by various chapters of the Nevada DAR. Vol. 1, 1953-1954. 89 pp. Typewritten.

Federal Death Records of Nevada, June 1, 1869-June 1, 1870. 36 pp. Indexed. The Genealogical Society, Salt Lake City, Utah, has a copy.

Historical Records Survey, WPA: *Inventory of the Church Archives of Nevada.* Roman Catholic Church, August 1939. 49 pp.

Historical Records Survey, WPA: *Inventory of Church Archives of Nevada.* Protestant Episcopal Church, January 1941. 69 pp.

Peterson, C. Stewart: *Bibliography of County Histories of the 3111 Counties in the 48 States.* Baltimore, 1946.

Polk, R.L. & Co.: *Nevada State Gazetteer and Business Directory.* 1907-1908. 1024 pp.

itary rosters, 's, and cords

State Rosters—Civil War: Nevada Adjutant General: Report of the Adjutant General (John Cradlebaugh) for 1865. January 1, 1866 (Carson City: 1866?). 55 pp.

Roster of Volunteers, in biennial report of the (Nevada) Adjutant General (C.E. Laughton, ex-officio). December 31, 1884, pp. 29-55.

Official records

Vital Records: Fee for birth and death certificate: $2.00.

State Custodian: Division of Vital Statistics, Department of Health, Welfare and Rehabilitation, Division of Health, Carson City, 89710.

Birth and Death Records: Subsequent to July 1, 1911: Above-named State Custodian. *Prior to July 1, 1911:* County Recorder of the County Seat where the birth or death occurred. *Delayed birth certificates:* By court proceedings only.

Marriage Licenses: County Clerk.

Marriage Records: County Recorder.

Court Records: Wills, administrations, and other probate matters: County Clerk, County Seat. *Other Civil Actions:* County Clerk, County Seat.

Divorce Records: County Clerk of county where divorce was granted. Cost of certified copy varies.

Land Records: Deeds, mortgages, leases, and other matters affecting title to land: County Recorder, County Seat.

Federal census records

1. See index for section on United States census.

2. Custody of mortality schedules, 1860, 1870, 1880: Nevada Historical Society, Reno.

3. The original 1880 United States census records for Nevada were transferred in 1956 by the National Archives to: Nevada State Museum, Box 495, Carson City.

State census

None.

New Hampshire

General information

Capital: Concord. Entered the Union: June 21, 1788.

Libraries, historical societies, and archives

For a complete list, see: Brown, Karl: *The American Library Directory.* Also, *Directory of Historical Societies and Agencies in the United States and Canada,* 1956.

Exeter Historical Society, County Records Building, Exeter.

Manchester Historical Association, 129 Amherst Street, Manchester.

Nashua Historical Society, Community Council, 7 Prospect Street, Nashua.

New Hampshire Historical Society, 30 Park Street, Concord.

New Ipswich Historical Society, New Ipswich.

Peterborough Historical Society, Historical Building, Peterborough.

Wakefield Historical Society, Wakefield.

Wolfeboro Historical Society, Historical House, South Main Street, Wolfeboro.

w Hampshire earch gestions

The New Hampshire State Library in Concord has an outstanding collection of genealogical material. In addition to printed sources, microfilm copies of most of the local records are available there.

The New Hampshire Historical Society is housed in one of the finest buildings of any historical society in the United States, and its collection outdoes the splendor of the building. In addition to printed sources, the society has a fine collection of manuscript material; for instance, unofficial records of early births may be obtained from the obstetrical records of Dr. Leland J. Graves, who practiced medicine in Langdon, Acworth, Alstead, Charlestown, and Walpole.

Dearborn, David C.: "New Hampshire Genealogy: A Perspective." *New England Historical and Genealogical Register,* October 1976.

Prager, Herta, and William W. Price: "A Bibliography on the History of the Courts of the Thirteen Original States, Maine, Ohio, and Vermont." *American Journal of Legal History.* Vol. 1, p. 355.

v Hampshire graphical

Communities, Settlements and Neighborhood Centers in the State of New Hampshire. Concord, 1954. 61 pp. An inventory prepared by the New Hampshire State Planning and Development Commission.

Farmer, John: *A Gazetteer of the State of New Hampshire.* 1823. 276 pp.

New Hampshire: *Manual for the General Court.* 1957. 781 pp.

erence ks

Granite Monthly. 1877—.

Gross, Mrs. Charles Carpenter: *New Hampshire Epitaphs: Colonial Gravestone Inscriptions in the State of New Hampshire.* 1942. 160 pp.

Hammond, Otis G.: *Check List of New Hampshire Local History.* 1925. 106 pp.

Historical Records Survey, WPA: *Guide to Church Vital Statistics Records in New Hampshire.* May 1942. 102 pp.

Libby, Charles Thornton: *Sybil Noyes and Walter Goodwin Davis: Genealogical Dictionary of Maine and New Hampshire.* 5 parts. 1928-1938.

Little, George Thomas: *Genealogical and Family History*

of State of Maine. 4 vols. 1909. Contains data on New Hampshire families. It must be used with more than ordinary care, as it contains many mistakes.

National Society of the Colonial Dames of America, New Hampshire: *Gravestone Inscriptions . . . in the State of New Hampshire.* 1913.

New Hampshire Historical Society: *Family Names in New Hampshire Town Histories.* Concord. 78 pp.

New Hampshire Planning and Development Commission: *Communities, Settlements, and Neighborhood Centers in the State of New Hampshire.* Concord, 1954. (Mimeographed; pp. 6, 61.)

New Hampshire: *Provincial, State and Town Papers,* 1867—.

New Hampshire (Colony): *Probate Records of the Province of New Hampshire,* 1907—.

New Hampshire Antiquarian Society: *Collections.* 4 numbers in 1 vol., 1874-1879.

New Hampshire Genealogical Record. 7 vols., 1903-1910.

New Hampshire Historical Society: *Collections,* 1824—.

New Hampshire Historical Society: *Proceedings,* 1874—.

New Hampshire Repository. 2 vols., 1846-1847.

Peterson, C. Stewart: *Bibliography of County Histories of the 3111 Counties in the 48 States.* Baltimore, 1946.

Stearns, Ezra Scollay: *Genealogical and Family History of the State of New Hampshire.* 4 vols. 1908.

United States Bureau of the Census: *Heads of Families at the First Census of the United States Taken in the Year 1790.* New Hampshire, 1907.

Military rosters, rolls, and records

Baker, Mary Ellen: *Bibliography of Lists of New England Soldiers.* Boston. New England Historic Genealogical Society, 1911. 56 pp.

Revolutionary War and War of 1812:

Hammond, Isaac Weare: *Rolls of the Soldiers of the Revolutionary War,* Concord, 1885-1889. 4 vols. (New Hampshire: Provincial and State Papers, vols. 14-17.)

New Hampshire Adjutant General: *Military History of New Hampshire from its Settlement in 1623 to the Year 1861.* (n.d.) Rolls for the War of 1812 commence in Part 2, page 5.

New Hampshire State Roster—Civil War: Adjutant General's Office: *Revised Register of the Soldiers and Sailors of New Hampshire in the Rebellion. 1861-1866.* Prepared by Augustus D. Ayling. Adjutant General. Concord. 1895. 1347 pp.

cial records

Vital Records: Commence in 1640, but are incomplete. Fee for birth, marriage, and death certificate: $2.00.

State Custodian: Department of Health and Welfare, Division of Public Health, Bureau of Vital Statistics, 61 South Spring Street, Concord, 03301.

Birth, Marriage, and Death Records: Subsequent to 1640: Above-named State Custodian. Also try Town Clerk of the town where the birth, marriage, or death occurred. *Delayed birth certificates:* State Custodian will furnish information.

Divorce Records: Since 1881: Division of Vital Statistics, State Department of Health, 61 South Spring Street, Concord, New Hampshire, or Clerk of the Superior Court which issued the decree. Cost of certified copy of divorce decree varies.

Marriage Licenses: Town Clerk.

Court Records: Wills, administrations, and other probate matters: Register of Probate, County Seat. *Other Civil Actions:* Clerk, Superior Court, County Seat.

Land Records: Deeds, mortgages, leases, and other matters affecting title to land: Register of Deeds, County Seat.

eral census
rds

1. See index for section on United States census.

2. Custody of mortality schedules, 1850, 1860, 1870, 1880: New Hampshire State Library, Concord.

3. The original 1880 United States census records for New Hampshire were transferred in 1956 by the National Archives to: National Society, Daughters of the American Revolution, Administration Building, 1776 D Street, N.W., Washington, D.C.

Hampshire
census
rds

Other than a short enumeration of heads of families in Peterborough, 1786, in State Papers, vol. 10, p. 686, no record of a state census taken by authority of the state government has ever been found.

New Jersey

eral
mation

Capital: Trenton. Entered the Union: December 18, 1787.

ries,
rical
ties,
rchives

For a complete list, see: Brown, Karl: *The American Library Directory.* Also, *Directory of Historical Societies and Agencies in the United States and Canada,* 1965.

Atlantic County Historical Society, Somers Mansion, Somers Point.

Burlington County Historical Society, James Fenimore Cooper House, 457 High Street, Burlington.

Camden County Historical Society, Park Boulevard and Euclid Avenue, Camden.

Cape May County Historical and Genealogical Society, Courthouse, Cape May.

Cumberland County Historical Society, Courthouse, Bridgeton.

Gloucester County Historical Society, Courthouse, Woodbury.

Haddonfield Historical Society, 231 Kings' Highway East, Haddonfield.

Historical Society of Hudson County, Free Public Library, Jersey Avenue, Jersey City.

Historical Society of Plainfield and North Plainfield, Nathaniel Drake House, 602 West Front Street, Plainfield.

Huguenot Society of New Jersey, New Jersey Historical Building, Newark.

Jersey City Free Public Library, 472-486 Jersey Avenue, Jersey City.

Monmouth County Historical Association, 70 Court Street, Freehold.

Newark Public Library, 5 Washington Street, Newark.

New Jersey Historical Society, 230 Broadway, Newark.

New Jersey State Library and Archives, Trenton 08625.

Passaic County Historical Society, Lambert Castle, Garret Mountain Reservation, Paterson.

Revolutionary Memorial Society of New Jersey, Wallace House, Washington Place, Somerville.

Salem County Historical Society, Alexander Grant House, 83 Market Street, Salem.

Trenton Historical Society, 410 Wallach Building, 86 East State Street, Trenton.

Union County Historical Society, Courthouse, Broad Street, Elizabeth.

Vineland Historical and Antiquarian Society, Seventh and Elmer Streets, Vineland.

New Jersey research suggestions

Schlam, Rebecca, and Kenneth W. Richards, comp.: *Genealogical Research: A guide to source materials in the New Jersey State Library and other state agencies.* New Jersey Division of the State Library, Archives, and History. Trenton, 1957.

Prager, Herta, and William W. Price: "A Bibliography on the History of the Courts of the Thirteen Original States, Maine, Ohio, and Vermont." *American Journal of Legal History,* vol. 1, p. 357.

Many New Jersey families, especially those of the northern part of the state, may be found in the *Shoemaker Genealogy.*

rence
s

Chambers, Theodore Frelinghuysen: *The Early Germans of New Jersey: Their History, Churches and Genealogies.* 1895.

Daughters of the American Revolution, chapters in the state of New Jersey: *Bible Records,* etc. 7 vols. 1948-1954. Typewritten.

Documents Relating to the Colonial History of the State of New Jersey, 1880—. (New Jersey Archives.)

Documents Relating to the Revolutionary History of the State of New Jersey. 5 vols. 1901-1917. (The second series of the New Jersey Archives.)

Genealogical Magazine of New Jersey: 1925—.

Gordon, Thomas F.: *A Gazetteer and History of the State of New Jersey.* 1834.

Genealogical Magazine of New Jersey. Vol. 1, 1925.

Hinshaw, William Wade: *Encyclopedia of American Quaker Genealogy.* Volume 2, 1938.

Historical Records Survey, WPA: *Calendar of the New Jersey State Library Manuscript Collection in the Cataloguing Room.* State Library, Trenton, 1939. 168 pp.

Historical Records Survey, WPA: *Guide to Vital Statistics Records in New Jersey.* Vol. I, Public Archives. 1941. 313 pp. Vol. 2, Church Archives. 1941. 588 pp.

Historical Records Survey, WPA: *Guide to Depositories of Manuscript Collections in the United States:* New Jersey. 1941. 62 pp.

Lee, Francis Bazley: *Genealogical and Memorial History of the State of New Jersey.* 4 vols. 1910. Inaccurate—must be used with care.

Lee, Francis Bazley: *New Jersey as a Colony and as a State.* 4 vols. 1902.

Littell, John: *Family Records; or Genealogies of the First Settlers of Passaic Valley.* 1851.

Nelson, William: *Calendar of New Jersey Wills, 1901—.* (See: *Documents Relating to the Colonial History of the State of New Jersey,* vol. 23.)

Nelson, William: *Church Records in New Jersey.* 1904.

Nelson, William: *Marriage Records, 1665-1800,* 1900. (See: *Documents Relating to the Colonial History of the State of New Jersey,* vol. 22.)

New Jersey Historical Society: *Proceedings, 1845—*. (An index to vols. 1-36 has been published.)

New Jersey Secretary of State: *Index of Wills.* 2 vols. 1705-1830. 1901.

New Jersey Secretary of State: *Index of Wills, Inventories,* etc., in the Office of the Secretary of State prior to 1901. 3 vols. 1912-1913.

Peterson, C. Stewart: *Bibliography of County Histories of the 3111 Counties in the 48 States.* Baltimore, 1946.

Somerset County Historical Quarterly. 8 vols. 1912-1919.

Stillwell, John Edwin: *Historical and Genealogical Miscellany: Data Relating to the Settlement and Settlers of New York and New Jersey.* 5 vols. 1903—.

United States: Historical Records Survey of the WPA: *Calendars of Manuscript Collections in New Jersey.* Calendar of the Stevens Family Papers, Stevens Institute of Technology Library, Hoboken. Newark, 1940. Mimeographed.

United States, WPA: *Bibliography of Research Projects Reports—Check List of Historical Records Survey Publications.* 1943.

Military rosters, rolls, and records

Revolutionary War: Stryker, William S.: *Official Register of Officers and Men of New Jersey in the Revolutionary War.* Trenton, 1872. For an index to this work see: Historical Records Survey, WPA: *Index of the Official Register of the Officers and Men of New Jersey in the Revolutionary War.* 1941. 142 pp.

War of 1812: New Jersey Adjutant General: *Records of Officers and Men of New Jersey in Wars, 1791-1815.* Trenton, 1909.

New Jersey state rosters

Civil War: New Jersey Adjutant General's Office: *Records of Officers and Men of New Jersey in the Civil War. 1861-1865.* Compiled in the office of the Adjutant General, William S. Stryker. Trenton, 1876. 2 vols.

Official records

Vital Records: Fee for birth, marriage, and death certificate: $2.00.

State Custodian: State Registrar of Vital Statistics, P.O. Box 1540, State House, Trenton, 08625.

Birth and Marriage and Death Records: Subsequent to 1848: Above-named State Custodian. General index of birth and marriages prior to 1901. Deaths arranged by towns and counties; births, marriages, and deaths alphabetically by individual years starting with 1901. For records from May 1848 through May 1878: Archives and History Bureau, State Library, Trenton, 08625. *Delayed birth certificates:* State Custodian will furnish information.

Divorce Records: Superior Court, Chancery Division, State House, Trenton. Cost of certified copy of divorce decree is $2.00.

Marriage Licenses: Licenses issued by registrar of vital statistics, who sometimes is Town Clerk, Township Assessor, Clerks of cities, boroughs, or towns.

Court Records: Wills, administrations, and other probate matters: Jurisdiction of matters of probate and administration is in prerogative, Orphans' and Surrogate's Courts. Write to clerks of these at county seat. *Other Civil Actions:* County Clerk, County Seat. Also: Supreme Court Clerk or Clerk in Chancery, State House Annex, Trenton.

Land Records: Deeds, mortgages, leases, and other matters affecting title to land: County Clerk, County Seat.

eral census
ords

1. See index for section on United States census.

2. Custody of mortality schedules, 1850, 1860, 1870, 1880: New Jersey State Library, Trenton.

3. The original 1880 United States census records for New Jersey were transferred in 1956 by the National Archives to: Rutgers University Library, New Brunswick.

Jersey
census
ords

Custodian: New Jersey State Library, State House Annex, Trenton.

1855 State Census: Thirteen counties in three volumes. Seven counties missing: Burlington, Cape May, Essex, Mercer, Middlesex, Ocean, and Salem. Information disclosed: Name, sex, race.

1865 State Census: Thirteen counties in four volumes. Eight counties missing: Cape May, Essex, Mercer, Morris, Ocean, Somerset, Sussex, Warren. Information disclosed: Name, sex, race.

1885 State Census: Twenty-one counties complete. Information disclosed: Name, sex, race, and approximate age.

1895 State Census: Twenty-one counties complete. Information disclosed: Name, sex, race.

1905 State Census: Twenty-one counties complete. Information disclosed: Name, sex, age (year and month), occupation, marital status, birthplace, parents' birthplace.

1915 State Census: Twenty-one counties complete. Information disclosed: Name, sex, age.

Availability of Records: All requests must be in writing or on a special form provided by the New Jersey State Library.

New Mexico

General information

Capital: Santa Fe. Organized as a Territory: September 9, 1850. Entered Union: January 6, 1912.

Libraries, historical societies, and archives

For a complete list, see: Brown, Karl: *The American Library Directory.* Also, *Directory of Historical Societies and Agencies in the United States and Canada,* 1956.

Historical Society of New Mexico, Palace of the Governor, Santa Fe.

Librarian, Museum of New Mexico Library, Santa Fe.

Reference books

Guide to Public Vital Statistics Records in New Mexico. 1942—. 135 pp.

Historical Records Survey, WPA: *Directory of Churches and Religious Organizations in New Mexico.* 1940. 385 pp.

Peterson, C. Stewart: *Bibliography of County Histories of the 3111 Counties in the 48 States.* Baltimore, 1946.

Twitchell, Ralph Emerson: *The Spanish Archives of New Mexico.* 2 vols. 1914.

Official records

Vital Records: Fee for birth and death certificate: $2.00.

State Custodian: Vital Records Unit, New Mexico Health and Social Service Department, P.O. Box 2348, Santa Fe, 87501.

Birth and Death Records: Subsequent to January 1, 1920: Above-named State Custodian. (There are some earlier records on file, but not complete.) *Delayed birth certificates:* By court proceedings only.

Divorce Records: Clerk of District Court in county where divorce was granted. Cost of certified copy varies.

Marriage Licenses: County Clerk.

Marriage Records: County Clerk.

Court Records: Wills, administrations, and other probate matters: Clerk, probate court, county seat. *Other Civil Actions:* County Clerk, County Seat.

Land Records: Deeds, mortgages, leases, and other matters affecting title to land: County Clerk, County Seat.

Federal census records

1. See index for section on United States census.

2. Custody of Mortality schedules, 1850, 1860, 1870: New Mexico Historical Society, Santa Fe.

3. The original 1880 United States census records for New Mexico were transferred in 1956 by the National Archives to: National Society, Daughters of the American Revolution, Administration Building, 1776 D Street, N. W., Washington, D.C.

ritorial sus

The National Archives has custody of a special census of New Mexico territory taken in 1885. The schedules include the name, age, sex, and color of every inhabitant, as well as information on occupation, civil condition, and place of birth.

'e census ords

No record of a census taken by authority of New Mexico has ever been located.

New York

neral rmation

Capital: Albany. (Once a part of New Netherlands.) Entered Union: July 26, 1788.

raries, orical ieties, l archives

For a complete list, see: Brown, Karl: *The American Library Directory.* Also, *Directory of Historical Societies and Agencies in the United States and Canada,* 1956.

Albany County Historical Association, Albany.

American-Scandinavian Foundation, 127 E. 73rd Street, New York.

Broome County Historical Society, Courthouse, Binghamton.

Buffalo Historical Society, Delaware Park, Buffalo.

Columbia County Historical Society, Route 9, Kinderhook.

Cortland County Historical Society, Courthouse, Cortland.

Fort Anne Historical and Genealogical Society, Fort Anne.

Green County Historical Society, Bronck House, West Coxsackie.

Hamilton Historical Society, Public Library Building, Hamilton.

Herkimer County Historical Society, 402 N. Main St., Herkimer.

Historical Branch of Palmyra King's Daughters, Free Library, 127 Cuyler Street, Palmyra.

Huguenot and Historical Association of New Rochelle, Thomas Paine Cottage, 277 North Avenue, New Rochelle.

Huguenot Society of America, 122 E. 58th Street, New York.

Huntington Historical Society, High Street, Huntington.

LeRoy Historical Society, 26 East Main Street, LeRoy.

Lewis County Historical Society, Lowville Free Library, Lowville.

Long Island Historical Society Library, 128 Pierrepont Street, Brooklyn.

Nassau County Historical Society, P. O. Box 207, Garden City, 11530.

New York Genealogical and Biographical Society, 124 East 58th Street, New York.

New York Historical Society, 170 Central Park West, New York.

New York Public Library, Genealogy Department, Fifth Avenue at 42nd Street, New York.

New York State Historical Association, 22 Main Street, Cooperstown.

New York State Library, Albany.

Grosvenor Library, Buffalo.

Oneida Historical Society, Munson-Williams Memorial Building, Park Avenue, John and Elizabeth Streets, Utica.

Onondaga Historical Association, 311 Montgomery Street, Syracuse.

Oyster Bay Historical and Genealogical Society, care of Rayham Hall, Oyster Bay.

Queens Borough Public Library, Jamaica.

Rochester Public Library, 115 South Avenue, Rochester.

Rochester Historical Society, Woodside, 485 East Avenue, Rochester.

Schenectady County Historical Society, 13 Union Street, Schenectady.

Schoharie County Historical Society, Old Stone Fort Museum, Schoharie.

Staten Island Historical Society, Court and Center Streets, Richmond, Staten Island.

Staten Island Italian Historical Society, 257 Bement Ave., West Brighton, Staten Island.

Suffolk County Historical Society, West Main Street, Riverhead, Long Island.

Syracuse Public Library, 335 Montgomery Street, Syracuse.

Washington County Historical Society, County Clerk's Office, Hudson Falls.

Westchester County Historical Society, Room 106, County Office Building, White Plains.

New York research suggestions

Local Historians: A provision of New York law provides for the office of a local historian. There is supposed to be a historian in every town, city, village, and county in the state.

The name and address of the historian in the locality in which you are interested may be obtained from the State Historian, State Education Building, Albany.

Church Records: The Vosburgh Collection of early New York State Protestant church records has been microfilmed. Heretofore these records were available only in a few libraries in their manuscript collections in typewritten form. Typewritten copies are available at the New York Genealogical and Biographical Society, 122 E. 58th Street, N.Y.; Library of Congress; and the New York State Library, Albany.

Marriage Licenses: Names of Persons for Whom Marriage Licenses were Issued by the Secretary of the Province of New York Previous to 1784. Albany 1860. 480 pp.

Seversmith, Herbert F.: "Long Island Genealogical Source Material." *National Genealogical Society Quarterly.* Vol. 36 (June 1948), pp. 61ff.

DAR records in the New York State Library, Albany: The Daughters of the American Revolution in the State of New York through their local chapters have copied and transcribed many local records. Copies of these records have been deposited at the New York State Library as well as the DAR genealogical library in Washington, D.C. These records are quite voluminous and run into several hundred typewritten volumes. The scope of these records is as follows: (1) *Vital Records of Towns,* (2) *Vital Records of Counties,* (3) *Gravestone Records,* (4) *Cemetery Records,* (5) *Family and Bible Records and other manuscript Genealogy.*

Church Records: These records are in the custody of the Manuscripts and History Section of the New York State Library, Albany.

Due to the lack of early vital records in New York State it is necessary to use substitutes such as the New York State Census Records, U. S. Census Records, and Church Records. For an excellent explanation of the value of "New York State Church Records," see the article bearing that title by Paul W. Prindle in *American Genealogist,* vol. 34 (July 1958), pp. 162-63.

Prager, Herta, and William W. Price: "A Bibliography on the History of the Courts of the Thirteen Original States, Maine, Ohio, and Vermont," *American Journal of Legal History,* vol. 2, p. 35.

Early New York Records: The Department of State, 164 State Street, Albany, has custody of some early land records. A card index has been prepared to these records.

The Manuscripts and History Section, New York State

Library, Albany, has custody of many early records, including manuscripts, church records, vital records, family records, and other miscellaneous material of great genealogical and historical value.

Quaker Records: In the following libraries: N. Y. Genealogical and Biographical Society, New York Public Library, New York Historical Society, and Long Island Historical Society. Over 1500 volumes of records, documents, etc., of the Society of Friends in New York, Pennsylvania, New Jersey, Connecticut, Massachusetts, etc., are in the Society's files in the office of the Custodian, 7 East 42nd Street, New York.

Geographical data

Historical and Statistical Gazetteer of New York State. R. P. Smith, publisher, 1860. 739 pp.

Reference books

Albany County: *Early Records of the City and County of Albany, and Colony of Rensselaerwyck,* 1869—.

Anjou, Gustave: *Ulster County, N. Y., Probate Records,* 1906—.

Bailey, Rosalie Fellows: *Guide to Genealogical and Biographical Sources for New York City* (Manhattan), 1783-1898. 1954.

Bergen, Teunis G.: *Register in Alphabetical Order, of the Early Settlers of Kings County, Long Island.* 1881.

Catalogue of American Genealogies in the Library of the Long Island Historical Society. New York, 1935. A bibliography of 8000 books and 850 typescripts and manuscripts.

Daughters of the American Revolution, New York, Manhattan chapter: *Old Homesteads and Historic Buildings, Genealogy and Family Lore.* 1930.

Disturnell, J[ohn]: *Gazetteer of the State of New York.* Albany, 1842.

Documents Relative to the Colonial History of the State of New York. 15 vols. 1853-1887.

Evjen, John Oluf: *Scandinavian Immigrants in New York, 1630-1674.* 1916.

Fernow, Berthold: *Calendar of Wills on File and Recorded in the Offices of the Clerk of the Court of Appeals, of the County Clerk at Albany, and of the Secretary of State, 1626-1836.* 1896.

Fernow, Berthold: *New Amsterdam Family Names and Their Origin.* 1898.

Flagg, Charles Allcott: *Bibliography of New York Colonial History.* 1901. (New York State Library, Bulletin 56.)

French, J. H.: *Gazetteer of New York.* 2 vols. 1860-61.

Hinshaw, William Wade: *Encyclopedia of American Quaker Genealogy.* Vol. 3, 1940.

Jacobson, Edna L.: *An Inventory of New York State and Federal Census Records.* New York State Library—May 1937.

MacWethy, Lou D.: *The Book of Names Especially Relating to the Early Palatines and the First Settlers in the Mohawk Valley.* 1933.

Morris, R. B.: *Select Cases of the Mayor's Court of New York City, 1674-1784.* Washington, 1935. (Vol. 2 of American Legal Records.)

New York: *Handbook of Historical and Patriotic Societies in New York State,* including List of Local Historians. Prepared by the Division of Archives and History, State Department of Education, Albany, 1926.

New York (Colony): *Calendar of New York Colonial Commissions, 1680-1770.* 1929.

New York: *Colonial Records, General Entries.* Vol. 1, 1664-1665. 1899.

New York: *Names of Persons for Whom Marriage Licenses Were Issued by the Secretary of the Province of New York, Previous to 1784.* Albany, 1860. For supplement see New York State Library Bulletin: History, No. 1.

New York: *New York Marriage Licenses.* c. 1916. Supplemented by *New York Genealogical and Biographical Record,* commencing in July 1915.

New York Genealogical and Biographical Society: *Collections.* 1890.

New York Historical Society: *Collections:* 11 vols., 1811-1859.

New York Historical Society: *Collections.* 1868—.

New York (City) Orphan Masters: *The Minutes of the Orphanmasters of New Amsterdam, 1655 to 1663.* 2 vols. 1902-1907.

New York State Historian: *Ecclesiastical Records, State of New York.* 7 vols. 1901-1916.

New York State Historian: *Handbook of Historical and Patriotic Societies in New York State, Including List of Local Historians.* 1926.

New York Surrogate's Court: *Abstracts of Wills on File in the Surrogate's Office, City of New York.* 1893-1913. (See: New York Historical Society: *Collections.* New York County.)

Callahan, E.B., ed.: *Documentary History of the State of New York.* 4 vols. 1849-51.

Pelletreau, William Smith: *Early Long Island Wills of Suffolk County, 1691-1703.* 1897.

Pelletreau, William Smith: *Early Wills of Westchester County, New York, from 1664 to 1784.* 1898.

Pelletreau, William Smith: *Historic Homes and Institutions and Genealogical and Family History of New York.* 4 vols. 1907. This work should be used with caution because of inaccuracies—information should be verified.

Peterson, C. Stewart: *Bibliography of County Histories of the 3111 Counties in the 48 States.* Baltimore, 1946.

Robison, Mrs. Jeannie Floyd: *Genealogical Records: Manuscript Entries of Births, Deaths, and Marriages, Taken from Family Bibles, 1581-1917.* 1917.

Spofford, Horatio Gates: *Gazetteer of the State of New York.* Albany, 1824.

Stillwell, John Edwin: *Historical and Genealogical Miscellany: Data Relating to the Settlement and Settlers of New York and New Jersey.* 1903.

Talcott, Sebastian Visscher: *Genealogical Notes of New York and New England Families.* 1883.

Toler, Henry Pennington: *The New Harlem Register.* 1903.

Turner, Orsamus: *History of the Pioneer Settlement of Phelps and Gorham's Purchase, and Morris' Reserve.* 1852.

Turner, Orsamus: *Pioneer History of the Holland Purchase of Western New York.* 1850.

United States Bureau of the Census: *Heads of Families at the First Census of the United States Taken in the Year 1790.* New York, 1908. In addition to the usual decennial census, censuses were taken in 1855 and 1865 in New York.

United States, WPA: *Bibliography of Research Projects Reports—Check List of Historical Records Survey Publications.* 1943.

Wright, Albert Hazen, and Willard Waldo Ellis: *A Check List of the County Atlases of New York.* Ithaca, 1943.

Military rosters, rolls, and records

Existing records of the Colonial wars, including the French and Indian War and the Revolutionary War, are in the custody of the Manuscripts and History Division, New York State Library, Albany. These records are not to be confused with similar records in the National Archives.

Revolutionary War:

New York State Comptroller's Office: *New York in the Revolution as Colony and State,* Albany, 2 vols. 1901-1904.

________. *New York in the Revolution as Colony and State.* Albany, 1898.

New York Secretary of State: *The Balloting Book, and*

Other Documents Relating to Military Bounty Lands, in the State of New York. Albany, 1825.

New York University: *New York in the Revolution.* Albany, 1887.

Public Papers of George Clinton, First Governor of New York 1775-1795, 1801-1804. 10 vols. 1899-1914. (Index: Vols. 9 and 10.)

Hastings, Hugh: State Historian: *Military Minutes of the Council of Appointment of the State of New York.* 1783-1821. Vols. i-iv, 1901-1902. (Index in Vol. iv.)

War of 1812:

New York Adjutant General's Office: *Index of Awards on Claims of the Soldiers of the War of 1812,* as audited and allowed by the Adjutant and Inspector Generals (of New York State) Pursuant to Chapter 176, of the Laws of 1859. Albany, 1860. (N.Y.S.L. Ms. & Hist. Sect. has errata list inserted in this volume.).

Public Papers of Daniel D. Tompkins, Governor of New York. 1807-1817. 3 vols. 1898-1902. (Index in Vol. 3.)

Hastings, Hugh: State Historian: *Military Minutes of the Council of Appointment of the State of New York.* 1783-1821. Vols. i-iv. 1901-1902. (Index in Vol. iv.)

Civil War:

New York Adjutant General's Office: *Annual Reports of the Adjutant General. . . . Registers of New York Regiments in the War of the Rebellion.* Albany, 1894—. 46 vols.

Phisterer, Frederick: *New York in the War of the Rebellion. 1861-1865.* 1912. (3rd ed.) 5 vols. and index.

:ial records

Vital Records:

Birth and Death Records: All of New York State (except New York City): Custodian, Bureau of Vital Records, Empire State Plaza, Tower Building, Albany, N.Y. 12237. Fee: $2.00. State Custodian has records subsequent to 1880. For records prior to 1914 in Albany, Buffalo, and Yonkers, or before 1880 in any other city, apply to Registrar of Vital Statistics in the city where birth or death occurred. For the balance of New York State (except New York City) write to State Custodian mentioned above.

New York City Births and Deaths for Boroughs of Manhattan, Brooklyn, Queens, Bronx, and Richmond: Bureau of Records, Department of Health, 125 Worth Street, New York, 10013. Fees for certificates: births, $3.00; deaths, $2.50. Records of the above-mentioned Custodian are subsequent to 1898.

Birth and Death Records for Old City of New York

(*Manhattan and Part of the Bronx*), *1865-97:* Municipal Archives and Records Retention Center of New York, 23 Park Row, New York, 10038.

Marriage Records, All of New York State (*except New York City*): Bureau of Vital Records, State Department of Health, Empire State Plaza, Tower Building, Albany, 12237, for records from January 1880 to December 1907 and also subsequent to May 1915. Fee, $2.00.

Marriage Records from January 1908 to April 1915: County Clerk in the county where license was issued, County Seat. Cost of certificates varies.

Marriage Records from January 1880 to December 1907: City Clerk in Albany and Buffalo, and the Registrar of Vital Statistics in Yonkers, if the marriage was performed in these cities. Cost of certificate, $2.00.

New York City Marriage Records: 1847-1865: Custodian: Municipal Archives and Records Retention Center, New York Public Library, 23 Park Row, New York, 10038, except Brooklyn record for this period, the custodian of which is the County Clerk's Office, Kings County, Supreme Court Building, Brooklyn, 11201. Cost of certificate: $4.00. *1866 to 1907:* City Clerk's Office in the borough in which the marriage was performed.* *1908 to May 12, 1943:* City Clerk's Office in the borough of the bride's residence.* *Non-residents:* City Clerk's Office in the borough in which the license was issued.* *May 13, 1943, to date:* City Clerk's Office in borough in which the license was issued.*

Bronx: Office of City Clerk, 1780 Grand Concourse, Bronx, 10457. Cost: $4.00 (Records for 1908-1913 for the Bronx are filed in the Manhattan office referred to below. Cost of certificate: $4.00.)

Brooklyn: Office of City Clerk, 208 Joralemon St., Brooklyn, N.Y. 11201. Cost: $4.00.

Manhattan: Office of City Clerk, Chambers and Centre Streets, New York, 10007. Cost: $4.00.

Queens: Office of City Clerk, 120-55 Queens Blvd., Borough Hall Station, Jamaica, 11424. Cost: $4.00.

Richmond: Office of City Clerk, Borough Hall, St. George, Staten Island, 10301. Cost: $4.00.

Birth, Marriage, and Death Records prior to 1880: Town Clerk or City Clerk. (*Exception:* New York City Boroughs: Refer to subject above.) *Note:* Vital records prior to 1880 are not complete.

Divorce Records: County Clerk of county where divorce was granted. Cost of certified copy of divorce decree varies.

*Cost of certificates: $4.00 if exact year of marriage is known; otherwise there is a charge of 50 cents for the second year's search, and 25 cents for each additional year.

Court Records: Wills, administrations, and other probate matters: Clerk, Surrogate's Court, County Seat. *Civil Actions:* Clerk of County Court, County Seat.

Land Records: Deeds, mortgages, leases, and other matters affecting title to land; County Clerk, or Register of Deeds, County Seat.

leral census ords

1. See index for section on United States census.

2. Custody of mortality schedules, 1850, 1860, 1870, 1880: New York State Library, Albany.

3. The original 1880 United States census records for New York were transferred in 1956 by the National Archives to: New York State Library, Albany.

v York state sus records

In 1855 the scope of the information included in these census records was broadened. Prior to 1855, only the name of the head of the family was listed, and other family members were represented by number and not by name. Beginning with the 1855 New York State census, in addition to listing the names, ages, etc., of persons, other important features were included, such as the relationship to the head of the family and the county in New York where born, or if born elsewhere, the name of the state or country. For this reason the 1855 New York State census is more helpful than the 1850 U.S. census, as the U.S. census did not state the relationship to the head of the family or some of the other features mentioned above until much later.

The custodians and location of the New York State census are as follows:

nmary of custodians xisting New York State sus records

(*The custodian is the County Clerk unless otherwise stated*)

ne of nty	*Location of County Clerk's Office or Other Custodian*	*Census Records*
.ny	Albany	1915, 1925. New York State Library has custody of 1855, 1865, 1875, 1892, and 1905.
gany	Belmont	1855, 1865, 1875, 1892, 1905, 1915, 1925.
x	Bronx	1915, 1925.
me	Binghamton	1825, 1835, 1855, 1865, Military Census for Vestal only 1875, 1892, 1905, 1915, 1925.
araugus	Little Valley	1835, 1855, 1865, 1875, 1892, 1905, 1915, 1925, Custodian: Cattaraugus County Memorial and Historical Building, Little Valley.

Name of county	*Location of County Clerk's Office or Other Custodian*	*Census Records*
Cayuga	Auburn	1865, 1875, 1892, 1905, 1915, 1925.
Chautauqua	Mayville	1845, 1855, 1875, 1892, 1915, 1925.
Chemung	Elmira	1855, 1865, 1892, 1905, 1915, 1925.
Chenango	Norwich	1855, 1865, 1905, 1925.
Clinton	Plattsburgh	1892, 1905, 1915, 1925.
Columbia	Hudson	1845 (Hudson); 1855, 1865, 1875, 1905, 1925.
Cortland	Cortland	1835, 1845, 1855, 1865, 1875, 1892, 1905, 1925.
Delaware	Delhi	1845, 1855, 1865, 1875, 1892, 1905, 1915, 1925.
Dutchess	Poughkeepsie	1865, 1875, 1892, 1915 (1925 towns of Hyde Park, Poughkeepsie, town and city, and Rhinebeck).
Erie	Buffalo	1855, 1865, 1875, 1892, 1905, 1915, 1925.
Essex	Elizabethtown	1855, 1875, 1892, 1905, 1925.
Franklin	Malone	1875, 1905, 1915, 1925.
Fulton	Johnston	1845, 1855, 1865, 1875, 1905, 1915, 1925.
Genesee	Batavia	1845, 1865, 1875, 1892, 1905, 1915, 1925.
Greene	Catskill	1855, 1865, 1875, 1892, 1915, 1925.
Hamilton	Lake Pleasant	1892, 1905, 1915, 1925.
Herkimer	Herkimer	1825, 1835, 1845, 1855, 1865, 1875, 1892, 1905, 1915, 1925.
Jefferson	Watertown	1835, 1855, 1865, 1875, 1905, 1915, 1925.
Kings	Brooklyn	1855, 1865, 1875, 1892, (1905 Election Dist. 1-39 only), 1915, 1925.
Lewis	Lowville	1825, 1835, 1855, 1865, 1875, 1892, 1905, 1915, 1925.
Livingston	Geneseo	1855, 1865, 1875, 1915, 1925.
Madison	Wampsville	1855, 1865, 1875, 1892, 1905, 1925.
Monroe	Rochester	(1855 Co. Clerk has towns only. Schedules fo city of Rochester at State Library), 1865, 187 1892, 1905, 1915, 1925.
Montgomery	Fonda	1825 Towns of Minden, Palatine, Hope, Lak Pleasant, Oppenheim, Stratford, Johnstown, Florida, Canajoharie, and Root only. 1835 Oppenheim only. 1845 Minden and Oppenheim only. 1855, 1865, 1875, 1892, 1905, 1915, 1925.
Nassau	Mineola	1915, 1925.
New York	Manhattan	1905, 1915, 1925. (1855 Commissioner of Records of New York County, Hall of Records Manhattan.)
Niagara	Lockport	1835, 1845, 1855, 1865, 1875, 1892, 1905, 1915, 1925.
Oneida	Utica	1875, 1915, 1925. Utica Public Library has schedules for most of the towns for 1835, 1855, and 1865.

of y	*Location of County Clerk's Office or Other Custodian*	*Census Records*
daga	Syracuse	1855, 1865, 1875, 1892, 1905, 1915, 1925.
o	Canandaigua	1855, 1865, 1875, 1892.
e	Goshen	1825, 1835, 1845, 1855, 1865, 1875, (1915 Town of Goshen missing), 1925.
ns	Albion	1855, 1865, 1875, 1892, 1905.
go	Oswego	1855, 1865, 1875, 1892, 1915, 1925.
o	Cooperstown	1855, 1865, 1875, 1892, 1905, 1915, 1925.
n	Carmel	1915, 1925.
ns	Jamaica	1892, 1915, 1925.
elaer	Troy	1855, 1865, 1875, 1905, 1925.
ond	Staten Island	1855, 1915, 1925 (1835 Staten Island Historical Society, Richmond).
and	New City	1865, 1875, 1892, 1915, 1925.
wrence	Canton	1905, 1915, 1925.
ga	Ballston Spa	1855, 1865, 1875, 1892, (1905 Towns of Saratoga Springs, Stillwater, Waterford, and Wilton), 1915, 1925.
ectady	Schenectady	1835, 1855, 1865, 1875, 1892, 1905, 1915, 1925.
arie	Schoharie	1825, 1835, 1865, 1875, 1892, 1905, 1915, 1925.
ler	Watkins Glen	1855, 1865, 1875, 1915, 1925.
a	Waterloo	1905, 1915, 1925.
en	Bath	1825, 1835, 1845, 1855, 1865, 1875, 1892, 1905, 1915, 1925.
	Riverhead	No records.
n	Monticello	1855, 1865, 1875, 1892, 1925.
	Owego	1855, 1865, 1875, 1892, 1905, 1915, 1925.
ins	Ithaca	1825, 1865, 1875, 1892, 1905, 1925. (1835 Town of Ulysses only, New York State Library.)
	Kingston	1845, 1855, 1865, 1875, 1905, 1915, 1925. Missing from 1875: Marlboro, New Paltz, Olive, Plattekill, Rochester, Rosendale, Saugerties, Shandaken, Showangunk, Waworsing, Woodstock.
n	Lake George	1855, 1865, 1875, 1905, 1925.
ngton	Hudson Falls	1825, 1835, 1855, 1865, 1875, 1892, 1905, 1915, 1925.
	Lyons	1855, Volume for Rose, Savannah, Sodus, Walworth, Williamson, Wolcott, missing: 1865, 1875, except Savannah; 1892, 1905, 1915, 1925.
nester	White Plains	1905, 1915, 1925.
ng	Warsaw	1875, Towns of Perry, Pike, Sheldon, Warsaw, Wethersfield; 1915, 1925.
	Penn Yan	1825, 1835, 1855, 1865, 1875, 1892, 1905, 1915, 1925.

New York State Census Records in the custody of the New York State Library, Albany:

1835: Coeymans and Westerlo, Albany County; Root, Montgomery County; Ulysses, Tompkins County.

1845: City of Hudson, Columbia County.

1855: City of Rochester and Albany County.

1865, 1875, 1892, and 1905: Albany County only.

1915 and 1925: The entire state of New York.

Other census records taken by the state of New York and formerly on file in the New York State Library were burned in the capitol fire in 1911, a few fragments only remaining for the enumerations of 1801, 1814, and 1821.

North Carolina

General information

Capital: Raleigh. Entered Union: November 21, 1789. Seceded from Union: May 20, 1861. Reentered Union: July 20, 1868.

Libraries, historical societies, and archives

For a complete list, see: Brown, Karl: *The American Library Directory.* Also, *Directory of Historical Societies and Agencies in the United States and Canada,* 1956.

Henderson County Historical Society, Hendersonville.

State Department of Archives and History, Box 1881, Raleigh.

North Carolina State Library, Raleigh, North Carolina. Among other items, contains 6967 volumes of newspapers.

North Carolina research suggestions

Corbitt, *The Formation of the North Carolina Counties, 1663-1943.* 1950.

The North Carolinian, a quarterly magazine voted to North Carolina research. Address: Box 531, Raleigh.

Articles of general interest

"The North Carolina State Department of Archives and History and Its Manuscript Collection," by Christopher Crittenden, *National Genealogical Society Quarterly,* March 1946, pp. 1-3.

"Eastern North Carolina as a Field for Genealogical Research," *National Genealogical Society Quarterly,* December 1945, pp. 101-104.

"A Bibliography on the History of the Courts of the Thirteen Original States, Maine, North Carolina, Ohio, and

Vermont," by Herta Prager and William W. Price, *American Journal of Legal History,* vol. 2, p. 43.

ence
s

Arthur, John Preston: *Western North Carolina; a History.* 1914.

Cemetery Records of North Carolina. 3 vols. Typed by the Genealogical Society, Salt Lake City, Utah. 1947-1955.

Clemens, William Montgomery: *North and South Carolina Marriage Records.* c. 1927.

DeMond, Robert O.: *The Loyalists in North Carolina during the Revolution.* 1940.

Draughon, Wallace R.: *North Carolina Genealogical Reference.* 1956.

Grimes, J. Bryan: *Abstract of North Carolina Wills,* in the Office of the Secretary of State. 1910. 670 pp.

Grimes, J. Bryan: *North Carolina Wills and Inventories,* in the Office of the Secretary of State. 1912. 587 pp.

Hinshaw, William Wade: *Encyclopedia of American Quaker Genealogy.* Vol. 1, 1936.

Historical Records Survey, WPA: *The Historical Records of North Carolina.* 3 vols.

Hunter, C. L.: *Sketches of Western North Carolina, Historical and Biographical.* 1877.

North Carolina: *The Colonial Records of North Carolina.* 10 vols. 1886-1890.

North Carolina Obituary Notices 1835-1877. Typewritten by the Genealogical Society, Salt Lake City, Utah. 1938 204 pp.

North Carolina Historical and Genealogical Register. 3 vols. 1900-1903. (For an index to this work see: *Ray's Index and Digest to Hathaway's North Carolina Historical and Genealogical Register.* 1945. 192 pp.)

Olds, Fred A.: *Abstracts of North Carolina Wills from about 1760-1800.* 1936. 360 pp. Typewritten. (Index to the foregoing compiled and typed by the Genealogical Society, Salt Lake City, Utah. 1948. 400 pp.)

Peterson, C. Stewart: *Bibliography of County Histories of the 3111 Counties in the 48 States.* Baltimore, 1946.

Ramsey, J. G. M.: *Annals of Tennessee to the End of the Eighteenth Century.* 1853. Reprinted 1926. Contains valuable information on North Carolina men.

United States Bureau of the Census: Heads of Families at the First Census of the United States Taken in the Year 1790. North Carolina, 1908.

Wheeler, John Hill: *Historical Sketches of North Carolina from 1584 to 1851.*.1851. Reprinted in 1925.

Military rosters, rolls, and records

Revolutionary War Rolls, etc.:

Blair, Anna: *A List of Revolutionary Soldiers Buried in North Carolina* (see Historical Collections of the Georgia Chapters, Daughters of the American Revolution, vol. 1 (1926), pp. 352-64).

Daughters of the American Revolution, North Carolina: *Roster of the Soldiers from North Carolina in the American Revolution.* Durham, 1932.

North Carolina: *Roster of the Continental Line from North Carolina.* 1783. (See the State Records of North Carolina, vol. 16, pp. 1002-1197. See also Index in vol. 4.)

War of 1812:

North Carolina, General Assembly: Adjutant General: *Muster Rolls of the Soldiers of the War of 1812 Detached from the Militia of North Carolina in 1812 and 1814.* Raleigh, 1851. Reprinted by Barber Printing Company, Inc., Winston-Salem, N.C., 1926. The roster is arranged by unit and is not indexed.

Civil War:

North Carolina General Assembly: *Roster of North Carolina Troops in the War Between the States.* Prepared by Order of Legislature of 1881, by J.W. Moore. 4 vols. Raleigh, 1882.

Confederate Military Records: The National Archives has compiled the *Consolidated Index* to Compiled Records of Confederate Soldiers. The index is on cards that give the name of the soldier, his rank, the unit in which he served, and often a statement concerning the origin or background of that unit. There are cross-reference cards for soldiers' names that appeared in the records under more than one spelling. This index is available for personal search or by an agent. It is microfilmed.

Confederate Pensioners: Department of Archives and History, Raleigh.

Official records

Vital Records: Fee for birth and death certificate, $2.00; for marriage certificate, $2.00.

State Custodian: Office of Vital Statistics, N. C. State Board of Health, P.O. Box 2091, Raleigh, 27602.

Birth and Death Records: Subsequent to October 1, 1913 Above-named State Custodian. *Prior to Oct. 1, 1913:* Try City Board of Health where birth or death occurred. For births and deaths not in a city, try Register of Deeds, County Seat. *Delayed birth certificates:* State Custodian will furnish information.

Divorce Records: Since January 1, 1958: Public Health Statistics Section, State Board of Health, P.O. Box 2091,

Raleigh. Cost of certified copy of divorce decree is $2.00. *Prior to 1958:* Clerk of Superior Court in county where divorce was granted. Cost of certified copy of divorce decree varies.

Marriage Licenses: Register of Deeds.

Marriage Records: County Register of Deeds, County Seat.

Court Records: Wills, administrations, and other probate matters: Clerk, Superior Court, County Seat. *Other Civil Actions:* County Clerk, County Seat.

Land Records: Deeds, mortgages, leases, and other matters affecting title to land: Register of Deeds, County Seat.

…eral census

1. See index for section on United States census.

2. Custody of mortality schedules, 1850, 1860, 1870, 1880: North Carolina State Department of Archives and History, Raleigh.

3. The original 1880 United States census records for North Carolina were transferred in 1956 by the National Archives to: Department of Archives and History, State of North Carolina, Raleigh.

…e census

North Carolina has no state census records.

North Dakota

…eral …mation

Capital: Bismarck. Organized as a territory: March 2, 1861. Entered Union: November 2, 1889.

…aries, …orical …eties, …archives

For a complete list, see: Brown, Karl: *The American Library Directory.* Also *Directory of Historical Societies and Agencies in the United States and Canada,* 1956.

North Dakota Historical Society, Liberty Memorial Building, Bismarck.

…rence …ks

Historical Records Survey, WPA: *Guide to Public Vital Statistics Records in North Dakota.* 1941. 77 pp.

Lounsberry, Clement A.: *North Dakota History and People.* 3 vols. 1917. (Vols. 2 and 3, biographical.)

Ogle, A. & Co.: *Compendium of History and Biography of North Dakota.* 1900. 1410 pp.

Peterson, C. Stewart: *Bibliography of County Histories of the 3111 Counties in the 48 States.* Baltimore, 1946.

State Historical Society: *Collections.* Vol. 1, 1906.

Military rosters, rolls, and records

Civil War—Dakota Territory Roster: U.S. Congress: Dakota Militia in the War of 1862. Washington, 1904. (U.S. 58th Congress, 2d Session, Senate Doc. No. 241.)

No official state publications known.

Official records

Vital Records: Fees: Birth and death certificate, $2.00. Money order should be made payable to the State Department of Health, Bismarck. Marriage certificates, usual fee is $1.00. Should be sent to the County Judge of the county in which the license was secured.

State Custodian: State Registrar of Vital Statistics. All requests should be addressed to: Division of Vital Statistics, State Department of Health, Bismarck, 58501. Local registrars' records are confidential, and they have no authority to issue copies.

Birth and Death Records: Subsequent to 1907: Above-named State Custodian. Approximate date and name of county should be furnished. Also try county auditor. *Prior to 1907:* The State Custodian has some earlier records on file; also try county auditor of the county seat. *Delayed birth certificates:* State Custodian will furnish information.

Divorce Records: Clerk of District Court in county where divorce was granted. Cost of certified copy of divorce decre varies.

Marriage License and Certificates: Original records are o file in the office of the County Judge of the county in which license to marry was obtained. Copies are on file in the Division of Vital Statistics, State Department of Health, Bismarck, North Dakota, beginning July 1, 1925.

Court Records: Wills, administrations, and other probate matters: Clerk, County Court, County Seat. *Other Civil Actions:* Clerk, District Court, County Seat.

Land Records: Deeds, mortgages, leases, and other matters affecting title to land: Register of Deeds, County Seat.

Federal census

1. See index for section on United States census.

2. Custody of mortality schedules, 1860, 1870: State Historical Society, Bismarck.

3. "The U.S. Census for 1850 of the Pembina District" is published in volume 1, *State Historical Collections,* 1906.

Territorial census records

Custodian: State Historical Society of North Dakota, Liberty Memorial Building, Bismarck.

1855 Territorial Census of Dakota Territory (for that part that is now North Dakota): Reports head of family, name, an age of each member, sex, occupation, where born, and where parents were born.

Dakota census ds

1905: Names only, not complete. *1915:* Name of each member of the family. In most cases the age is not given. *1925:* Name, age, and citizenship of each member of the family.

Ohio

ral nation

Capital: Columbus. Entered the Union: March 1, 1803.

ries, ical ties, and ves

For a complete list, see: Brown, Karl: *The American Library Directory.* Also, *Directory of Historical Societies and Agencies in the United States and Canada,* 1956.

Akron Public Library, 11 S. Summit Street, Akron.

Allen County Historical and Archaeological Society, Memorial Hall, Lima.

Canton Public Library, Canton.

Cincinnati Public Library, Vine at 8th, Cincinnati.

Cleveland Public Library, 325 Superior Avenue, Cleveland.

Dayton Public Library, Cooper Park, 215 E. 3rd St., Dayton.

Firelands Historical Society, Firelands Memorial Building, West Main Street, Norwalk.

Historical & Philosophical Society of Ohio, University of Cincinnati Library Building, Cincinnati.

Hudson Library and Historical Society, Hudson.

Mahoning Valley Historical Society, Youngstown Public Library, 305 Wick Avenue, Youngstown.

Ohio Historical Society, Interstate 71 and 17th Ave., Columbus, 43211.

Ohio State Archaeological and Historical Library, 15th Avenue and High Street, Columbus.

Ohio State Library, Columbus.

Librarian, William Howard Doane Library, Denison University, Granville, Ohio. This library has material pertinent to Licking County and surrounding counties.

Ross County Historical Society, 45 West Fifth St., Chillicothe.

Stark County Historical Society, Box 483, Canton.

Toledo Public Library, 325 Michigan Avenue, Toledo.

Western Reserve Historical Society Library, 10825 East Blvd., Cleveland. This library ranks among the best in the U.S. for its genealogical collection.

Genealogical periodicals

The Firelands Pioneer, published by the Firelands Historical Society. Vol. 1, 1858.

Ohio Archaeological and Historical Quarterly. Vol. 1, 1888.

The Ohio Genealogical Quarterly, published by the Columbus Genealogical Society. 7 vols. 1937-1943.

Articles of general interest

Dickore, Marie: ''Genealogical Resources in the Cincinnati, Ohio Area,'' *National Genealogical Society Quarterly.* Vol. 43 (March 1955), pp. 1ff.

Dolle, Mrs. P. A.: ''Ohio's Records,'' *Genealogical Forum* (Portland, Oregon). Vol. 6, pp. 52-53.

Hinebaugh, Preston: ''Research Facilities in Ohio,'' *Genealogical Forum* (Portland, Oregon). Vol. 4, p. 34.

Prager, Herta, and William W. Price: ''A Bibliography on the History of the Courts of the Thirteen Original States, Maine, North Carolina, Ohio, and Vermont,'' *American Journal of Legal History.* Vol. 2, p. 45.

Raber, Nellie M.: ''An Ohio Tax List of 1804, Giving Resident Proprietors of the Western Reserve and a Key to the Location of Their Farms,'' *National Genealogical Society Quarterly.* September 1943, pp. 65-73. (First of a series.)

Reference books

Bell, Annie Walker Burns: *Pension Applications.* Record of Abstracts of Soldiers Who Applied for Pensions While Residing in Ohio. Washington, D. C. (n.d.) 100 pp.

Dailey, Mrs. Orville D.: *The Official Roster of the Soldiers of the American Revolution Who Lived in the State of Ohio.* Published by the Ohio State DAR, 1938. Vol. 2. 436 pp.

Henderson, Frank D.: *The Official Roster of the Soldiers of the American Revolution Buried in the State of Ohio.* 1929. 445 pp.

Hildreth, S. P.: *Bibliographical and Historical Memoirs of the Early Pioneers of Ohio,* with Narratives of Incidents and Occurrences in 1775. Cincinnati, 1852.

Historical Records Survey, WPA: *Inventory of the State Archives of Ohio.* 1941. 71 pp.

Kilbourn, John: *The Ohio Gazetteer.* 8th ed., 1826. 231 pp.

Peterson, C. Stewart: *Bibliography of County Histories of the 3111 Counties in the 48 States.* Baltimore, 1946.

Summers, Ewing, ed.: *Genealogical and Family History of Eastern Ohio.* 1903. 792 pp.

United States Department of State: *Territorial Papers of the United States.* Clarence E. Carter, ed. 1934. Vols. 2 and 3: *Territory Northwest of the Ohio River,* 1787-1803. (For a summary of this source see *National Genealogical Society Quarterly,* 37:93ff.)

tary rosters, s and ords

Ohio Adjutant General's Records: Records of the Ohio Adjutant General's Department Division of Soldier's Claims. Veteran's Affairs, State House, Columbus. The military records of Ohio soldiers in all wars from the War of 1812, to and including World War I, are in the custody of this office. This office also maintains a card index of soldiers of all wars buried in Ohio cemeteries, including the American Revolution. Ohio has never paid pensions to war veterans.

Revolutionary War: Ohio Adjutant General's Office: *Official Roster of the Soldiers of the American Revolution Buried in the State of Ohio.* 1929.

War of 1812: Adjutant General of Ohio: *Roster of Ohio Soldiers in the War of 1812.* 1916. 157 pp.

Civil War: Ohio Roster Commission: *Official Roster of the Soldiers of the State of Ohio in the War of the Rebellion, 1861-1866.* Compiled under the direction of the Roster Commission, and published by authority of the General Assembly. 12 vols. Akron, 1886-1895.

cial records

Vital Records: Fee for birth and death certificate: $1.00.

State Custodian: Division of Vital Statistics, Room G 20, Ohio Departments Building, Columbus, 43215.

Birth and Death Records: Subsequent to December 20, 1908: Above-named State Custodian. *Prior to December 20, 1908:* City Board of Health if in a city, or Clerk of Probate Court at the County Seat where the event occurred. *Delayed birth certificates:* By court proceedings only.

Divorce Records: Clerk of Court of Common Pleas in county where divorce was granted.

Marriage Licenses: Clerk, Probate Court, County Seat.

Marriage Records: Clerk, Probate Court.

Court Records: Wills, administrations, and other probate matters: Clerk, Probate Court, County Seat. *Other Civil Actions:* Clerk, Court of Common Pleas, County Seat.

Land Records: Deeds, mortgages, leases, and other matters affecting title to land: County Recorder, County Seat.

deral census ords

1. See index for section on United States Census.

2. Custody of the mortality schedules of the U.S. Census: The Ohio State Library, Reference Department, Columbus, has the custody of the following mortality schedules:

1850: Hamilton and Wyandot counties.

1860: All counties.
1880: Adams and Geauga counties.

3. The original 1880 United States census records for Ohio were transferred in 1956 by the National Archives to: Ohio State Museum, Ohio State Historical Society, Columbus.

Ohio state census records

Ohio has no state census records.

Oklahoma

General information

Capital: Oklahoma City. Organized as a territory: May 2, 1890. Entered Union: November 16, 1907.

Libraries, historical societies, and archives

For a complete list, see: Brown, Karl: *The American Library Directory.* Also, *Directory of Historical Societies and Agencies in the United States and Canada,* 1956.

Oklahoma Historical Society, Historical Building, Lincoln Blvd. at 20th St., Oklahoma City.

Tulsa Public Library, Tulsa.

Reference books

Chronicles of Oklahoma.

Cook, Mrs. John P.: *Collection of Bible and Family Records.* Assembled by DAR Chapters of Oklahoma. 1946-1954.

Historical Records Survey, WPA: *A List of Records of the State of Oklahoma.* 1938.

Historical Records Survey, WPA: *Guide to Public Vital Statistics Records in Oklahoma.* 1941. 85 pp.

Historical Records Survey, WPA: *Preliminary List of Churches and Religious Organizations in Oklahoma.* 1942. 340 pp.

Illustrated Oklahoma State Gazetteer and Business Directory. R.L. Polk and Co. 1913-1914.

Peterson, C. Stewart: *Bibliography of County Histories of the 3111 Counties in the 48 States.* Baltimore, 1946.

Portrait and Biographical Record of Oklahoma. Chapman Publishing Co., 1901. 1298 pp.

Military rosters, rolls, and records

Military records: Oklahoma Adjutant General. Little information prior to 1900.

fficial records

Vital Records: Fee for birth and death certificate: $2.00.

State Custodian: Division of Vital Statistics, State Dept. of Public Health, P.O. Box 53551, Oklahoma City, 73105.

Birth and Death Records: Subsequent to 1907: Above-named State Custodian. *Delayed birth certificates:* By court proceedings only.

Divorce Records: County Clerk in county where divorce was granted. Cost of certified copy varies.

Marriage Licenses: Clerk, County Court at the County Seat.

Marriage Records: Subsequent to May 2, 1890: Above-named State Custodian. Incomplete, try Clerk, County Court at the county seats. *Prior to May 2, 1890:* Clerk, County Seat.

Court Records: Wills, administrations, and other probate matters: Clerk, County Court, County Seat. *Other Civil Actions:* Clerk, County Court, County Seat.

Land Records: Deeds, mortgages, leases, and other matters affecting title to land: County Clerk, County Seat.

ederal census

See index for section on United States Census. Mortality schedules: None taken.

erritorial nsus records

The Bureau of the Census has custody of a Special Census of Oklahoma Territory for Seminole County for 1907. Schedules include name, color, age, sex, and relationship to the head of the family of every inhabitant. These records may be examined only by employees of the Census Bureau.

klahoma state nsus records

None taken by the state of Oklahoma, except those for Indians of the Five Civilized Tribes, which were made about 1902. There are some other censuses of Indians on microfilm, which were the result of later land openings.

Oregon

eneral ormation

Capital: Salem. Organized as a territory: August 13, 1848. Entered Union: February 14, 1859.

braries, storical cieties, and chives

For a complete list, see: Brown, Karl: *The American Library Directory*. Also, *Directory of Historical Societies and Agencies in the United States and Canada,* 1956.

Oregon Historical Society, 235 S.W. Market Street, Portland.

Oregon State Library, State Library Building, Salem.

Oregon State Archives, State Library Building, Salem.

Portland Library Association, 8015 W. 10th Avenue, Portland.

Reference books

Clarke, S. A.: *Pioneer Days of Oregon History.* 1905.

Gaston, Joseph: *The Centennial History of Oregon, 1811-1912.* 3 vols. Chicago, 1912. (Vols. 2 and 3, biographical.)

Genealogical Forum of Portland, Oregon: "Genealogical Material in Oregon Donation Land Claims Abstracted from Applications." Vol. 1, 1957.

Historical Records Survey, WPA: *Guide to the Manuscript Collections of the Oregon Historical Society.* 1940. 133 pp.

Historical Records Survey, WPA: *Directory of Churches and Religious Organizations, State of Oregon.* 1940. 303 pp.

Historical Records Survey, WPA: *Guide to Public Vital Statistics Records in Oregon.* 1942. 78 pp.

Historical Records Survey, WPA: *Guide to Depositories of Manuscript Collections in the United States.* 1940. 42 pp.

Historical Records Survey, WPA: *Descriptions of County Offices in Oregon and a Check List of Their Records.* 1937.

"Index to Oregon Donation Land Claim Files in the National Archives," in *The Genealogical Forum of Portland, Oregon.* Beginning with vol. 3, September 1953, up to and including vol. 7, November 1957. Invaluable for tracing Oregon pioneer families.

McArthur, Lewis A.: *Oregon Geographic Names.* 1944. 581 pp.

Oregon State Archives: *Pioneer Families of the Oregon Territory 1850.* Bulletin No. 3, Pub. No. 17. 1951. 44 pp. Modern states of Oregon, Washington, Idaho, and part of Wyoming. A list of heads of families and of individuals of other surnames recorded in the U.S. Census of 1850.

Peterson, C. Stewart: *Bibliography of County Histories of the 3111 Counties in the 48 States.* Baltimore, 1946.

Military rosters, rolls, and records

State Rosters—Civil War: Report of the Adjutant General (C.A. Reed) of the State of Oregon for the Years 1865-66. Salem, 1866. 353 pp.

Oregon Adjutant General Records: The earliest records of this office commence with the Indian wars of 1843, which continued intermittently for fifty years. These consist of muster rolls of the various volunteer militia companies and letter correspondence. Available for personal search. Office of the Adjutant General, Salem, Oregon.

ial records

Vital records: Fee for certified birth, marriage, and death certificate: $3.00.

State Custodian: Statistics Section, State Board of Health, P.O. Box 231, Portland, Oregon 97207.

Birth and Death Records: Subsequent to September 1903, including delayed birth certificates filed since that date: Above-named State Custodian. Prior birth and death records: Benton County, 1893—; Clackamas County, 1850—; Wasco County, 1865-1891; Wheeler County, 1899—; Yamhill County, 1873—. Prior death certificates only: City Bureau of Health, Portland, January 1, 1881. *Delayed birth certificates:* State Custodian will furnish information.

Divorce Records: Since 1925: Above-named State Custodian. Cost of certified copy of divorce decree is $3.00. *Prior to 1925:* County Clerk of the county where divorce was granted. Cost of certified copy varies.

Marriage Certificates: County Clerk at County Seat, from 1849 or 1850 or from creation of county. Must obtain certified copies from him. Return of Marriage Certificate Reports subsequent to 1906: State Custodian. Since 1925 serves as master index to surname of husband and maiden name of wife.

Marriage Records and Divorce Decrees: County Clerk at County Seat from 1849 or 1850 or from creation of county.

Court Records: Wills, administrations, and other probate matters: County Clerk, County Seat. *Other Civil Actions:* County Clerk, County Seat.

Land Records: Deeds, mortgages, leases, and other matters affecting title to land: County Clerk, County Seat.

eral census

1. See index for section on United States census.

2. Custody of mortality schedules, 1850, 1860, 1870, 1880: Oregon State Library, Salem.

3. The original 1880 United States census records for Oregon were transferred in 1956 by the National Archives to: Oregon State Library, Salem.

gon
itorial
state
sus records

Custodian: Oregon State Archives, Oregon State Library, State Library Building, Salem.

1845 Census: Included the following counties: Champoeg (now Marion), Clackamas, Clatsop, Tuality (now in Washington), Yamhill. Lists single men and heads of families by name.

1849 Census: Included the following counties: Champoeg (now Marion), Clackamas, Clatsop, Lewis (now in Washington), Linn, Polk, Tuality (now in Washington),

Vancouver (now in Washington), and Yamhill. Lists heads of families and in some counties all of the members.

1853 Census: Included the following counties: Marion, Umpqua (now Douglas), and Washington. Lists names of heads of families.

1854 Census: Included Benton, Clatsop, and Jackson counties. Lists names of heads of families except Jackson County, in which heads and members of the families are listed.

1855 Census: Included Coos and Jackson counties. Names of members of the family are listed.

1856 Census: Included Clackamas, Curry, Jackson, Polk, and Washington counties. Names of heads of families listed.

1857 Census: Included Coos and Douglas counties. Members of the household were listed for Coos, heads of families for Douglas.

1858 Census: Included Coos County only. Members of the household listed.

1859 Census: Included Clatsop County only. Names of heads of household listed.

1865 Census: Included Marion and Umatilla counties. Names of heads of families listed.

1885 Census: Included Umatilla County only. Names of heads of families listed.

1895 Census: Included Marion and part of Multnomah counties. Names of members of the family listed.

1905 Census: Marion County only. Names of members of the family listed.

Pennsylvania

General information

Capital: Harrisburg. Entered Union: December 12, 1787. (Pennsylvania, New York, New Jersey, and Delaware comprise what was once New Netherlands.)

Libraries, historical societies, and archives

For a complete list, see: Brown, Karl: *The American Library Directory.* Also, *Directory of Historical Societies and Agencies in the United States and Canada,* 1956.

American Swedish Historical Foundation, 1900 Pattison Avenue, Philadelphia.

Blair County Historical Society, Hollidaysburg.

Bucks County Historical Society, Doylestown.

Carnegie Library, 4400 Forbes Street, Pittsburgh.

Chester County Historical Society, 225 North High Street, West Chester.

Crawford County Historical Society, Public Library, Meadville.

Division of Public Records, Pennsylvania Historical and Museum Commission, 221 Educational Building, Harrisburg. Military records, and records of naturalization, immigration, and microfilms of certain county records and federal censuses. For further information see subsequent paragraphs on immigration records.

Genealogical Society of Pennsylvania, 1300 Locust Street, Philadelphia.

Friends Historical Association, Swarthmore College, Swarthmore.

Hamilton Library and Historical Association of Cumberland County, North Pitt Street, Carlisle.

Historical Society of Berks County, 940 Centre Avenue, Reading.

Historical Society of Dauphin County, John Harris Mansion, 219 South Front Street, Harrisburg.

Historical Society of Montgomery County, 18 East Penn Street, Norristown.

Historical Society of Pennsylvania, 1300 Locust St., Philadelphia.

Historical Society of York County, 225 East Market Street, York.

Lackawanna Historical Society, 232 Monroe Ave., Scranton.

Lancaster County Historical Society, 307 N. Duke St., Lancaster.

Monroe County Historical Society, Stroud Community House, Ninth and Main Streets, Stroudsburg.

Northampton County Historical and Genealogical Society, Fourth and Ferry Streets, Easton.

Pennsylvania Free Library, Genealogy Division, Logan Square, Philadelphia.

Pennsylvania State Library, Harrisburg.

Pennsylvania Historical Association, Pennsylvania State College, State College.

Pennsylvania Historical Commission, State Museum Bldg., Harrisburg.

Snyder County Historical Society, Susquehanna University Library, Selinsgrove.

Susquehanna County Historical Society and Free Library Association, Library Building, Montrose.

Valley Forge Historical Society, Bishop White Memorial Building, Valley Forge.

Wyoming Historical and Geological Society, 69 So. Franklin St., Wilkes-Barre.

Pennsylvania research suggestions

For a record of more than 2640 names of persons who were parties to court proceedings during the period when Virginia claimed jurisdiction over what is now Allegheny, Fayette, Greene, Washington, and Westmoreland counties, Pennsylvania, search Waldenmaier, Inez, ed.: *Index to the Virginia Court Records of Southwestern Pennsylvania, 1775-1780.* 55 pp.

For Pennsylvania research, refer to "Sources of Information," *Genealogical Quarterly Magazine,* 3rd series, January-December 1900, pp. 155ff.

Bell, Raymond M.: "Sources for Genealogy and Local History of the Scotch-Irish of Central Pennsylvania," *National Genealogical Society Quarterly.* Vol. 39 (December 1945), pp. 114-17.

County Government and Archives in Pennsylvania. Harrisburg, 1947. 576 pp.

Gerberich, Albert H.: "Geographical Aspects of Pennsylvania German Genealogical Study," *National Genealogical Society Quarterly.* Vol. 34 (December 1946), pp. 113-117.

Gordon, Thomas F.: *A Gazetteer of Pennsylvania.* 1975. 508 pp.

Helman, Frances Strong. "Trailing Ancestors Through Pennsylvania," *National Genealogical Society Quarterly.* Vol. 39 (March 1951), pp. Iff.

Prager, Herta, and William W. Price: "A Bibliography on the History of the Courts of the Thirteen Original States, Maine, Ohio, and Vermont," *American Journal of Legal History.* Vol. 2, p. 47.

Rubincam, Milton: "Genealogical Research Materials Relating to Pennsylvania," *American Genealogist.* Vol. 34 (October 1958), pp. 193-98.

Reference books

Blair, Williams T: *The Shoemaker Book.* 1924.

Browning, Charles Henry: *Welsh Settlement of Pennsylvania.* 1912.

Colonial Records of Pennsylvania. 16 vols., 1851-1853.

Daughters of American Revolution: "Location of Unpublished Manuscript Material," *National Historical Magazine.* March 1940, p. 38.

Dorman, John F.: *Virginia Revolutionary Pension Applications.* 1958. Discloses relatives and other persons named in the pension files.

Eddy, Henry Howard: *Guide to the Published Archives of Pennsylvania.* 1949.

Egle, William Henry: *Pennsylvania Genealogies: Scotch-Irish and German.* 1886.

Egle, William Henry: *Some Pennsylvania Women during the War of the Revolution.* 1898.

Eliot, Margaret S., and Sylvester K. Stevens, eds.: *Guide to Depositories of Manuscript Collections in Pennyslvania.* Bulletin 774, No. 4 of Historical Commission Series. Published by Pennsylvania Historical Commission, 1939.

Genealogical Society of Pennsylvania: *Publications.* 1895.

Hinshaw, William Wade: *Encyclopedia of American Quaker Genealogy.* Vol. 2, 1938. Pennsylvania and New Jersey.

Historical Journal: A Quarterly Record of Local History and Genealogy, Devoted Principally to Northwestern Pennsylvania. 2 vols. 1888-1894.

Historical Record of Wyoming Valley. 14 vols. 1887-1908.

Historical Register: *Notes and Queries, Historical and Genealogical, Relating to Interior Pennsylvania.* 2 vols. 1883-1884.

Indiana State Library, Genealogy Section: *Guide to Genealogical Material in the Pennsylvania Archives.* 1937.

Keith, Charles Penrose: *Chronicles of Pennsylvania from the English Revolution to the Peace of Aix-la-Chapelle, 1688-1748.* 2 vols. 1917.

Keith, Charles Penrose: *The Provincial Councillors of Pennsylvania Who Held Office between 1733 and 1776.* 1883.

Kittochtinny Historical Society: *Papers.* 1900—.

Kittochtinny Magazine: *A Tentative Record of Local History and Genealogy West of the Susquehanna.* 1905.

Lancaster County Historical Society: *Historical Papers and Addresses.* 1897—.

Meginness, John Franklin: *Biographical Annals of Deceased Residents of the West Branch Valley of the Susquehanna.* 1889.

Meginness, John Franklin: *Otzinachson: A History of the West Branch Valley of the Susquehanna.* 1857. Reprinted 1889.

Myers, Albert Cook: *Immigration of the Irish Quakers into Pennsylvania, 1682-1750. 1902.*

Myers, Albert Cook: *Quaker Arrivals at Philadelphia, 1682-1750.* 1902.

Northampton County Historical and Genealogical Society: *Publications.* 1926—.

The Penn Germania. 1900—.

Pennsylvania Archives, 1852—.

Pennsylvania German Society: *Proceedings and Addresses.* 1891—.

Pennsylvania Magazine of History and Biography. 1877—

Peterson, C. Stewart: *Bibliography of County Histories of the 3111 Counties in the 48 States.* Baltimore, 1946.

Philadelphia Department of Records: *Guide to the Municipal Archives of the City and County of Philadelphia.* 1957. Compiled by Charles E. Hughes, Jr., city archivist, and Allen Weinberg, archival examiner.

Rupp, Israel Daniel: *A Collection of Upwards of Thirty Thousand Names of German, Swiss, Dutch, French, and Other Immigrants in Pennsylvania from 1727 to 1776.* 1931.

Strassburger, Ralph Beaver: *Pennsylvania German Pioneers:* A Publication of the Original Lists of Arrivals in the Port of Philadelphia from 1727 to 1808. 3 vols. 1934. (Consult: Pennsylvania German Society *Proceedings,* vols. 42-44.)

United States, WPA: *Bibliography of Research Projects Reports—Check List of Historical Publications.* 1943.

United States Bureau of the Census: *Heads of Families at the First Census of the United States Taken in the Year 1790.* Pennsylvania, 1908.

United States, WPA: *Historical Records Survey: Check List of Philadelphia Newspapers 1740-1937 in Philadelphia Libraries.* Philadelphia, 1937.

Waldenmaier, Inez, ed.: *Index to the Virginia Court Records of Southwestern Pennsylvania, 1775-1780.* 55 pp.

Western Pennsylvania Historical Magazine. 1918—.

Wilkinson, N.B., and S.K. Stevens: *Bibliography of Pennsylvania History.* 1958. (Section III lists genealogical sources.)

Wyoming Historical and Geological Society: *Proceedings and Collections.* 1858.

Military rosters, rolls, and records

Revolutionary War: Pennsylvania Archives, 2d series, vols. 1, 3, 11, 13-15. 3rd series, vol. 23. 5th series, vols. 1-8. 6th series, vols. 1-2, 15.

War of 1812: Pennsylvania records covering the War of 1812 are published in the Pennsylvania Archives, 6th Series, vols. 7, 8, and 9. (Service records and pension papers.) The original documents available for examination are in the custody of the Division of Public Records, Pennsylvania Historical and Museum Commission, Room 222, Educational Building, Harrisburg. No searches are performed for correspondents except to verify military and naval service.

Pennsylvania Military Records: The 138 volumes of Pennsylvania Archives contain considerable data on Pennsylvania men enrolled in military units during the Revolution, especially volumes of the 5th, 6th and 7th series, which contain extensive lists of soldiers. In most cases the Division of Public Records, Pennsylvania Historical and Museum Commission, Room 222, Educational Building, Harrisburg, can certify military service from the original records, if the name in full, place of residence at time entering service, and name of war are given. For a certificate under seal, the fee is $1.00. The Division of Public Records publishes the *Guide to the Published Archives of Pennsylvania,* 1949, available from the Bureau of Publications, 10th and Market Streets, Harrisburg.

For military records of persons who served with Pennsylvania units after 1861, inquiry should be addressed to the Old Records Section, Department of Military Affairs, 29 North Office Building, Harrisburg.

nsylvania e rosters

Civil War:

Annual Report of the Adjutant-General (A.L. Russell) for 1863. Harrisburg, 1864. 675 pp. (Bound with report for 1862.)

Annual Report of the Adjutant-General (A.L. Russell) for 1864. Harrisburg, 1865. 269 pp.

Annual Report of the Adjutant-General (A.L. Russell) for 1865. Harrisburg, 1866. 319 pp.

Annual Report of the Adjutant-General (A.L. Russell) for 1866. Harrisburg, 1867. 1221 pp.

For military records of persons who served with Pennsylvania units after 1861, inquiry should be addressed to the Old Records Section, Department of Military Affairs, 29 North Office Building, Harrisburg.

cial records

Vital Statistics: Prior to 1885, only in a few exceptional cases were Pennsylvania births, marriages, and deaths officially recorded. For the earlier years the genealogist must rely chiefly upon unofficial sources such as newspaper files, church registers, entries made in family Bibles, and gravestone inscriptions.

Inquiries regarding marriages performed in Pennsylvania

after September 30, 1885, and births and deaths occurring between 1893 and 1906 should be directed to the Clerk of the Orphans' Court for the appropriate county. In a few Pennsylvania cities, registers of births and deaths occurring between 1880 and 1906 are to be found. Inquiries regarding these should be directed to the Clerk of the city involved.

For the years 1852-1854, registers of births, deaths, and marriages were kept by the Register of Wills at each county seat, and in most cases a duplicate was sent to the state capital. For certain counties these duplicate registers, unindexed and slow to use, are now in the custody of the Division of Public Records, where they may be consulted. It is impossible for the staff to comply with requests to search out specific information from these unindexed materials.

Marriage licenses and marriage bonds were the exception rather than the rule in Pennsylvania prior to 1885, since notice through the publication of banns could make a license unnecessary. Even in cases where licenses were used, seldom were the names of licensees recorded, and no return was required from the person officiating. Very few records of marriages have survived from the older periods. (See also Miscellaneous Records and Sources, below.)

State Custodian: Pennsylvania State Department of Health, Vital Statistics, P.O. Box 1528, Newcastle, 16103. Fee for birth and death certificate: $2.00.

Birth and Death Records (See also Miscellaneous Records and Sources below): *Subsequent to January 1, 1906:* Above-named State Custodian. Pittsburgh births—write City Health Department, City-County Building, Pittsburgh 15219. They have birth records prior to 1906. *Prior to January 1, 1906:* If the birth, marriage, or death occurred prior to this date, write to the following: City Board of Health, if in a city; in unincorporated area, Clerk, Orphans Court, at the County Seat. Certain of the larger cities had municipal registration beginning on various dates. Records for Philadelphia extend back to July 1, 1860; for Pittsburgh to the year 1870. *Delayed birth certificates:* State Custodian will furnish information.

Divorce Records: Prothonotary, Courthouse, in county where divorce was granted. Cost of a certified copy of divorce decree varies.

Marriage Records: Clerk, Orphans' Court, County Seat.

Court Records: Wills, administrations, and other probate matters: Register of Wills, County Seat.

Land Records: Deeds, mortgages, leases, and other matters affecting title to land: Recorder of Deeds, County Seat. Land Records (Commonwealth, including Pennsylvania military grants) are on record at the Bureau of

Land Records, Department of Internal Affairs, Capitol Building, Harrisburg.

Oaths of Allegiance, 1777-1789: The Oath of Allegiance required of adult male residents during the Revolutionary upheaval was a matter of county record, and normally the lists were maintained by recorders of deeds at the respective courthouses. Few records of this type have survived.

Immigration — Naturalization Records: Index to Records of Aliens' Declaration of Intention and/or Oaths of Allegiance 1789-1880 in U.S. Circuit Court, U.S. District Court, Supreme Court of Pennsylvania, Quarter Sessions Court, Court of Common Pleas. Compiled by WPA (Project No. 20837). Sponsored by the Pennsylvania Historical Commission. 11 vols. Indexed alphabetically. Contains names, country of former allegiance, court of record, and date of declaration. These records contain information similar to passenger lists. (New York Public Library has one set.)

Works Progress Administration: Pennsylvania Historical Survey, *Maritime Records Port of Philadelphia.* Sponsor: Pennsylvania Historical Commission, Harrisburg. Section 2, Alphabetical Index of Naturalization Records, 1789-1880. Vol. 1 to 11. Typescript. These records contain information similar to shipping lists. (New York Public Library has one set.)

The Division of Public Records has custody of the official passenger lists showing arrivals at the port of Philadelphia during the period 1727-1808. Those lists, which date before the American Revolution, concern immigrants from the continent of Europe only, not persons previously subjects of Great Britain. Almost every one of the individuals included in the early lists was either German or Swiss.

These lists of immigrants have been published completely in the three volumes of Strassburger and Hinke's *Pennsylvania German Pioneers* (Norristown, 1934). Sets of this publication can still be purchased from the Pennsylvania German Society, Norristown, and it may be consulted at most large libraries and historical societies. Volume 2 carried facsimiles of all signatures occurring in the original lists.

The Division of Public Records has in custody also official lists of aliens naturalized by Pennsylvania courts during the years 1740-1773. All information contained in these lists is available in printed form, some in Pennsylvania Archives, Second Series, vol. 2, and others in M. S. Giuseppi's *Naturalizations of Foreign Protestants in the American and West Indian Colonies* (Pursuant to Statute 13 George II, c. 7), published as volume 24 of the Publications of the Huguenot Society of London (London, 1921).

By special Act of Assembly, aliens were on occasion granted a type of naturalization more limited than that granted by the courts. The numerous special acts passed for the purpose of naturalizing citizens are found in vols. 2 to 7 of the Statutes at Large of Pennsylvania, a series to be found in every extensive library of law and in many general libraries.

Aliens living in Pennsylvania at the time of the Declaration of Independence became naturalized automatically and no record resulted. Those arriving in later years could be naturalized according to processes prescribed from time to time. During the years 1777 to 1791, new arrivals simply took an oath of allegiance. The taking of this oath was a matter of record in the county of residence, but most of these records have since been lost. The only "test oaths" now preserved by the Commonwealth pertain exclusively to the city and county of Philadelphia. Beginning in 1791, records of naturalization are strictly county and federal records that never have been in the custody of any state official.

Miscellaneous Records and Sources: For nearly all the vital records it is necessary to rely on church records as a substitute, some of which may be found in the Archives of Pennsylvania. A number of unpublished church records are in the Pennsylvania State Historical Society, Philadelphia. It is well to know that ministers in early times were itinerant, holding services on succeeding Sundays in as many different churches; therefore, a family might have their children baptized in a number of different churches though their residence never changed. Also try the Pennsylvania State Library, Harrisburg, for vital statistics.

Harllee, William Curry: *Kinfolks, A Genealogical and Biographical Record of Thomas and Elizabeth* (*Stuart*) *Harllee.* 1934. Vol. 1 contains a chapter concerning state and county records, and the derivation of the counties of a number of states, including Pennsylvania.

Federal records

1. See index for section on United States census.

2. Custody of mortality schedules, 1850, 1860, 1870, 1880: Pennsylvania State Library, Harrisburg.

3. The original 1880 United States Census records for Pennsylvania were transferred in 1956 by the National Archives to: University of Pittsburgh Library, University of Pittsburgh, Pittsburgh.

Pennsylvania state census records

Beginning with the Pennsylvania Constitution of 1776, an enumeration of taxable inhabitants and slaves within the Commonwealth was required. The *Inventory of County Archives of Pennsylvania* discloses these original records among others filed in county offices. The Archives Section of the Pennsylvania State Library reports that duplicates of a small percentage of these enumerations are on file in that office.

Rhode Island

neral ormation

Capital: Providence. Entered Union: May 29, 1790.

raries, torical cieties, d archives

For a complete list, see: Brown, Karl: *The American Library Directory.* See also: *Directory of Historical Societies and Agencies in the United States and Canada,* 1956.

Providence Public Library, 150 Empire Street, Providence.

Rhode Island Historical Society, 52 Power St., Providence.

Rhode Island State Library, Providence.

Rhode Island State Archives, 314 State House, Providence.

Westerly Public Library, Westerly.

ode Island earch ggestions

Arnold's *Vital Records of Rhode Island* (referred to in the list of reference books below) has been published in a microcard edition by the Godfrey Memorial Library, Middletown, Conn.

Prager, Herta, and William W. Price: "A Bibliography on the History of the Courts of the Thirteen Original States, Maine, Ohio, and Vermont," *American Journal of Legal History,* vol. 2, p. 148.

ference oks

Arnold, James Newell: *The Records of the Proprietors of the Narragansett, Otherwise Called the Fones Records.* 1894.

Arnold, James Newell: *Vital Record of Rhode Island, 1636-1850.* 21 vols. 1891.

Austin, John Osborne: *The Genealogical Dictionary of Rhode Island,* Comprising Three Generations of Settlers Who Came before 1690, 1887. (See also Austin's 4-page supplement of additions and corrections.)

Chapin, Howard Miller: *Rhode Island in the Colonial Wars.* A List of Rhode Island Soldiers and Sailors in King George's War, 1740-1748. 1920.

Chapin, Howard Miller: *Rhode Island in the Colonial Wars.* A List of Rhode Island Soldiers and Sailors in the Old French and Indian War, 1755-1762. 1918.

Chapin, Howard Miller: *Rhode Island Privateers in King George's War,* 1739-1748. 1926.

Historical Records Survey, WPA: *Guide to the Public Vital Statistics Records . . . in the State of Rhode Island, and Providence Plantations.* 1941. 280 pp.

Historical Records Survey, WPA: *Guide to Church Vital Statistic Records in the State of Rhode Island.* 1942. 171 pp.

Historical Records Survey, WPA: *Directory of Churches and Religious Organizations of Rhode Island.* December 1931. 128 pp.

Hopkins, Charles Wyman: *The Home Lots of the Early Settlers of the Providence Plantations.* 1886.

Moriarty, G. Andrews: "Additions and Corrections to Austin's Genealogical Dictionary of R. I." (1887). See *American Genealogist,* 19:129—. (First of a series.)

Narragansett Historical Register. 9 vols. 1882-1891.

Newport Historical Society: *Bulletin.* 1912—.

Peterson, C. Stewart: *Bibliography of County Histories of the 3111 Counties in the 48 States.* Baltimore, 1946.

Rhode Island Court of Trials: *Rhode Island Court Records:* Records of the Court of Trials of the Colony of Providence Plantations, 1647-1670. 2 vols. 1920-1922.

Rhode Island General Assembly: *Census of the Inhabitants of the Colony of Rhode Island and Providence Plantations, Taken . . . in 1774—.* 1858.

Rhode Island General Assembly: *Records of the Colony* [and of the State] of Rhode Island, and Providence Plantations. 10 vols. 1856-1865. (1636-1792.)

Rhode Island Historical Magazine, 7 vols. 1880-1887. (First 4 vols., known as *The Newport Historical Magazine.*)

Rhode Island Historical Society: *Collections.* 1827—.

Rhode Island Historical Society: *Proceedings.* 34 vols. 1872-1914.

Rhode Island Historical Society: *Publications.* 8 vols. 1893-1900.

Rhode Island Historical Tracts. 1877—.

Rhode Island Land Evidences. Vol. 1, 1648-1696. Abstracts, 1921.

Smith, Joseph Jencks: *Civil and Military List of Rhode Island, 1647-1800.* 1900.

Smith, Joseph Jencks: *Civil and Military List of Rhode Island, 1800-1850.* 1901—.

Smith, Joseph Jencks: *New Index to the Civil and Military Lists of Rhode Island.* 1907.

United States Bureau of the Census: *Heads of Families at the First Census of the United States Taken in the Year 1790.* Rhode Island, 1908.

ry rosters, and ds

Revolutionary War: Baker, Mary Ellen: "Bibliography of Lists of New England Soldiers," *New England Historic Genealogical Society.* 1911. 56 pp.

Cowell, Benjamin: *Spirit of '76 in Rhode Island.* 1850. (Indexed in James N. Arnold's *Vital Records of Rhode Island,* vol. 12, pp. 91-298.)

War of 1812: No roster of men who served from Rhode Island has been published. The record of the men who served is in manuscript form in the custody of the State Record Commissioner, State House, Providence.

State Roster—Civil War: Rhode Island General Assembly: Official Register of Rhode Island Officers and Soldiers Who Served in the United States Army and Navy from 1861 to 1866. Providence, 1866.

al records

Vital Records: Fee for birth, marriage, and death certificate: $2.00.

State Custodian: Rhode Island Department of Health, Division of Vital Statistics, Room 101, Davis St., Providence, 02908.

Birth, Marriage, and Death Records: Subsequent to 1853: Above-named State Custodian. *Prior to 1853:* Town Clerk or City Clerk, or City Registrar of Providence. *Delayed birth certificates:* State Custodian will furnish information.

Divorce Records: Clerk of Superior Court in county where divorce was granted. Cost of certified copy of divorce decree varies.

Marriage Licenses: Town Clerk, or City Clerk, or City Registrar of Providence.

Court Records: Wills, administrations, and other probate matters: Clerk, Probate Court, of City or Town. *Other Civil Actions:* Clerk, Superior Court, County Seat.

Land Records: Deeds, mortgages, leases, and other matters affecting title to land: Town Clerk, or City Clerk.

ral census

1. See index for section on United States Census.

2. Custody of mortality schedules, 1850, 1860, 1870, 1880: Rhode Island State Library, Providence.

3. The original 1880 United States census records for Rhode Island were transferred in 1956 by the National Archives to: National Society, Daughters of the American Revolution, Administration Building, 1776 D Street, N.W., Washington, D.C.

Rhode Island state census records

Custodian: Rhode Island State Archives, 314 State House, Providence.

Colonial Census of 1774: *Census of the Inhabitants of the Colony of Rhode Island and Providence Plantations.* Taken by Order of the General Assembly in the Year 1774. Arranged and edited by John Russell Bartlett, Secretary of State. Providence, 1858.

Censuses of 1776 and 1777: A representative of the Rhode Island State Archives wrote as follows on November 21, 1962: "The Census of 1776 is incomplete and as far as I know has never been printed. The military Census of 1777 is in manuscript form here in the Archives, with several towns missing and has not been printed to my knowledge."

Census of 1875: Includes name, age, color, sex, marital status, relationship to the head of the house, place of birth, parentage, education, occupation, and address by street numbers.

Census of 1885: Name, sex, relationship, color, age, conjugal status, place of birth, parentage, occupation, education, by district.

South Carolina

General information

Capital: Columbia. Entered Union: May 23, 1788. Seceded from Union: December 20, 1860. Reentered Union: July 18, 1868.

Libraries, historical societies, and archives

For a complete list, see: Brown, Karl: *The American Library Directory.* Also, *Directory of Historical Societies and Agencies in the United States and Canada,* 1956.

Historical Commission of Charleston, 92 East Bay Street, Charleston.

South Carolina Archives Dept., World War Memorial Building, Columbia.

South Carolina Historical Society, Fireproof Building, Charleston.

South Carolina State Library, Columbia.

South Carolina geographical data

Wakefield, Roberta: "Evolution of South Carolina Counties," *National Genealogical Society Quarterly.* Vol. 32, pp. 51-52.

South Carolina research suggestions

The South Carolina Archives Department, World War Memorial Building, Columbia, published on February 1, 1957, a pamphlet containing a list of its publications and microfilms. Included are Confederate war records, vital records from old newspaper files, land records, etc. Prices for these publications and microfilms are reasonable.

Articles of General Interest:

Prager, Herta, and William W. Price: "A Bibliography on the History of the Courts of the Thirteen Original States, Maine, Ohio, and Vermont," *American Journal of Legal History.* Vol. 2, p. 149.

Wakefield, Roberta P.: "Genealogical Source Material in South Carolina," *National Genealogical Society Quarterly.* Vol. 40 (September 1952), p. 1.

Clemens, William Montgomery: *North and South Carolina Marriage Records, from the Earliest Days to the Civil War.* c. 1927.

Daughters of the American Revolution: *Genealogical Records,* compiled by various chapters of the DAR in South Carolina. 7 vols. 1953-54.

Davis, Harry Alexander: *Some Huguenot Families of South Carolina and Georgia,* 1927. (See also the three supplements to this work.)

Peterson, C. Stewart: *Bibliography of County Histories of the 3111 Counties in the 48 States.* Baltimore, 1946.

Rogers, Mrs. John D.: *Indexes to the County Wills of South Carolina formed before 1853.* 1939. Typewritten.

Salley, Alexander Samuel: *Death Notices in the South Carolina Gazette, 1732-1775.* 1917.

Salley, Alexander Samuel: *Marriage Notices in the South Carolina Gazette and County Journal* (*1765-1775*), *and in the Charlestown Gazette* (*1778-1780*). 1904.

Salley, Alexander Samuel: *Marriage Notices in the South Carolina and American General Gazette from May 30, 1766 to February 28, 1781, and its successor, The Royal Gazette (1781-1782).* 1914.

Salley, Alexander Samuel: *Marriage Notices in the South Carolina Gazette and Its Successors* (1732-1801). 1902.

Salley, Alexander Samuel: *Marriages in the Courier, 1803-1808.*

Salley, A. S., Jr.: *South Carolina Troops in Confederate Service.* 3 vols. 1913-1930.

Salley, A. S., Jr.: *Records in the British Public Record Office Relating to South Carolina.* 5 vols. 1928-1947.

South Carolina Historical and Genealogical Magazine. 1900—.

South Carolina Historical Society: *Collections.* 1857—.

South Carolina Historical Society: *Proceedings.* 1931—.

South Carolina Historical Commission: *Bulletins.* 1915—.

South Carolina Historical Commission: *Warrants for Lands in South Carolina, 1672-1679.* 1910.

South Carolina — Historical Commission: *The Colonial Records of South Carolina.* 4 vols. 1951-55.

United States Bureau of the Census: *Heads of Families at the First Census of the United States Taken in the Year 1790.* 1908.

United States Department of State: "Territorial Papers of the United States." Clarence E. Carter, ed. Vol. 4: "Territory South of the River Ohio." (For a summary of this source see *National Genealogical Society Quarterly,* vol. 37, pp. 93ff.)

Young, Pauline: *A Genealogical Collection of South Carolina Wills and Records.* 2 vols. 1955.

Young, Pauline: *"Early Settlers" of South Carolina.* Vol. 1, 1945. 50 pp.

Miscellaneous source

Harllee, William Curry: *Kinfolks, A Genealogical and Biographical Record of Thomas and Elizabeth* (*Stuart*) *Harllee.* 1934. (Vol. 1 contains a chapter concerning state and county records and the derivation of the counties of a number of states, including South Carolina.)

Military rosters, rolls, and records

Revolutionary War: South Carolina Treasury: Stub Entries of Indents Issued in Payment of Claims against South Carolina Growing Out of the Revolution. Columbia, 1910.

War of 1812: There is no printed roster of the South Carolina men who served in the War of 1812; however, a fairly complete list copied from records in Washington is in the custody of Mrs. J. S. Land, Custodian, Confederate Relic Room and Museum, State House, Columbia.

Confederate Military Records: The National Archives has compiled the *Consolidated Index to Compiled Records of Confederate Soldiers.* The index is on cards that give the name of the soldier, his rank, the unit in which he served, and often a statement concerning the origin or background of that unit. There are cross-reference cards for soldiers' names that appeared in the records under more than one spelling. This index is available for personal search or by an agent. It is microfilmed.

The South Carolina Archives Department, World War Memorial Building, Columbia, has custody of South Carolina Confederate War Records.

Official records

Vital Records: Fee for birth, marriage, and death certificates: $2.00.

State Custodian: South Carolina State Board of Health, Bureau of Vital Statistics, 2600 Bull St., Columbia, 29201.

Birth and Death Records: Subsequent to January 1, 1915: Above-named State Custodian. *Prior to January 1, 1915:* For the city of Charleston only, write to Health Department, Charleston; or County Clerk, County Seat. *Delayed birth certificates:* Clerk of Court, County Seat, will furnish information.

Divorce Records: Clerk of Court in county where petition was filed. Cost of certified copy of divorce decree varies.

Marriage Licenses: Clerk, Probate Court.

Marriage Records: Clerk, Probate Court, or subsequent to July 1, 1911, above-named state custodian.

Court Records: Wills, administrations, and other probate matters: Clerk, Probate Court, County Seat. *Other Civil Actions:* Clerk, Circuit Court, County Seat.

Land Records: Deeds, mortgages, leases, and other matters affecting title to land: Register of Mesne Conveyances, County Seat.

eral census

1. See index for section on United States census.

2. Custody of mortality schedules, 1850, 1860, 1870, 1880: South Carolina State Library, Columbia.

3. The original 1880 United States census records for South Carolina were transferred in 1956 by the National Archives to: South Carolina Archives Department, World War Memorial, Columbia.

e census ords

Census records taken by State Authority: None.

South Dakota

eral rmation

Capital: Pierre. Organized as a territory: March 2, 1861. Entered Union: November 2, 1889.

aries, orical ieties, l archives

For a complete list, see: Brown, Karl: *The American Library Directory.* Also, *Directory of Historical Societies and Agencies in the United States and Canada,* 1956.

State Historical Society, Memorial Hall, Pierre.

erence oks

Ogle, Geo. A. & Co.: *Memorial and Biographical Records.* 1897. 680 pp.

Peterson, C. Stewart: *Bibliography of County Histories of the 3111 Counties in the 48 States.* Baltimore, 1946.

Smith, George Martin, ed.: *History of South Dakota, Its History, Its People.* 1915. (Vols. 4 and 5, biographical.)

South Dakota Historical Review. 2 vols. 1935-37.

Military rosters, rolls, and records

Civil War — Dakota Territory Roster: U.S. Congress: *Dakota Milita in the War of 1862.* Washington, 1904. 88 pp. (U.S. 58th Congress, 2d Session, Senate Doc. No. 241.)

Official records

Vital Records: Fee for birth, marriage, and death certificates: $2.00.

State Custodian: South Dakota Department of Health, Division of Public Health Statistics, Pierre, 57501.

Birth, Marriage, and Death Records: Subsequent to July 1, 1905: Above-named State Custodian. *Prior to July 1, 1905:* Director of Vital Statistics, Pierre, South Dakota. *Delayed birth certificates:* County Clerk, County Seat has forms.

Divorce Records: Division of Public Health Statistics, State Department of Health, Pierre; or Clerk of Court in county where divorce was granted. Cost of certified copy of divorce decree varies.

Marriage Licenses: Director of Vital Statistics, Department of History, Pierre.

Court Records: Wills, administrations, and other probate matters: County Clerk, County Seat. *Other Civil Actions:* County Clerk, County Seat.

Land Records: Deeds, mortgages, leases, and other matters affecting title to land: Register of Deeds, County Seat.

Federal census

1. See index for section on United States census.

2. Custody of mortality schedules, 1860, 1870: State Library, Pierre.

3. The original 1880 United States census records for South Dakota were transferred in 1956 by the National Archives to: South Dakota State Historical Society, Pierre.

Territorial census of 1885 of Dakota territory

(Includes what is now North Dakota and South Dakota.)

The State Historical Society of North Dakota, Liberty Memorial Building, Bismarck, has custody of the 1885 census of Dakota Territory. This census reports the heads of family, name and ages of each member, sex, occupation, where born, and where parents were born.

Territorial and state census records

Custodian: South Dakota State Historical Society, Department of History, Memorial Building, Pierre.

1860 Territorial Census: Published in Volume 9, *Collections of the South Dakota Historical Society.*

1880 Territorial Census: The custodian has both originals and microfilm.

1885 Territorial Census: Covers the following counties: Beadle, Butte, Charles Mix, Edmunds, Fall River, Faulk, Hand, Hanson, Hutchinson, Hyde, Lake, Lincoln, Marshall, McPherson, Moody, Roberts, Sanborn, Spink, Stanley, Turner.

Information disclosed in the foregoing censuses: Listed by families in general, place of birth of individual and father and mother, occupation, age.

1905, 1915, 1925, 1935, and 1945 State Census: These censuses are recorded on cards. Information disclosed: Name, age, location, occupation, marital status, color, place of birth, place of birth of father and mother. Subject of search is readily located through this card system.

Tennessee

eral mation

Capital: Nashville. Entered Union: June 1, 1796. Seceded from Union: June 24, 1861. Reentered Union: July 24, 1866.

ries, rical ties, archives

For a complete list, see: Brown, Karl: *The American Library Directory*. Also, *Directory of Historical Societies and Agencies in the United States and Canada,* 1956.

Cossilt Reference and Research Library, Front & Monroe Street, Memphis.

East Tennessee Historical Society, Lawson McGee Library, Knoxville.

Tennessee Historical Commission, State Library, Nashville.

Tennessee Historical Society, War Memorial Building, Nashville.

Tennessee State Library, Capitol, Nashville.

West Tennessee Historical Society, 246 S. Watkins St., Memphis.

essee arch estions

Article of General Interest:

"Genealogical Resources of Tennessee," by Charles E. Allred, *Genealogical Forum of Portland, Oregon,* vol. 4, pp. 42-44.

rence s

Acklen, Jeannette T.: *Tennessee Records, Bible Records, Marriage Bonds* (etc.). 2 vols. 1933.

Allison, John, ed.: *Notable Men of Tennessee.* 2 vols. 1905.

Armstrong, Zella: *Notable Southern Families.* 6 vols. 1928. Use also for Virginia.

Cartwright, Betty, and Lillian Gardiner: *North Carolina Land Grants in Tennessee, 1778-1791.* 1958.

Chattanooga *Sunday Times,* Chattanooga, Tennessee: "Leaves from the Family Tree." *Genealogical column,* December 17, 1933-June 27, 1937. (Discontinued.)

East Tennessee Historical Society *Publications* (Knoxville). 1929—.

Historical Records Survey, WPA: *Guide to Collections of Manuscripts in Tennessee.* 1940. 27 pp. March 1941. 38 pp

Historical Records Survey, WPA: *Guide to Public Vital Statistics in Tennessee.* 1941. 146 pp.

Houston, Martha Lou: *Tennessee Census Reports.* 1939—. (Copied from original census records.)

Peterson, C. Stewart: *Bibliography of County Histories of the 3111 Counties in the 48 States.* Baltimore, 1946.

Ramsey, J. G. M.: *The Annals of Tennessee to the End of the Eighteenth Century.* 1853. Reprinted 1926. In connection with this, use Fain's *Critical and Analytical Index.* This work contains valuable information about North Carolina men who were in the Revolutionary War and later went to Tennessee.

Temple, O. P.: *Notable Men of Tennessee, 1833-1875.* 1912.

Tennessee Historical Magazine. 1915—.

United States Department of State: *Territorial Papers of the United States.* Clarence E. Carter, ed. Vol. 4: Territory South of the River Ohio. (For a summary of this source see: *National Genealogical Society Quarterly,* 37:93ff.)

WPA War Services Section: *Guide to Church Vital Statistics in Tennessee.* 1942. 510 pp.

Whitley, Mrs. E. J. R.: *Revolutionary Soldiers Granted Land in Tennessee.* 1939.

Whitley, Mrs. E. J. R.: *Tennessee Genealogical Records.* 10 vols. 1932—.

Military rosters, rolls, and records

Revolutionary and War of 1812: Armstrong, Zella: *Twenty-Four Hundred Tennessee Pensioners, Revolution, War of 1812.* 1937. 121 pp.

Allen, Penelope Johnson: *Tennessee Soldiers in the Revolutionary War in the Counties of Washington and Sullivan.* 1935. 71 pp.

Confederate Military Records: The National Archives has compiled the *Consolidated Index to Compiled Records of Confederate Soldiers.* The index is on cards that give the name of the soldier, his rank, the unit in which he served, and often a statement concerning the origin or background of that unit. There are cross-reference cards for soldiers' names that appeared in the records under more than one spelling. This index is available for personal search or by an agent. It is microfilmed.

:ial records

Vital Records: Fee for birth, marriage, and death certificates: $2.00.

State Custodian: Vital Records, Department of Public Health, Cordell Hull Building, Nashville, Tennessee 37219.

Birth and Death Records: Since January 1, 1914, and from July 1908 to June 1912: Above-named State Custodian. Prior to statewide registration: A few counties have records of births and deaths. In general the records are quite incomplete and are not indexed. They are on file with the County Court Clerk at the County Seat.

For records in four largest cities, write to respective City Health Departments:

Chattanooga City Health Department: Birth records: January 1, 1882, to 1914. Death records: March 1872 to 1914.

Knoxville Bureau of Health: Birth records: 1881 to 1914. Death records: 1881 to 1914.

Memphis City Health Department: Birth records: 1874 to 1914. Death records: 1840 to 1914.

Nashville City Health Department: Birth records: 1871 to 1914. Death records: July 1874 to 1914.

Delayed birth certificates: State Custodian will furnish information.

Divorce Records: Since July 1945: Division of Vital Statistics, State Department of Public Health, Cordell Hull Office Building, Nashville 37219. Cost of certified copy of divorce decree is $2.00. Prior to July 1945: Clerk of Court where divorce was granted. Cost of certified copy of divorce decree varies.

Marriage Records and Marriage Licenses: County Clerk. Effective July 1, 1945, the central registration of marriages for entire state began. A certificate of every marriage occurring after that date in the state is recorded with State Registrar of Vital Statistics, Nashville; licenses are filed with the County Clerk where marriage occurred.

Court Records: Wills, administrations, and other probate matters: County Clerk, County Seat. *Other Civil Actions:* County Clerk, County Seat; Circuit Court Clerk, County Seat; Clerk and Master, Chancery Court, County Seat.

Land Records: Deeds, mortgages, leases, and other matters affecting title to land: Register of Deeds, County Seat.

Federal census

1. See index for section on United States census:

2. Custody of mortality schedules, 1850, 1860, 1870, 1880: DAR, Washington, D.C.

3. The original 1880 United States census records for Tennessee were transferred in 1956 by the National Archives to: Tennessee State Library and Archives, Nashville.

Tennessee state census records

The state of Tennessee has never conducted a state census and therefore has no state census records.

Texas

General information

Capital: Austin. Entered Union: December 29, 1845. Seceded from Union: March 2, 1861. Reentered Union: March 30, 1870.

Libraries, historical societies, and archives

For a complete list, see: Brown, Karl: *The American Library Directory.* Also, *Directory of Historical Societies and Agencies in the United States and Canada,* 1956.

Dallas Public Library, Dallas.

Dallas Local History and Genealogy Society, c/o Dallas Public Library, Commerce at Harwood, Dallas.

Houston Public Library, 500 McKinney Street, Houston.

Librarian, Cody Memorial Library, Southwestern University, Georgetown, Texas. This library has a collection containing information on Southern families in addition to Texas.

San Antonio Public Library, 210 W. Market Street, San Antonio.

Texas State Historical Association, Box 8011 University Station, Austin.

Texas State Library, Austin.

West Texas Historical Association, Box 152, Abilene.

Reference books

Biggerstaff, Mrs. Malcolm B.: *Four Thousand Tombstone Inscriptions from Texas.* 1745-1870. (1952) IX, 99 pp. and index.

Historical Records Survey, WPA: *Guide to Public Vital Statistics in Texas.* 1941. 177 pp.

Historical Records Survey, WPA: *Texas Newspapers*

1813-1939. 1941. 293 pp. A Union list of newspaper files available in offices of publishers, libraries, and a number of private collections.

Peterson, C. Stewart: *Bibliography of County Histories of the 3111 Counties in the 48 States.* Baltimore, 1946.

Ray, Worth S.: *Austin Colony Pioneers Including History of Texas and Their Earliest Settlers.* 3 vols. (n.d.) Original Typewritten Copy: Genealogical Society, The Church of Jesus Christ of Latter-day Saints, Salt Lake City, Utah.

Shaw & Blaylock: *Abstract of Land Titles of Texas,* comprising the titled, patented, and located lands in the state. 2 vols. and supplement. 1878.

Taylor, Virginia H.: *The Spanish Archives of the General Land Office of Texas.* 1955. 258 pp.

ry rosters, and rds

Confederate Military Records: The National Archives has compiled the *Consolidated Index to Compiled Records of Confederate Soldiers.* The index is on cards that give the name of the soldier, his rank, the unit in which he served, and often a statement concerning the origin or background of that unit. There are cross-reference cards for soldiers' names that appeared in the records under more than one spelling. This index is available for personal search or by an agent. It is microfilmed.

ial records

Vital Records: Fee for birth and death certificate: $2.00.

State Custodian: Texas State Department of Health, State Bureau of Vital Statistics, Austin, 78701.

Birth and Death Records: Subsequent to 1903: Above-named State Custodian. *Prior to 1903:* Write to City Clerk of the city where birth or death occurred or to County Clerk at the county seat where birth or death occurred. *Delayed birth certificates:* County Clerk has forms.

Divorce Records: Clerk of District Court in county where divorce was granted. Cost of certified copy of divorce decree varies.

Marriage Licenses: County Clerk.

Marriage Records: County Clerk of the county where the marriage license was issued.

Court Records: Wills, administrations, and other probate matters: County Clerk, County Seat. *Other Civil Actions:* County Clerk, County Seat.

Land Records: Deeds, mortgages, leases, and other matters affecting title to land: County Clerk, County Seat.

ral census

1. See index for section on United States census.
2. The original 1880 United States census records for

Texas were transferred in 1956 by the National Archives to: Texas State Library, Austin.

3. The Texas State Library, Archives Division, Camp Hubbard, Austin, has copies of the U.S. censuses of Texas for 1850, 1860, 1970, 1880. Mortality schedules, 1850, 1860, 1870, 1880.

Texas state census records

Although state censuses were taken in 1847, 1848, 1851, and 1858, the records have never been found.

Utah

General information

Capital: Salt Lake City. Organized as a territory: September 9, 1850. Entered Union: January 4, 1896.

Libraries, historical societies, and archives

For a complete list, see: Brown, Karl: *The American Library Directory.* Also, *Directory of Historical Societies and Agencies in the United States and Canada,* 1956.

Daughters of Utah Pioneers, Daughters of Pioneers Building, Salt Lake City 84103.

The Genealogical Society, 50 East North Temple, Salt Lake City 84150. American, English, Scandinavian, German collections. Outstanding microfilm collection of official records, parish registers, and other church records. Large collection of manuscript genealogies.

Sons of Utah Pioneers, Salt Lake City.

Utah State Historical Society, 603 East South Temple, Salt Lake City 84102.

Cache County Library, Logan.

Reference books

Eshom, Frank: *Pioneers and Prominent Men of Utah,* 1913. Valuable information of Utah pioneers, but it should be used with care due to mistakes.

Jensen, Andrew: *LDS Biographical Encyclopedia.* 4 vols. 1901. Indexed. Valuable for information on Utah pioneers.

Peterson, C. Stewart: *Bibliography of County Histories of the 3111 Counties in the 48 States.* Baltimore, 1946.

Utah Genealogical and Historical Magazine. 1910-1940.

Utah Pioneer Biographies, Compiled by different individuals and deposited with the Genealogical Society, Salt Lake City. 35 vols.

Military rosters, rolls, and records

All Indian war records and two rolls of Civil War service are in the custody of the State Historical Society, 603 East South Temple Street, Salt Lake City, Utah 84102.

cial records

Vital Records: Fee for certified copy of birth and death certificate: money order for $3.00.

State Custodian: Utah Department of Health, Division of Vital Statistics, 554 South 3rd East, Salt Lake City, Utah 84102.

Birth and Death Records: Subsequent to 1905: Above-named State Custodian. *Prior to 1905:* County Clerk, County Seat. Births and deaths for Salt Lake City, 1890-1904, City Board of Health, 610 S. 2nd East, Salt Lake City, 84111. Ogden also has City Board of Health for birth and death records. *Delayed birth certificates:* No provision for delayed birth certificates by statute; but by administrative practice, delayed certificates are issued. Address above State Custodian.

Divorce Records: Clerk of District Court in county where divorce was granted. Cost of certified copy of divorce decree varies.

Marriage Licenses and Marriage Records: County Clerk at the County Seat.

Court Records: Wills, administrations, and other probate matters: County Clerk, County Seat. *Other Civil Actions:* County Clerk, County Seat.

Land Records: Deeds, mortgages, leases, and other matters affecting title to land: County Recorder, County Seat.

eral census

1. See index for section on United States census.

2. Custody of mortality schedules, 1850, 1860, 1870: Genealogical Society, 50 East North Temple, Salt Lake City, Utah 84150.

3. The original 1880 United States census records for Utah were transferred in 1956 by the National Archives to: National Society, Daughters of the American Revolution, Administration Building, 1776 D Street, N. W., Washington, D.C.

torial and census rds

Censuses of the territory of Utah were taken in the years 1851 and 1895. The state constitution provided for a decennial census to commence in 1905. No record has been found of any census taken in accordance with the constitutional provision.

Vermont

eral mation

Capital: Montpelier. Entered the Union: March 4, 1791.

Libraries, historical societies, and archives

For a complete list, see: Brown, Karl: *The American Library Directory.* Also, *Directory of Historical Societies and Agencies in the United States and Canada,* 1956.

Bennington Battle Monument and Historical Association, Bennington.

Isle La Motte Historical Society, South End Schoolhouse, Isle La Motte.

Orleans County Historical Society, Old Stone House, Brownington.

Sheldon Museum, Archaeological and Historical Society, Museum Building, Park Street, Middlebury.

Vermont Historical Society, Supreme Court Building, Montpelier.

Vermont Historical Society Library and Museum, Montpelier.

Vermont State Library, Montpelier.

Woodstock Historical Society, Woodstock.

Reference books

Barden, Merritt Clark: *Vermont Once No Man's Land.* 1928. A genealogical summary of the families who lived along the New York border in Vermont.

Comstock, John M.: *The Congregational Churches of Vermont and Their Ministers, 1762-1914.* 1915.

Crocker, Henry: *History of the Baptists in Vermont.* 1913.

DeGoesbriand, Louis: *Catholic Memoirs of Vermont and New Hampshire.* 1886.

Dodge, Prentiss Cutler: *Encyclopedia, Vermont Biography.* 1912.

Hemenway, Abby Maria: *The Vermont Historical Gazetteer.* 5 vols. 1868-1891. In 1923 an index was published covering the five volumes.

Historical Records Survey, WPA: *Index to the Burlington Free Press in the Billings Library.* 6 vols. University of Vermont, 1941. 1848-1865.

Historical Records Survey, WPA: *A Directory of Churches and Religious Organizations in the State of Vermont.* 1939. 122 pp.

Jeffrey, William Hartley: *Successful Vermonters: A Modern Gazetteer of Lamoille, Franklin, and Grand Isle Counties.* 1907.

Peterson, C. Stewart: *Bibliography of County Histories of the 3111 Counties in the 48 States.* Baltimore, 1946.

Protestant Episcopal Church in the United States of America, Vermont Diocese: *Documentary History of the Protestant Episcopal Church in the Diocese of Vermont.* 1870.

Ullery, Jacob G.: *Men of Vermont, An Illustrated Biographical History*. 1894.

United States Bureau of the Census: *Heads of Families at the First Census of the United States Taken in the Year 1790: Vermont*. 1907. Taken in April-September 1791.

United States Bureau of the Census: *Heads of Families at the Second Census of the U.S. Taken in the Year 1800.* Published by Vermont Historical Society, 1938.

United States, WPA: *Bibliography of Research Projects Reports*—Check List of Historical Records Survey Publications. 1940.

Vermont: *Records of the Governor and Council of the State of Vermont, 1775 to 1836.* 8 vols. 1873-1880.

Vermont Secretary of State: *A List of the Principal Civil Officers of Vermont from 1777 to 1918.* 1918.

Vermont Antiquarian. 3 vols. 1902-1905.

Vermont Historical Society: *Collections.* 2 vols. 1870-1871.

Vermont Historical Society: *Proceedings.* 1860—.

Vermont Marriages, 1903.

Vermont Year-Book, 1818—. Formerly called Walton's *Vermont Register.* Valuable for brief information regarding the history of each town.

Williams, Henry Clay: *Biographical Encyclopedia of Vermont of the Nineteenth Century.* 1835.

ary rosters, , and rds

Baker, Mary Ellen: *"Bibliography of Lists of New England Soldiers."* New England Historic Genealogical Society, Boston. 1911. 56 pp.

Revolutionary War:

Crockett, Walter Hill: "Revolutionary Soldiers Interred in Vermont." Vermont Historical Society, *Proceedings,* 1903-1904, pp. 114-65; 1905-1906, 189-203.

"Green Mountain Boys" and "Men with Ethan Allen at Ticonderoga." *The Vermont Antiquarian,* vol. 3, pp. 138-143.

Goodrich, John E.: *Rolls of the Soldiers in the Revolutionary War 1775-1783.* Rutland, 1904.

War of 1812:

Vermont Adjutant General: *Roster of Soldiers in War of 1812-1814.* Prepared and published under the direction of Herbert T. Johnson, Adjutant General. 1933.

Clark, Byron N.: *A List of Pensioners of the War of 1812.* 1904.

Civil War: Vermont Adjutant General: *Revised Roster of Vermont Volunteers and Lists of Volunteers Who Served in the Army of the United States during the War of the Rebellion 1861-1866.* Compiled by authority of the General Assembly under direction of Theodore S. Peck, Adjutant General. Montpelier, 1892. Indexed.

Official records

Vital Records: Fee for birth, marriage, and death certificates: Secretary of State, $1.50. Town or City Clerk, $2.00.

State Custodian: Vital Records, Secretary of State, Montpelier, 05602.

Birth, Marriage, and Death Records: (See also Miscellaneous Records and Sources.) Custodian: Address above State Custodian. (Also try Town or City Clerk if State Custodian does not have the record.) The State Custodian is supposed to have on file returns or certified copies of all of the birth, marriage, and death records of the Town Clerk's offices. Custodian: Town Clerk of the town where birth, marriage, or death occurred, or, if in a city, City Clerk. Town Clerks are the custodians of the official records of births, marriages, and deaths from the commencement of the registration of vital records. *Delayed birth certificates:* By court proceedings only.

Divorce Records: County Clerk of county where divorce was granted, or office of the Secretary of State. Cost of certified copy of divorce decree is $1.50.

Marriage Licenses: Town Clerk.

Court Records: Wills, administrations, and other probate proceedings: The state is divided into Probate Districts with a Probate Court in each district. Each county comprises one or more Probate District. The following counties constitute a single district: Caledonia, Chittenden, Essex, Franklin, Grand Isle, Lamoille, Orleans, and Washington. For records concerning towns in these counties write to the Register, Probate Court, at the County Seat. In Addison, Bennington, Orange, Rutland, Windham, and Windsor counties, there is more than one probate district. For a summary of which towns of these counties are in which probate districts, see: "Vermont Probate Districts," by Grace W. W. Reed and Winifred Lovering Holman, *American Genealogist,* April 1951, pp. 65-68. See also "A Bibliography on the History of the Courts of the Thirteen Original States, Maine, Ohio, and Vermont," by Herta Prager and William W. Price. *American Journal of Legal History,* vol. 2, p. 152. *Other Civil Actions:* Clerk, County Court, County Seat.

Land Records: Deeds, mortgages, leases, and other matters affecting title to land: Town Clerk or City Clerk. Deeds and conveyances of land in an unorganized town, gore, or grant are recorded by the clerk of the county in which such lands lie.

Microfilm Copies of Official Records: The Public Records Commission, State Library Building, Montpelier, has custody of microfilm copies of original and official land and probate records from the various towns and probate districts.

eral census

1. See index for section on United States census.

2. Custody of mortality schedules, 1850, 1860, 1870, and 1880: Vermont State Library, Montpelier. The Vermont Historical Society has typewritten and indexed copies of the mortality schedules for 1850 and 1860.

3. The original 1880 United States census records for Vermont were transferred in 1956 by the National Archives to: Director of Public Records, State of Vermont, State House, Montpelier.

-statehood
sus records

Cumberland County, Vermont, Census, 1771. This brief census was printed in the *Semi-Weekly Eagle,* Brattleboro, Vermont, January-July 1850. The Vermont Historical Society, Montpelier, has a typewritten copy. Information disclosed: Heads of families. This census was taken when Vermont was a part of New York. Cumberland County included what is now parts of Windsor and Windham counties.

Gloucester County, Vermont Census, 1771: Towns of Newbury, Mooretown (now Bradford), Barnet, Ryegate, Lunenburgh, Guildhall, Thetford, and Stafford (Strafford?).

Census of 1765: Towns of Pownal, Bennington, Arlington, Sunderland, and Manchester. See pp. 361-362, 433, *The Documentary History of the State of New York,* by E. B. O'Callaghan, M. D., vol. 4, 1851. See also the Boston *Transcript,* September 20, 1937. These census records were also taken when Vermont was a part of New York. Information included: Heads of families.

te Census

None.

Virginia

neral
ormation

Capital: Richmond. Entered Union: June 25, 1788. Seceded from Union: April 17, 1861. Reentered Union: January 27, 1870.

raries,
storical
cieties,
d archives

For a complete list, see: Brown, Karl: *The American Library Directory.* Also, *Directory of Historical Societies and Agencies in the United States and Canada,* 1956.

Albemarle County Historical Society, University of Virginia Library, Charlottesville.

Archives Division, Virginia State Library, Richmond.

Norfolk Public Library, 345 W. Freemason Street, Norfolk.

Richmond Public Library, 101 E. Franklin Street, Richmond.

Virginia Historical Society, Lee House, 707 E. Franklin Street, Richmond.

Virginia State Library, Richmond.

Virginia research suggestions

The Virginia Genealogist. Washington, D.C., quarterly.

The Virginia Gazette, Williamsburg. Publishes a weekly genealogical column.

The Virginia Herald, published in Fredericksburg 1786-1836, contained considerable data of genealogical value, such as marriages, births, deaths, suits, removals to Kentucky and the western country, etc.

"Seventeenth Century Virginia Parochial and County Court Records," *Virginia Magazine of History and Biography.* April 1948.

Prager, Herta, and William W. Price: "A Bibliography on the History of the Courts of the Thirteen Original States, Maine, Ohio, and Vermont," *American Journal of Legal History.* Vol. 2, p. 153.

Reference books

Armstrong, Zella: *Notable Southern Families.* 6 vols. 1928.

Barton, R. T.: *Virginia Colonial Decisions. 1728-1741.* 1909. 2 vols.

Boogher, William Fletcher: *Gleanings of Virginia History: An Historical and Genealogical Collection, Largely from Original Sources.* 1903.

Brock. Robert Alonzo: *Documents, Chiefly Unpublished, Relating to the Huguenot Emigration to Virginia.* 1886.

Brock, Robert Alonzo: *Virginia and Virginians,* 2 vols. 1888.

Casey, Joseph J.: *Personal Names in Hening's Statutes at Large of Virginia and Shepherd's Continuation.* 1933 and 1896.

Clemens, William Montgomery: *Virginia Wills before 1799.* 1924.

Crozier, William Armstrong: *Early Virginia Marriages.* 1907.

Crozier, William Armstrong: *A Key to Southern Pedigrees.* 1911.

Crozier, William Armstrong: *Virginia Colonial Militia, 1651-1776.* 1905.

Crozier, William Armstrong: *Virginia Heraldica,* being a Registry of Virginia Gentry Entitled to Coat Armor, with Genealogical Notes of the Families. 1908.

Crozier, William Armstrong: *Westmoreland County.* 1913. Abstracts of Westmoreland County wills, 1655-1794.

Crozier, William Armstrong: *Williamsburg Wills.* 1906.

Daughters of the American Revolution: "A List of Parishes and the Ministers in Them." *National Historical Magazine.* Vol. 76 (June 1938), p. 75. See also *William and Mary Quarterly,* vol. 5 (1897), p. 200.

Fothergill, Augusta Bridgland: *Wills of Westmoreland County, Virginia, 1654-1800.* 1925.

Hiden, Martha W.: "Seventeenth Century Virginia Parochial and County Court Records." *Virginia Magazine of History and Biography.* April 1948.

Johnston, David Emmons: *A History of Middle New River Settlements and Contiguous Territory.* 1906.

Johnston, Frederick: *Memorials of Old Virginia Clerks,* Arranged Alphabetically by Counties with Complete Index of Names, and Dates of Service from 1634 to the Present Time. 1888.

Long, Charles Massie: *Virginia County Names:* Two Hundred and Seventy Years of Virginia History. 1908.

McWhorter, Lucullus Virgil: *The Border Settlers of Northwestern Virginia from 1768 to 1795.* 1915.

Meade, William: *Old Churches, Ministers, and Families of Virginia.* 2 vols. 1897. Editions were published in 1857, 1861, and 1878; indexes published by J. M. Toner in 1898, and J. C. Wise in 1910.

Peterson, C. Stewart: *Bibliography of County Histories of the 3111 Counties in the 48 States.* Baltimore, 1946.

Researcher: A Magazine of History and Genealogical Exchange. 2 vols. 1926-1928.

Stanard, William Glover: *The Colonial Virginia Register:* A List of Governors, Councillors and Other Higher Officials, and also of Members of the House of Burgesses, and the Revolutionary Conventions of the Colony of Virginia. 1902.

Stanard, William Glover: *Some Emigrants to Virginia.* 1911 and 1915 ed., enlarged.

Stewart, Robert Armistead: *Index to Printed Virginia Genealogies,* 1930. Not indexed as to given and surnames as in Swem's *Virginia Historical Index.*

Swem, Earl Gregg: *Virginia Historical Index.* 2 vols. 1934-1936. Personal names and subjects in seven important Virginia magazines and other sources are indexed by librarian of the College of William and Mary.

Torrence, Clayton: *Virginia Wills and Administration, 1632-1800.* 1931.

Tyler's *Quarterly Historical and Genealogical Magazine.* 1919—.

United States Bureau of the Census: *Heads of Families at the First Census of the United States Taken in the Year 1790.* Virginia, 1908. Federal census schedules of Virginia for 1790 are missing; the lists of the state enumerations made in 1782, 1783, 1784 and 1785, while not complete, have been substituted.

United States, WPA: *Bibliography of Research Projects Reports*—Check List of Historical Records Survey Publications. 1940.

Valentine, Edward Pleasants: *The Edward Pleasants Valentine Papers.* 4 vols. 1927.

Van Meter, Benjamin Franklin: *Genealogies and Sketches of Some Old Families Who Have Taken Prominent Part in the Development of Virginia and Kentucky Especially.* 1901.

Virginia State Library: *Annual Reports.* With bibliographies.

Virginia State Library: *Bulletin.* Some of the bulletins contain bibliographies.

Virginia Historical Society: *Collections.* 12 vols. 1833-1892.

Virginia Magazine of History and Biography. 1893—.

Waldenmaier, Inez: *A Finding List of Virginia Marriage Records before 1853.* 1957. Pp. 3, 42. Mimeographed.

Wayland, John Walter: *Virginia Valley Records.* 1930.

William and Mary College Quarterly Historical Magazine. 1892—.

Military rosters, rolls, and records

The Virginia State Library, Richmond, has a collection of indexed records concerning service by Virginia soldiers in the Colonial Wars, Revolutionary War, War of 1812, and the War Between the States. Service to correspondents by the library is limited to examining their indexes for specifically named soldiers.

Revolutionary War Rolls, Etc.:

Brumbaugh, Gaius Marcus: *Revolutionary War Records,* 1936. Virginia Army and Navy forces with bounty land warrants for Virginia military district of Ohio and Virginia, military scrip from federal and state archives.

Burgess, Louis Alexander: *Virginia Soldiers of 1776.* 3 vols. Richmond, 1927.

Stewart, Robert Armistead: *Roster of the Virginia Navy of*

the Revolution (included in *The History of Virginia's Navy of the Revolution,* 1934, pp. 137-271.)

Virginia State Library, Department of Archives and History: *List of the Revolutionary Soldiers of Virginia.* Richmond, 1913.

War of 1812:

Ritchie, William F.: "Commonwealth of Virginia," Public Printer: *Payrolls of the Virginia Militia in the War of 1812.* 1851.

Muster Rolls of the Virginia Militia in the War of 1812. 1852. (A supplement to the *Payrolls.*)

Civil War:

The Roster of Confederate Pensioners of Virginia Showing Payments . . . to all Pensioners Enrolled under the Several Acts of Assembly, issued as a part of the state Auditor's Reports in 1925-1926, has been superseded by an index housed in the office of the Pension Clerk, Department of Accounts and Purchases, Richmond.

The National Archives has compiled the *Consolidated Index to Compiled Records of Confederate Soldiers.* The index is on cards that give the name of the soldier, his rank, the unit in which he served, and often a statement concerning the origin or background of that unit. There are cross-reference cards for soldiers' names that appeared in the records under more than one spelling. This index is available for personal search or by an agent. It is microfilmed.

ial records

Vital Records: Fee for birth, marriage, and death certificates: $2.00

State Custodian: Commonwealth of Virginia, Department of Health, Bureau of Vital Records and Health Statistics, P.O. Box 1000, Richmond, 23208.

Birth and Death Records: Subsequent to June 14, 1912: Above-named State Custodian. Incomplete records from 1853 to 1896 and death records are arranged for search but not indexed, place and time essential for a satisfactory search. *Delayed birth certificates:* State Custodian will furnish information.

Divorce Records: Since 1918: Bureau of Vital Statistics, State Department of Health, P.O. Box 1000, Richmond, 23208. Cost of certified copy of divorce decree is $2.00. Also try Clerk of Court of county or city where divorce was granted. Cost of certified copy of divorce decree varies.

Marriage Licenses: Clerk of the Circuit Court of the County or Clerk of Hustings Court of the county or city where license was issued.

Marriage Records: Subsequent to 1853: Above-named State Custodian. (Some missing years for some counties.) *Prior to 1853:* Clerk of Circuit Court of county or Clerk of Hustings Court of the city where license issued. A number of cities in Virginia, and one county, commenced registration of vital records prior to June 14, 1912, as follows:

Name	Date Birth Records Commenced	Date Death Records Commenced
Richmond	Jan. 1, 1900	Jan. 1, 1900
Lynchburg	Aug. 1, 1910	Aug. 1, 1910
Norfolk	1892	1892
Roanoke	1891	1891
Newport News	1896	1896
Portsmouth	Jul. 1, 1900	Jan. 31, 1881
Petersburg	Jan. 1, 1910	Jan. 1, 1900
Elizabeth City County	1900	1900

Court Records: Wills, administrations, and other probate matters: County Clerk, County Seat. *Other Civil Actions:* County Clerk, County Seat.

Land Records: Deeds, mortgages, leases, and other matters affecting title to land: County Clerk, County Seat.

Federal census

1. See index for section on United States census.

2. Custody of mortality schedules, 1850, 1860, 1870, 1880: Virginia State Library, Richmond.

3. The original 1880 United States census records for Virginia were transferred in 1956 by the National Archives to: Library, University of Pittsburgh, Pittsburgh.

4. The Virginia State Library, Richmond, has microfilm copies of the U. S. Census for the period of 1830-1880.

Virginia state census records

There are no state census records other than the 1782-1785 state enumerations (heads of families) included in the published first U. S. Census of 1790.

Washington

General information

Capital: Olympia. Organized as a territory: March 2, 1853. Entered Union: November 11, 1889.

Libraries, historical societies, and archives

For a complete list, see: Brown, Karl: *The American Library Directory*. Also, *Directory of Historical Societies and Agencies in the United States and Canada,* 1956.

Daughters of the Pioneers of Washington, State Library, Olympia.

Seattle Public Library, 4th Avenue at Madison Street, Seattle.

State Archives, Social Security Building, Olympia.

State Capitol Historical Association, 211 West 21st Street, Olympia.

State Historical Society, State Historical Building, 315-323 North Stadium Way, Tacoma.

Washington State Library, Olympia.

rence
:s

Hawthorne, Julian, ed: *History of Washington.* 2 vols. 1893.

Hines, H. K.: *An Illustrated History* [and Biographies] *of the State of Washington.* 1893.

Historical Records, WPA: *Guide to Public Vital Statistics Records in Washington.* 1941. 131 pp.

Historical Records Survey, WPA: *Guide to Church Vital Statistics Records in Washington.* 1942. 93 pp.

Peterson, C. Stewart: *Bibliography of County Histories of the 3111 Counties in the 48 States.* Baltimore, 1946.

Washington State Historical Society: *Building a State:* Washington, 1889-1939. 1940. An index to Washington Donation Land Claims appears on pages 403-452.

ry rosters,
and
rds

Custodian: Adjutant General, Camp Murray, Fort Lewis.

Very few records were maintained on the militia of Washington territory or state prior to 1886, except that records are now available on the militia regiments from Washington Territory that participated in the Cayuse War of 1847-48, the Indian wars of Washington and Oregon, 1855-56, and during the Civil War (stationed in the territory).

ial records

Vital Records: Fee for birth, marriage, and death certificates, $3.00.

State Custodian: State Department of Health, Bureau of Vital Statistics, P.O. Box 709, Olympia, 98504.

Birth and Death Records: Subsequent to July 1, 1907: For those born outside of first class cities (Seattle, Spokane, and Tacoma): Address above-named State Custodian. *Prior to July 1, 1907:* If the birth or death in Seattle, Spokane, or Tacoma, write to City Health Department of those cities. If birth or death elsewhere and in county areas, write County Auditor, County Seat. *Delayed birth certificates:* State Custodian will furnish information.

Divorce Records: County Clerk of county where divorce was granted. Cost of certified copy of divorce decree varies.

Marriage Licenses: County Clerk, County Seat. Record is in the clerk's office of county where marriage took place, regardless of county where license was issued. A copy may be deposited with the latter.

Marriage Records: County Clerk.

Court Records: Wills, administrations, and other probate matters: County Clerk, County Seat. *Other Civil Actions:* County Clerk, County Seat.

Land Records: Deeds, mortgages, leases, and other matters affecting title to land: County Auditor, County Seat.

Federal census

1. See index for section on United States census.

2. Custody of mortality schedules, 1860: Washington State Library, Olympia.

3. The original 1880 United States census records for Washington were transferred in 1956 by the National Archives to: Washington State Library, Temple of Justice, Olympia.

Washington state census records

Census Years: 1871, 1883, 1885, 1887, 1889, 1892. Most counties included. Custodian: Washington State Library, Olympia. Information included: At least names head of family.

West Virginia

General information

Capital: Charleston. Entered the Union: June 20, 1863.

Libraries, historical societies, and archives

For a complete list, see: Brown, Karl: *The American Library Directory.* Also, *Directory of Historical Societies and Agencies in the United States and Canada.* 1956.

Daughters of the American Pioneers Historical Society, Parkersburg.

Jefferson County Historical Society, Shepherdstown.

Marion County Historical Society, County Library, Fairmont.

West Virginia Department of Archives and History, Charleston.

West Virginia Historical Society, Charleston.

West Virginia geographical data

Kenny, Hammil: *West Virginia Place Names.* 1945. 768 pp.

Sims, Edgar B.: *Making a State.* 1956. Formation of the counties, maps, an index to land grants for Fincastle, Giles, and Rockingham counties.

ɪrence ks

Butcher, B. L.: *Upper Monongahela Valley, Genealogical and Personal History of.* 3 vols. 1912.

Hale, J. P.: *Trans-Allegheny Pioneers.* 1886.

Historical Records Survey, WPA: *West Virginia County Formations and Boundary Changes.* 1939. 249 pp.

Historical Records Survey, WPA: *Inventory of Public Vital Statistics Records in West Virginia.* 1941. 76 pp. Births, marriages, and deaths.

Historical Records Survey, WPA: *Inventory of the Vital Statistics Records in West Virginia.* 1942. 278 pp. Vol. 2, Church Archives.

Myers, S.: *History of West Virginia.* 2 vols. 1915.

Peterson, C. Stewart: *Bibliography of County Histories of the 3111 Counties in the 48 States.* Baltimore, 1946.

Sims, Edgar B.: *Sims Index to Land Grants in West Virginia.* 1951. 50,000 names of persons to whom grants were made in territory now West Virginia, 1746—.

Sims, Edgar B.: *Making a State, 1956.* Contains an index to land grants for Fincastle, Giles, and Rockingham Counties.

Tetrick, W. Guy: *Obituaries from Newspapers of Northern West Virginia.* 1933.

United States, WPA: *Bibliography of Research Projects Reports* — Check List of Historical Records Survey Publications. 1943.

West Virginia Wills. 4 vols. 1936.

West Virginia: *Biennial Report of the State Department of Archives and History.* Includes a bibliography of West Virginia in two parts, for period ending June 30, 1938. (Bibliography of Manuscripts and Genealogical Books.) Also contains a directory of newspapers in West Virginia, 1790-1905.)

ary rosters, , and ɪrds

Revolutionary Rolls:

"Graves of Revolutionary Soldiers," *National Historical Magazine.* Daughters of the American Revolution. June 1940, pp. 36-7.

Perkins, E. P.: *West Virginia Revolutionary Pensions.* Vol. 1, 1935.

Reddy, Anne W.: *West Virginia Revolutionary Ancestors Whose Services Were Non-Military and Whose Names, therefore, Do Not Appear in Revolutionary Indexes of Soldiers and Sailors.* 1930.

State Rosters — Civil War: West Virginia Adjutant General's Office: Annual Report of the Adjutant General (F. P. Peirpoint) of the State of West Virginia for the Year Endin Dec. 31, 1865. Sheeling, 1866.

Official records

Vital Records: Fee for birth and death certificates: $1.00

State Custodian: Division of Vital Statistics, State Department of Health, Charleston, 25305.

Birth and Death Records: Subsequent to 1917: Above-named State Custodian.

Prior to 1917: County Clerk, at County Seat. *Delayed bir certificates:* State Custodian will furnish information.

Divorce Records: Clerk of Circuit Court, Chancery side, i county where divorce was granted. Cost of certified copy of divorce decree varies.

Marriage Licenses: County Clerk.

Marriage Records: County Clerk, County Seat where marriage license was issued.

Court Records: Wills, administrations, and other probate matters: County Clerk, County Seat. *Other Civil Actions:* County Clerk, County Seat.

Land Records: Deeds, mortgages, leases, and other matters affecting title to land: County Clerk, County Seat.

Federal census

1. See index for section on United States census.

2. Custody of mortality schedules, 1850, 1860, 1870, 1880: Department of Archives and History, State of West Virginia, Charleston.

3. The original 1880 United States census records for West Virginia were transferred in 1956 by the National Archives to: Library, University of Pittsburgh, Pittsburgh, Pa

State census

No record of a state census has been found.

Wisconsin

General information

Capital: Madison. Organized as a territory: April 20, 1836 Entered Union: May 29, 1848.

Libraries, historical societies, and archives

For a complete list, see: Brown, Karl: *The American Library Directory.* Also, *Directory of Historical Societies and Agencies in the United States and Canada,* 1956.

Douglas County Historical Society, 1827 John Avenue, Superior.

Milwaukee Public Library, 814 W. Wisconsin Ave., Milwaukee.

Oconto County Historical Society, Beyer Homestead, 917 Park Avenue, Oconto.

State Historical Society of Wisconsin, 816 State Street, Madison.

Swiss-American Historical Society, 1 W. Main St., Madison.

onsin rch estions

Gleason, Margaret: ''Genealogical Materials at the State Historical Society of Wisconsin,'' *National Genealogical Society Quarterly,* vol. 43 (December 1955), pp. 131ff.

Van Alstyne, W. Scott, Jr.: ''Land Transfer and Recording in Wisconsin,'' *Wisconsin Law Review,* 1955, pp. 44-76, 223-253.

ence

Griswold, Ada Tyng: *Annotated Catalogue of Newspaper Files* in the Library of the State Historical Society of Wisconsin. 1911.

Historical Records Survey, WPA: *Directory of Churches and Religious Organizations in Wisconsin.* 1941. 358 pp.

Historical Records Survey, WPA: *Guide to Public Vital Statistics Records in Wisconsin.* 1941. 247 pp.

Historical Records Survey, WPA: *Guide to Church Vital Statistics Records in Wisconsin.* 1942. 255 pp.

Hunt, John Warren: *Wisconsin Gazetteer.* 1853.

Peterson, C. Stewart: *Bibliography of County Histories of the 3111 Counties in the 48 States.* Baltimore, 1946.

Quarterly Magazine of Wisconsin, Genealogical Society, Delafield, Wisconsin Vol. 1, 1940.

Schafer, Joseph: *Wisconsin Domesday Book.* Vol. 1, 1923. Maps showing land owners, genealogical notes.

United States Department of State: *Territorial Papers of the United States.* 1934. Vols. 2 and 3: *Territory Northwest of the Ohio River,* 1787-1803. (For a summary of this source see *National Genealogical Society Quarterly,* 37:93—.)

ry rosters, and ds

State Rosters — Civil War:

Wisconsin Adjutant General's Office: *Roster of Wisconsin Volunteers of the Rebellion,* 1861-1865. Compiled by Authority of the Legislature under Direction of Jeremiah M. Rusk, Governor, and Chandler P. Chapman, Adjutant General. Madison, Wisconsin, 1886. 2 vols.

Official records

Vital Records: Statewide index of all marriages, divorces births, and deaths since Oct. 1, 1907; prior to that indexed by counties separately. Fee for birth, marriage, and death certificate: $4.00

State Custodian: State of Wisconsin, Department of Health and Social Services, Division of Health, Section of Vital Records, 1 West Wilson Street, P.O. Box 309, Madiso 53701.

Birth Records: Subsequent to 1860: Above-named State Custodian. (1860 for some counties, 1800 for other counties, incomplete until 1907.) *Prior to 1907:* Try Registr of Deeds, County Seat. *Delayed birth certificates:* State Custodian will furnish information.

Marriage Licenses: Marriage certificates: State Bureau c Vital Statistics, or County Clerk.

Marriage Records: Subsequent to 1860: Above-named State Custodian. (1860 for some of the older counties, but incomplete prior to 1907.) *Prior to 1907 and 1860:* Registr of Deeds, County Seat.

Death Records: Subsequent to 1880: Above-named Sta Custodian. Incomplete prior to 1907. *Prior to 1880 or 1907* Registrar of Deeds, County Seat.

Divorce Records: Bureau of Vital Statistics, State Board Health, Madison. Cost of certified copy of divorce decree is $4.00.

Court Records: Wills, administrations, and other probate matters: County Clerk, County Seat. *Other Civil Actions:* County Clerk, County Seat.

Land Records: Deeds, mortgages, leases, and other matters affecting title to land: Registrar of Deeds, County Seat.

Federal census

1. See index for section on United States census.
2. Custody of mortality schedules, 1850, 1860, 1870, 1880: State Historical Society, Madison.
3. The original 1880 United States census records for Wisconsin were transferred in 1956 by the National Archive to: State Historical Society, 816 State Street, Madison.

Territorial and state census records

Wisconsin Territorial Census Records: Custodian: State Historical Society, 816 State Street, Madison.

Territorial censuses were taken in 1836, 1838, 1842, 1846, and 1847. The counties of Dubuque and Des Moine now in Iowa, were part of the territory of Wisconsin in 1836 and were included in the census of that year. (See Iowa.) Information included: 1836-38. Head of family only, and totals of males and females over and under 21.

1842: Name of township, head of family, white males, white females, total. Arranged by counties.

1846: Head of family, white males and females, total, arranged by counties. June 1, 1846.

1847: Head of family, white males and females, total. Arranged by counties. December 1, 1847.

nsin state s records

Custodian: State Historical Society, 816 State St., Madison.

1855 Census: Head of family, white male and female, foreign birth, arranged by counties and townships within counties. June 1, 1855.

1865 Census: Total population of townships, villages, etc., and county totals only.

1875 Census: Head of family, white, male and female. Arranged by counties. June 1, 1875.

1885 Census: Head of family, white male and female, information on foreign birth, arranged by counties, townships, and villages within counties. June 20, 1885.

1895 Census: Head of family, white male and female, place of birth, arranged by counties, townships, villages. June 20, 1895.

1905 Census: Custodian, Secretary of State, Madison.

Information included: Head of family, members of household, relationship to head of family, race, sex, age, marital status, place of birth, occupation. Arranged by villages, towns, and counties. June 1, 1905. Secretary of State furnishes application forms for search. Cost of search varies.

Wyoming

al ation

Capital: Cheyenne. Organized as a territory: July 25, 1868. Entered Union: July 10, 1890.

es, cal ies, chives

For a complete list, see: Brown, Karl: *The American Library Directory.* Also, *Directory of Historical Societies and Agencies in the United States and Canada,* 1956.

Wyoming State Archives and Historical Department, State Office Building, Cheyenne.

Wyoming State Library, Cheyenne.

Reference books

Historical Records Survey, WPA: *A Directory of Churches and Religious Organizations in the State of Wyoming.* 1939. 64 pp.

Peterson, C. Stewart: *Bibliography of County Histories of the 3111 Counties in the 48 States.* Baltimore, 1946.

Wyoming Official Directory.

Official records

Vital Records: Fee for birth, marriage, and death certificates: $2.00.

State Custodian: Vital Records Services Division of Health and Medical Services, State Office Building, Cheyenne, 82002.

Birth and Death Records: Subsequent to July 1909: Above-named State Custodian. *Prior to July 1909:* County Clerk, County Seat. *Delayed birth certificates:* State Custodian will furnish information.

Divorce Records: Since May 1941: Division of Vital Statistics, State Department of Public Health, Cheyenne. Cost of certified copy of divorce decree is $2.00. *Prior to May 1941:* Clerk of District Court in county where divorce was granted. Cost of certified copy of divorce decree varies.

Marriage Licenses: County Clerk.

Marriage Records: County Clerk. Also State Board of Health, Division of Vital Statistics, Cheyenne, since May 1941.

Court Records: Wills, administrations, and other probate matters: County Clerk, County Seat. *Other Civil Actions:* County Clerk, County Seat.

Land Records: Deeds, mortgages, leases, and other matters affecting title to land: County Clerk, County Seat.

Federal census

1. See index for section on United States census.

2. Custody of mortality schedules, 1870, 1880: State Archives and Historical Department, Cheyenne.

3. The original 1880 United States census records for Wyoming were transferred in 1956 by the National Archives to: State Library and Historical Bldg., Wyoming State Historical Department, Cheyenne.

Wyoming state census records

Census of 1905 is in the custody of the Secretary of State, Cheyenne; it is indexed by counties. This census is incomplete and in poor condition. Censuses of 1915 and 1925 cannot be located.

Trust Territories of the United States

American Samoa

records *Birth, marriage, and death certificates:* Office of the Territorial Registrar, Pago Pago, American Samoa 96799. Cost of certificates: $1.00. Records since 1900.

Guam

records Fee for birth, marriage, and death certificates: $1.00.

Custodian: Office of Vital Statistics, Department of Public Health and Social Services, Government of Guam, P.O. Box 2816, Agana, Guam 96910.

Divorce Records: Clerk, Superior Court of Guam, Agana, Guam. (Cost of decree varies.)

Trust Territory of the Pacific Islands

records Cost of certificates varies.

Custodian: Clerk of the Court in the District where the birth, marriage, death, or divorce occurred.

Department of Medical Services, Saipan, Mariana Islands 96950.

Virgin Islands

records Cost of birth, marriage, and death certificates: $2.00.

Custodian: Bureau of Research and Statistical Services, V. I. Department of Health, Charlotte Amalie, St. Thomas, Virgin Islands 00801.

Marriage Records: Clerk of the Municipal Court, Municipal Court of the Virgin Islands, Charlotte Amalie, St. Thomas, Virgin Islands 00801. St. Thomas and St. John: Judge of Police Court, Charlotte Amalie, St. Thomas, Virgin Islands, 00801.

Divorce Records: Clerk, U.S. District Court, Christiansted, St. Croix, Virgin Islands 00820. Cost of Decree: $2.40.

Canal Zone (Panama)

records Fee for birth, marriage, and death certificates: first copy, no fee; each additional copy, $2.00.

Custodian: Vital Statistics, Health Bureau, Balboa Heights Canal Zone.

Birth Records: Subsequent to May 4, 1904: Above-name Custodian.

Marriage Records: Subsequent to September 1905: Clerk United States District Court, Ancon, Canal Zone.

Death Records: Subsequent to May 4, 1904: Above-named Custodian.

Court Records: Divorces, wills, administrations, and othe probate matters: Clerk, U.S. District Court. *Other Civil Actions:* Clerk, U.S. District Court.

Land Records: Deeds, mortgages, leases, and other matters affecting title to land: Clerk, U.S. District Court, Ancon, Canal Zone.

American Indian Research and Records

Probably more valuable than private records and records of the various State official records are the records of the Bureau of Indian Affairs, located in the regional branches of the National Archives. These records include birth, death, marriage, censuses of tribes, school and other records beginning in the mid-nineteenth century. The locations and addresses of the regional branches are listed in National Archives *"General Information Leaflet No. 22."* Another outstanding source for Indian research is the *Guide to Genealogical Records in the National Archives,* by Meredith B. Colket, Jr., and Frank E. Bridgers. Both publications are available from the National Archives, Washington, D.C. 20408.

Puerto Rico

Vital records

Custodian: Bureau of Demographic Statistics, Department of Health, San Juan, Puerto Rico 00908.

Marriage: Records were established in the various municipalities of the island in 1885, and the municipal judge were in charge of these records until 1911, when a new law placed them under the control of the Municipal Secretaries, who are the only persons with authority to issue copies of al marriages certificates filed with them. A duplicate of each certificate was sent to the Department of Health for statistica purposes. On July 21, 1931, the Vital Statistics Registry Act came into effect giving the Commissioner of Health full control and supervision. This law is an adoption of the "Model Law for the Registration of Births and Deaths of the United States" and provides for the registration of marriages prescribing a penalty for failure to report. Copies of certificates registered from July 21, 1931 can only be obtained from the Bureau of Vital Statistics of the Department of Health.

Custodian: The Chief of the Bureau of Vital Statistics of the Department of Health has charge of the original certificates of birth, marriage, and death registered since July 21, 1931. Certificates registered prior to this date are filed under the custody of the Municipal Secretary of every town.

Marriages, Births, and Deaths: Records began to be kept in the Department of Health in July 21, 1931. Before that date only *copies* of certificates registered in each municipality were received in the Bureau of Vital Statistics of the Department of Health and used for statistical purposes. Provisions have been made for indexing all records. *Delayed birth certificates:* By special court proceedings.

Divorce Records: Clerk of Superior Court where decree was granted.

Census of 1935: The Bureau of the Census has custody of a social and population census of Puerto Rico for 1935. These schedules are written in Spanish, and contain name, residence, position in the family, sex, color, age, marital status, occupation, and place of birth. These records may not be examined except by an authorized employee of the census bureau.

Canada

Public Archives of Canada, Ottawa, Canada: The Public Archives of Canada operates under the authority of the Public Archives Act of 1912, and under the administration of the Department of the Secretary of State of the Dominion Government. The material in the custody of the Archives consists of the following:

Maps: Thirty thousand on file dating from 1500.

Photographs, Prints, Engravings, and Paintings: Approximately 70,000, which are catalogued and indexed.

Reference Library: Approximately 50,000 volumes. There is also a small historical museum.

Manuscripts: The manuscripts fall under three main headings:

1. Old records transferred from various government departments.

2. Transcripts made in Europe and America.

3. Collection of single items acquired by gift or purchase.

The official and semiofficial correspondence, generally termed state papers, comprises the official letters of government to and from Canada for both the French and English regimes. These official papers are supplemented by collections of private papers of families who were closely associated with government in Canada. Of equal importance with these official state papers are the manuscripts including Minutes of the Executive Councils of Upper and Lower Canada from 1764 to 1867, and Minutes of the Land Boards dealing with the granting of land in Upper and Lower Canada and general correspondence dealing with the laying out of lands, the building of roads and bridges, and other matters dealing with local administration.

Census: The Public Archives of Canada, at Ottawa, have the custody of the Canadian census from 1851 to 1871. Subsequent to 1871, the census is in the custody of the Dominion Statistician, Dominion Bureau of Statistics, Ottawa.

Church Records: Generally found in the parish church. The Public Archives of Canada, however, acquired copies in some cases, consisting of older records from the provinces of Quebec, Nova Scotia, and New Brunswick. In addition, the archivists in the provinces also have a certain number of parish registers in their custody. It is necessary to write to the Public Archives of Canada at Ottawa or to the provincial archivists to ascertain if they have the records you are seeking in a particular case.

Canadian Historical Societies and Libraries: Ninety-nine are listed in *Historical Societies in the United States and Canada,* published by the American Association for State and Local History, Washington, D. C., 1944.

Canadian Vital Records

Laws require that all births, marriages, and deaths be reported to the clerks of the counties and cities and forwarded to the Provincial Registrar General of the province where the birth, marriage, or death occurred. Cost of certified copies: $2.00. A resume of custody and location of vital and other official records of the various provinces follows.

Alberta, Canada

records

The province was inaugurated in 1905 when a Provincial Bureau of Vital Statistics was formed, and continued the records of the government of the Northwest Territories.

Custodian: Bureau of Vital Statistics, Department of Health, Edmonton, Alberta.

Births, Marriages, and Deaths: These have been registered since 1886 (Northwest Territories). Estimated 50 percent complete. From 1905 to 1915 the records are reasonably complete and are indexed. Subsequent to 1915 to date, the records are practically complete and are indexed. Probate records and civil court records and register of land transfers are on file in local registry offices. Provincial Archivist: Provincial Library, Edmonton, Alberta. Inspector of Land Titles: Calgary, Alberta.

British Columbia, Canada

records

Provincial Custodian: Registrar of births, marriages, and deaths, Parliament Building, Victoria, British Columbia.

Births, Marriages, and Deaths: Subsequent to September 1, 1872, write to above-named custodian.

Adoptions: Copies of all adoption orders entered in the various Supreme Court Registries are filed in Victoria and have been integrated with the birth records where the birth occurred in the province.

Baptisms, Marriages, and Burials Prior to 1872: An incomplete record of church registers for the province, which go back as far as 1836, is at Victoria with the above-named custodian.

Yukon Records: Records in Yukon are in the custody of Commanding Officer, Royal Canadian Mounted Police, Dawson. These records are complete and fully indexed. Deaths commenced in 1898 and births in 1899.

Court Records: Probate records, land records, civil court records are on file in local offices.

Provincial Archivists: Provincial Library, Victoria, British Columbia.

Manitoba, Canada

records

Provincial Custodian: Recorder of Vital Statistics, Department of Health and Public Welfare, Winnipeg, Manitoba.

Births, Marriages, and Deaths: Records dated from 1812, but incomplete in certain districts. Write above-named custodian.

Probate Records, Land Records, and Civil Court Records: In the custody of local offices.

Provincial Archivist: Provincial Librarian, Winnipeg, Manitoba.

New Brunswick, Canada

Vital records

Provincial Custodian: Registrar-General of New Brunswick, Fredericton, New Brunswick.

Births, Marriages, and Deaths: Records subsequent to January 1, 1920, in the custody of the above-named custodian. Records of the city of St. John that were not destroyed by the great fire of 1877 are in the custody of B. L. Gerow, Attorney, St. John, New Brunswick.

Early Marriages: These were recorded in Registers of Civil Status, which are kept by the ministers, priests, etc., of the various religious denominations in the province. These registers are kept in duplicate, one copy of which is filed annually with the prothonotary of the Superior Court in the district in which registers are kept. Some records date back to 1887. Books of records from 1887 to 1919 have been transferred from Division Registrar to Secretary of Sub District Board of Health (one for each county). Original certificates remain unfiled and unindexed in legislative buildings.

Probate Records, Land Records, and Civil Court Records: In the custody of local offices. Registers of lands, bills of sale, mortgages, land transfers, must be registered within 30 days with the Registrars of Deeds in each district. For certain older land records consult also the New Brunswick Museum, St. John, New Brunswick.

Provincial Archivist: The Provincial Librarian, Department of Education, Fredericton, New Brunswick.

Newfoundland, Canada

Vital records

Custodian: Registrar General, Vital Statistics, Department of Health and Welfare, St. John's, Newfoundland. Also: All clergymen are registrars and keep complete church records of births, deaths, and marriages, copies of which are furnished the Registrar-General at St. John's, quarterly for districts outside of St. John's and monthly for the city of St. John's.

Birth Records: Registration commenced on March 15, 1891, and are complete and are fully indexed.

Marriage Records: Records commence June 2, 1891, and are complete and fully indexed.

Death Records: Records commence on May 1, 1891, and

are complete and fully indexed. Prior to 1891 vital statistics were in the custody of the various local clergymen of their respective denominations.

Land Records, Wills, Administrations, Civil Court Records: Registrar of the Supreme Court, St. John's, Newfoundland. (This is the only registry in Newfoundland.)

Libraries and Historical Societies: Gosling Memorial Library, St. John's, Newfoundland; Newfoundland Historical Society, St. John's, Newfoundland.

Nova Scotia, Canada

l records

Provincial Custodian: Registrar-General, Bureau of Vital Statistics, Halifax, Nova Scotia.

Births and Deaths: Records commence in 1864; discontinued from 1876 to 1908, the approximate date and name of county needed to make a satisfactory search. (Write to above custodian.)

Marriages: Marriage records date from 1763 but are incomplete until 1864. (Write to above custodian.)

Marriage Licenses: Issued by the Deputy Issuer of Marriage Licenses in the district where the marriage was performed.

Probate Records, Land Records, and Civil Court Records: In the custody of local offices.

Provincial Archivist: Halifax, Nova Scotia.

Ontario, Canada

l records

Provincial Custodian: Registrar-General, Parliament Building, Toronto, Ontario.

Births and Deaths: Records commence in 1869. Write above custodian.

Marriages: Records commence in 1869. There are incomplete records from 1812 to 1869, which are indexed. Write above custodian.

Marriage Licenses: Licenses issued by municipal clerks or their deputies, the municipal clerk being the clerk of the city, town, or village. Local custodians, known as Division Registrars (Municipal Clerks as above), collect records of births, marriages, and deaths and transmit them monthly to the Registrar General.

Probate Records, Land Records, and Civil Court Records: In the custody of local officers.

Provincial Archivist: Parliament Building, Toronto, Ontario.

Inspector of Registry Offices: Parliament Building, Toronto, Ontario.

Prince Edward Island, Canada

Vital records

Provincial Custodian: Registrar General, Provincial Building, Charlottetown, Prince Edward Island.

Birth and Death Records: Subsequent to June 1906, ther are incomplete records; subsequent to 1920, they are more complete. Indexed. Prior to the time records were kept by Provincial Custodian, births and deaths were partially kept by the various churches in the Province. Write above custodian.

Marriage Records: Registration commenced in 1831. Records are complete in Surrogate's Office, Charlottetown, Prince Edward Island, to June 1906, when transferred to Office of Registrar General, fully indexed in both offices. Indexed as to the name of the male only. Ministers are required to make a return of any marriage performed within 48 hours of the ceremony.

Probate Records, Land Records, and Civil Court Records In the custody of local offices. Registrar of Deeds, etc., Charlottetown, Prince Edward Island.

Provincial Archivist: The Librarian, Legislative Library, Charlottetown, Prince Edward Island.

Quebec, Canada

Vital records

Provincial Custodian: Registrar, Parliament Building, Quebec; or Director of the Department of Health, City of Quebec; or the prothonotary of the chief town of the judicial district.

Certificates of marriages, births, and deaths are made ou in duplicate by the priests, rabbis, and clergymen of authorized denominations. The certificate of marriage in this province is the copy or the extract of the entry thereof in a register of civil status. The certificates themselves are not necessarily made in duplicate, but the registers in which the entries are made are always kept in duplicate by those authorized therefor, and one duplicate register is deposited by the custodian with the prothonotary of the district within which it is kept. In requesting copies of public records, state whether it is for a Catholic or non-Catholic, designating the particular congregation or church to which the parties belong, and whether for a citizen of Canada or an alien.

Marriages: Records date back as far as 1642. A general index for non-Catholics is available from 1760 to date. The index for Catholics being much larger, it is not yet complete If name and date are given to the prothonotary of a district, the information can be given very quickly.

Births: Records commence in 1894. Write the above

custodian. In requesting search, give name and date and also state whether the person is Catholic or not.

Deaths: The records of death in the Province of Quebec are handled not by the civil authorities, but by the religious authorities. When no clergyman is present at the death or burial of a non-Catholic, a record of such death may be obtained from the doctor's certificate filed with the Provincial Bureau of Health. Otherwise, such records may be had from the private records of the Mount Royal Cemetery Company, 1207 Drummond St., Montreal, Quebec. Deaths, like marriages and births, are recorded in registers of civil status kept by those specially authorized by law therefor.

Probate Records, Land Records, and Civil Court Records: In the custody of local offices.

Provincial Archivist: Quebec, Province of Quebec.

Saskatchewan, Canada

al records

Provincial Custodian: Division of Vital Statistics, Parliament Building, Regina, Saskatchewan.

Birth Records: Provincial custodian above-named has custody of the birth records, which commence in 1854; they are fully indexed.

Marriage Records: Records commence in 1878, are completely indexed, and above-named custodian has custody of them.

Death Records: Records commence in 1882 and are completely indexed. Write to above-named Custodian.

Probate Records, Land Records, and Civil Court Records: In the custody of local offices.

Provincial Archivist: University of Saskatchewan, Saskatoon, Saskatchewan.

Yukon Territory

l records

Custodian: Registrar of Vital Statistics, Territorial Treasurer's Office, Whitehorse.

Cuba

l records

Marriage: Civil Registry Law was enacted January 1, 1885. Previous to this date matrimonies were celebrated and recorded in the churches. The republic was established in

1902. The civil register is maintained from data sent in by municipal and provisional courts and original records made and kept on file in the proper municipal courts of the provinces.

Custodian: The officials in charge of the civil register in Cuba are: (1) The director of the Registry and Notaries, Department of Justice, Havana; and (2) The municipal judges in their capacities as custodians of the civil registers, at the municipal courts of the following provinces: Habana, Pinar del Rio, Matanzas, Santa Clara, Camaguey, and Oriente.

Births and Deaths: Previous to January 1, 1885, baptisms were noted in the birth records kept by churches, and deaths were also kept in the church records. Since that date they are kept in accordance with the provisions of the Civil Registry Law. At the end of each Birth and Death Record Book of the Civil Registry, there will be found indexed the inscriptions contained therein.

England and Wales

Vital records

Birth, Marriage, and Death Records: Since July 1, 1837: General Register Office, St. Catherine's House, 10 Kingsway, London, WC 2B 6 JP, England. *Prior to July 1, 1837:* This being before civil registration, the only source is registration of baptism, marriage, and death records of the established church and some nonconformist church records. These records are located in some 1400 parishes in England and Wales. Fortunately many of these parish registers have been transcribed, and some are in printed form.

Locating Parish Registers: The Society of Genealogists, 37 Harrington Gardens, London, S.W. 7, has a large collection of printed and typescript parish registers. Many libraries in the United States have printed copies and there are some microfilm copies of some of these registers. There are several valuable guides that aid in the location of printed and manuscript copies of parish registers:

Catalogue of the Parish Register Copies in the Possession of the Society of Genealogists. Second edition, 1937.

National Index of Parish Register Copies, compiled by Kathleen Bloomfield and H. K. Percy-Smith. Society of Genealogists. London, 1939.

An excellent guide to the location of the parishes of England and Wales is *Key to the Ancient Parish Registers of England and Wales,* by Arthur Meredyth Burke. London, 1908.

If the parish registers you are interested in have not been copied, it is necessary to search the original registers in the parish.

Marriages before 1837: Most persons of financial means were married by license prior to 1837. The license was issued by an official of the established church. These licenses contain valuable genealogical information. Custodians: the London Diocesan Registry; the Office of the Vicar General; and the Faculty Office of the Archbishop of Canterbury, all located at No. 1, The Sanctuary, London, S.W. 1. For Wales, the National Library of Wales, Aberystwyth, and libraries at Cardiff, Swansea, and the University of North Wales should be consulted.

us records

There are census returns every ten years beginning 1841, in the custody of the Public Record Office, Somerset House, London, W.C. 2, England. A successful search cannot be made without definite information concerning the person, the subject of the search, as to name and residence.

The Public Record Office Chancery Lane, London, contains national records since the Norman Conquest. There are many types of court records and other documents of great genealogical value. It is recommended that a professional genealogist or searcher be employed for any research undertaken at this office.

ate
rds, wills,
nistrations

England and Wales: To find a proved will before January 1, 1858, the date on which the Court of Probate Act, 1857 (20-21 Vict. C.77), came into operation, it is best to search first—if the testator was a person of substance—the index to the wills proved in the Prerogative Court of Canterbury, at Somerset House. Failing this, the will is probably to be found in the registry of the district in which it was proved. Wills proved prior to 1858 were all distributed among the district registries when these institutions came into existence. This is a broad rule that can be laid down to guide a searcher. For wills since 1858, write to: Principal Probate Registry, Somerset House, W.C. 2, London. Because of the fact that wills vary in length, one has to inquire as to the cost before sending money.

List of Probate Registers: The 29 District Probate Registries, established by the act of 1857, are located at the following cities: Bangor, Birmingham, Blandford, Bodmin, Bristol, Carlisle, Carmarthen, Chester, Durham, Exeter, Gloucester, Ipswich, Lancaster, Leicester, Lewes, Lincoln,

Liverpool, Llandaff, Manchester, Newcastle upon Tyne, Norwich, Nottingham, Oxford, Peterborough, Shrewsbury, Taunton, Wakefield, Winchester, and York.

For wills and estates prior to 1858 use the *Index Library Volumes,* published by the British Record Society; after one has obtained the name and number of an estate, the above data on probate records will disclose the proper place to write. Also write to the County Record Office of the county involved, as the early probate records may be deposited there. Prior to 1858 wills and administrations that were at Somerset House are now in the Public Record Office, Chancery Lane, London.

Reference books

Additional information about British records may be obtained from the following sources:

Whitaker's Almanac, published annually and found in most libraries.

The Genealogist's Handbook, published by the Society of Genealogists, 37 Harrington Gardens, London, S.W. 7.

Burke, Arthur Meredyth: *Key to the Ancient Parish Registers of England and Wales.* London, 1908.

Catalogue of the Parish Register Copies in the possession of the Society of Genealogists. Second ed. 1937. Published by the Society of Genealogists, London.

National Index of Parish Register Copies, compiled for the Society of Genealogists by Kathleen Bloomfield and H.K. Percy-Smith. London, 1939.

Wills and Their Whereabouts, compiled mostly from original sources by B. G. Bouwens. 1951.

British Record Society: *The Index Library.* Consult indexes to wills of various counties.

Born, Lester K: British Manuscript Project. A checklist of the microfilms prepared in England and Wales for the American Council of Learned Societies, 1941-1945. Library of Congress, Washington, 1955.

Principal libraries—genealogy and heraldry

Guildhall Library, King Street, London E.C. 2.

Kensington Public Library, Central Library, Kensington High Street, London, W. 8.

Public Libraries, Central Library, Guildhall Square, Portsmouth.

Historical Society of Lancashire and Cheshire, Royal Institution, Colquitt Street, Liverpool 1.

Public Libraries, Central Library, St. Peter's Square, Manchester 2.

Oxfordshire County Library, 14 Norham Gardens, Oxford.

William Salt Library, Eastgate Street, Stafford.

Public Library, Central Library, Beddington and Wallington, Surrey.

Cullum Reference Library, Cornhill, Bury St., Edmunds, Suffolk.

Society of Genealogists, 37 Harrington Gardens, London, S.W. 7.

Chetham's Library, Hunt's Bank, Manchester 3.

Lancashire County Library, Headquarters, County Hall, Pitt Street, Preston, Lancashire.

aries— history ections

Bedfordshire:

Bedfordshire County Library, The Embankment, Bedford.

Luton Museum and Art Gallery, Wardown Park, Luton.

Berkshire:

Berkshire County Library, Abbey Street, Reading.

Public Libraries, Blagrave Street, Reading.

Buckinghamshire:

Buckinghamshire County Library, Highbridge Road, Aylesbury.

Milton Cottage Trust, Milton's Cottage, Chalfont St., Giles.

Cambridgeshire:

Cambridgeshire County Library, Shire Hall, Castle Hill, Cambridge.

Isle of Ely County Library, Gordon Avenue, March.

Wisbech Museum and Literary Institution, Wisbech.

Cheshire:

Public Library, George Street, Altrincham.

Mayer Public Library, Rebington, Wirral,

Public Library, Borough Road, Birkenhead.

Cheshire County Library, 91 Hoole Rd, Chester.

Public Library, St. John Street, Chester.

Public Library, Carnegie Street, Ellesmere Port.

Historic Society of Lancashire and Cheshire, Royal Institution, Colquitt Street, Liverpool 1, England.

Public Library, Egerton Street, Runcorn.

Astley Cheetham Public Library, Trinity Street, Stalybridge.

Public Libraries, Central Library, Wellington Road South, Stockport.

Cornwall:

Public Library, Camborne.

Devon and Cornwall Record Society, c/o Hon. Secretary, University of Exeter, Exeter, Devon., England.

Public Library, Municipal Buildings, Falmouth.

Public Library, Morrab Road, Penzance.

Public Library, Clinton Road, Redruth.

Cornwall County Library, County Hall, Truro.

Public Library, Pydar Street, Truro.

Royal Institution of Cornwall, County Museum, River Street, Truro.

Cumberland:

Cumberland County Library, 1-2 Portland Sq., Carlisle.

Public Library, Tullie House, Carlisle.

Public Libraries, Central Library, Market Square, Lancaster, Lancs., England.

Public Library, Catherine Street, Whitehaven.

Public Library, Finkle Street, Workington.

Derbyshire:

Public Library, Terrace Road, Buxton.

Public Library, Stephenson Memorial Hall, Chesterfield.

Derbyshire County Library, St. Mary's Gate, Derby.

Public Library, Wardwick, Derby.

Public Library, Market Place, Ilkeston.

Public Library, Alexandra Road, Swadlincote.

Devonshire:

North Devon Athenaeum, The Square, Barnstaple.

St. Mary's Abbey, Buckfast.

Devon and Cornwall Record Society, c/o Hon. Secretary, University of Exeter, Exeter.

Devon and Exeter Institution, The Close, Exeter.

Devon County Library, Barley House, St. Thomas, Exeter.

Public Library, Central Library, Tavistock Road, Plymouth.

War Memorial Library, Angel Hill, Tiverton.

Public Library, Lymington Road, Torquay.

Dorsetshire:

Dorset County Library, County Hall, Dorchester.

Public Libraries, South Road, Poole.

Public Library, Westway Road, Weymouth and Melcombe Regis.

Durham:

Edward Pease Public Library, Crown Street, Darlington.

Durham Cathedral Library, Durham.

Durham County Library, 24 Old Elvet, Durham.

University of Durham (Durham Colleges), 38 North Bailey, Durham.

Public Libraries, Prince Consort Road, Shipcote, Gateshead 8.

Public Libraries, Borough Road, Sunderland.

Public Libraries, Clarence Road, West Hartlepool.

Essex:

Essex County Library, Goldlay Gardens, Chelmsford.

Public Library, Central Library, Duke Street, Chelmsford.

Public Library, Shewell Road, Colchester.

Public Library, Valence House, Becontree Ave., Dagenham.

Thurrock Public Library, Orsett Road, Grays.

Public Libraries, Central Library, Oakfield Road, Ilford.

East Ham Public Libraries, Central Library, High Street South, London E. 6.

Leyton Public Libraries, Central Library, High Road, Leyton, London, E. 10.

Walthamstow Public Library, High Street, Walthamstow, London, E. 17.

West Ham Public Libraries, Central Library, Water Lane, Stratford, London, E. 15.

Public Library, Victoria Avenue, Southend-on-Sea.

Gloucestershire:

Bristol Cathedral, Bristol 1.

Bingham Public Library, Dyer Street, Cirencester.

Public Libraries, Brunswick Road, Gloucester.

Hampshire:

Public Libraries, Central Library, Walpole Road, Gosport.

Public Libraries, Central Library, Guildhall Sq., Portsmouth.

Public Library, Jewry Street, Winchester.

Isle of Wight (See *Wight, Isle of*)

Herefordshire:

Herefordshire County Libraries, Widemarsh St., Hereford.

Public Library, Broad Street, Hereford.

Hertfordshire:

Public Library, Turner's Hill, Cheshunt.

Hertfordshire County Library, County Hall, Hertford.

Hitchin Museum, Paynes Park, Hitchin.

Herefordshire:

Herefordshire County Libraries, Widemarsh St., Hereford.

Public Library, Broad Street, Hereford.

Hertfordshire:

Public Library, Turner's Hill, Cheshunt.

Hertfordshire County Library, County Hall, Hertford.

Hitchin Museum, Paynes Park, Hitchin.

Huntingdonshire:

Huntingdonshire County Library, Gazeley House, Huntingdon.

Isle of Man:

Public Library, Ridgeway St., Douglas.

Kent:

Public Libraries, Central Library, Beckenham Road, Beckenham.

Public Libraries, Central Library, Broadway, Bexleyheath, Bexley.

Public Library, Maison Dieu House, Dover.

Public Libraries, Central Library, High Street, Gillingham.

Public Library, Windmill Street, Gravesend.

Woolwich Public Libraries, Central Library, Calderwood Street, London, S.E. 18.

Kent County Library, Springfield, Maidstone.

Public Library, Faith Street, Maidstone.

Public Libraries, Victoria Road, Margate.

Public Library, Northgate, Rochester.

Lancashire:

Public Library, York Street, Atherton.

Public Library, Knott Street, Darwen.

Public Libraries, Central Library, Market Square, Lancaster.

Public Library, Railway Road, Leigh.

Historic Society of Lancashire and Cheshire, Royal Institution, Colquitt Street, Liverpool 1.

Public Libraries, Central Library, St. Peter's Sq., Manchester 2.

Public Libraries, Central Library, Rodney St., Wigan.

Leicestershire:

Leicestershire Public Library, New Street, Leicester.

Leicestershire Archaeological and Historical Society, The Guildhall, Guildhall Lane, Leicester.

Museums and Art Gallery, New Walk, Leicester.

Public Libraries, Bishop Street, Leicester.

Public Libraries, Granby Street, Loughborough.

Lincolnshire:

Public Library, Municipal Buildings, West St., Boston.

Public Library, St. Peter's Hill, Grantham.

Public Library, Victoria Street, Grimsby.

Lincolnshire (Lindsey and Holland) County Library, Fairfield House, Newland, Lincoln.

Public Library, Free School Lane, Lincoln.

Public Library, High Street, Scunthorpe.

Lincolnshire (Kesteven) County Library, Westholme, Sleaford.

Spalding Gentlemen's Society, Broad Street and Red Lion Street, Spalding.

Middlesex:

Middlesex County Libraries, Headquarters, School Road, Hounslow.

Norfolk:

Public Library, Central Library, Hall Quay, Great Yarmouth.

Public Library, London Road, King's Lynn.

Public Library, St. Andrew Street, Norwich.

Northamptonshire:

Public Library, Sheep Street, Kettering.

Northamptonshire County Library, Angel Street, Northampton.

Northamptonshire Record Society, Lamport Hall, Northampton.

Public Libraries, Abington Street, Northampton.

Public Library, Newton Road, Rushden.

Northumberland:

Public Library, High Street, Gosforth.

Public Libraries, Central Library, New Bridge Street, Newcastle upon Tyne, 1.

Public Library, Park Avenue, Whitley Bay.

Nottinghamshire:

Public Library, Nottingham Road, Arnold.

Nottinghamshire County Library, County Hall, Trent Bridge, Nottingham.

University of Nottingham, University Park, Nottingham.

Oxfordshire:

Oxfordshire County Library, 14 Norham Gardens, Oxford.

Ashmolean Museum of Art and Archaeology, Beaumont Street, Oxford.

Shropshire:

Public Library, The Guildhall, Oswestry.

Public Library, Castle Gates, Shrewsbury.

Shropshire County Library, Wyle Cop, Shrewsbury.

Somersetshire:

Public Libraries, Bridge Street, Bath.

Public Library, Binford Place, Bridgwater.

Somerset County Library, Mount Street, Bridgwater.

Public Libraries, Central Library, College Green, Bristol 1, England.

Glastonbury Antiquarian Society, Lake Village Museum, Old Town Hall, Magdelen Street, Glastonbury.

Public Library, Corporation Street, Taunton.

Public Library, The Boulevard, Weston-Super-Mare.

Public Library, King George Street, Yeovil.

Staffordshire:

Public Libraries, Central Library, Moor Street, Brierley Hill.

Public Library, The Green, Stafford.

Staffordshire County Library, 27 Earl Street, Stafford.

William Salt Library, Eastgate Street, Stafford.

Public Libraries, Pall Mall, Hanley, Stoke on Trent.

Public Library, Walsall Street, Wednesbury.

Suffolk:

Cullum Reference Library, Cornhill, Bury St. Edmunds.

West Suffolk County Library, Shire Hall, Bury St. Edmunds.

East Suffolk County Library, County Hall, Ipswich.

Public Libraries, Central Library, Northgate St., Ipswich.

Surrey:

Public Library, Central Library, Beddington and Wallington.

Public Libraries, Central Library, Banstead Road, Coulsdon and Purley.

Public Library, Town Hall, Katharine Street, Croydon.

Surrey County Library, 140 High Street, Esher.

Public Library, 187 High Street, Guildford.

Haslemere Educational Museum, High Street, Haslemere.

Public Libraries, Fairfield Road, Kingston-on-Thames.

Minet Public Library, 52 Knatchbull Road, London, S.E. 5.

Wimbledon Public Library, Hill Road, London, S.W. 19.

Sussex:

Public Library, Church Street, Brighton 1.

West Sussex County Library, County Hall, Chichester.

Public Libraries, Central Library, 24 Grand Parade, Eastbourne.

Horsham Museum, Causeway House, Horsham.

Public Library, Church Road, Hove.

East Sussex County Library, Southdown House, St. Anne's Crescent, Lewes.

Public Library, Chapel Road, Worthing.

Warwickshire:

Public Libraries, Central Library, Ratcliff Place, Birmingham 1.

Public Libraries, Libraries Administration, Cow Lane, Coventry.

Public Library, Avenue Road, Leamington Spa.

Dugdale Society, Shakespeare's Birthplace, Stratford upon Avon.

Public Library, Church Street, Warwick.

Warwickshire County Library, The Butts, Warwick.

Westmorland:

Public Library and Westmorland County Library, Stricklandgate, Kendal.

Wight, Isle of:

County Seely Library, Upper St. James Street, Newport.

Wiltshire:

Public Library, Chipper Lane, Salisbury.

Public Libraries, Regent Circus, Swindon.

Wiltshire County Library, Prospect Place, Trowbridge.

Worcestershire:

Public Libraries, Ratcliff Place, Birmingham 1, England.

Public Libraries, Central Library, Dudley.

Public Library, Market Street, Kidderminster.

Public Library, Foregate Street, Worcester.

Worcestershire Record Office, Worcester. (Worcestershire records dating from 1135.)

Yorkshire:

East Riding County Library, County Hall, Beverly.

Public Library, Champney Road, Beverly.

Public Libraries, Central Library, Darley Street, Bradford 1.

Public Library, King Street, Bridlington.

Public Libraries, Halifax Road, Brighouse.

Public Libraries, Central Library, Barnsley Road, Goldthorpe, Dearne.

Museum and Art Gallery, Waterdale, Doncaster.

Public Library, Wellington Road, Dewsbury.

Public Library, Belle Vue, Halifax.

Public Library, Victoria Avenue, Harrogate.

Hull Subscription Library, King Edward Street, Hull.

Public Libraries, Albion Street, Hull.

Public Library, Station Road, Ilkley.

Public Library, Central Library, Leeds 1.

Public Library, Central Library, Victoria Square, Middlesbrough.

North Riding County Library, Grammar School Lane, Northallerton.

Public Libraries, Central Library, Surrey Street, Sheffield 1.

Public Library, Drury Lane, Wakefield.

West Riding County Library, County Library Headquarters, George Street, Wakefield.

Public Library, Hollings Mill Lane, Sowerby Bridge.

Wales

National Library of Wales, Aberystwyth, Cardiganshire.

Breconshire:

Breconshire County Libraries, County Library Headquarters, 32 High Street, Brecon.

Caernarvonshire:

Caernarvonshire County Library, Castle Street, Caernarvon.

Cardiganshire:

Cardiganshire Joint Library, Corporation Street, Aberystwyth.

Carmarthenshire:

Carmarthenshire County Library, 7 Spilman St., Carmarthen.

Denbighshire:

Denbighshire County Library, 46 Clwyd Street, Ruthin.

Public Library, Queen Square, Wrexham.

Flintshire:

Flint County Library, Chester Street, Mold.

Public Library, Wellington Road, Rhyl.

Merionethshire:

Merioneth County Library, Penarlag, Dolgelley.

Montgomeryshire:

Montgomeryshire County Library, Newton.

Pembrokeshire:

Pembrokeshire County Library, Education Offices, Haverfordwest.

Radnorshire:

Radnorshire County Library, County Hall, Llandrindod Wells.

Scotland

…, marriage, death …rds

Subsequent to 1855: General Registry Office, New Register House, Edinburgh 2.

Prior to 1855: Also available at the above-named General Registry Office are old parish registers dating prior to 1855, which were formerly kept under the administration of the Established Church of Scotland.

Wills, probate records

Since 1858: Principal Probate Registry, Somerset House, London, or the District Probate Registry in the district of residence in Scotland. Prior to 1858, the District Probate Registry in the district where the decedent resided.

Census records

Census returns commence in 1841 and have been taken every ten years thereafter. Application forms may be obtained from the Registrar General, New Register House, Edinburgh 2.

Heraldry

Information concerning Scottish coats of arms should be directed to the Court of the Lord Lyon, Old Register House, Edinburgh.

The Scots Ancestry Research Society, 4-A North David Street, Edinburgh, will undertake genealogical research at a reasonable cost.

Genealogical libraries

Scottish Genealogy Society, 13 Rothesay Terrace, Edinburgh 3.

Public Libraries, The Mitchell Library, North Street, Glasgow.

Burgh and County Public Library, Castle Wynd, Inverness.

Burgh Museum, The Observatory, Corberry Hill, Dumfries.

Libraries—local history collections

Scottish Central Library, Lawnmarket, Edinburgh 1.

Aberdeenshire:

Aberdeen County Library, 14 Crown Terrace, Aberdeen.

Public Library, Rosemount Viaduct, Aberdeen.

Angus:

Angus and Kincardineshire County Library, County Library Repository, High St., Montrose.

Ayrshire:

Ayr County Library, County Building, Ayr.

Public Libraries, Dick Institute, Elmbank Drive, Kilmarnock.

Public Library, 12 Main St., Ayr.

Banffshire:

Banffshire County Library, Central Repository, 70 Mid St., Keith.

Berwickshire:

Public Library, Marygate, Berwick-on-Tweed.

Berwickshire County Library, 49 Newton St., Duns.

Buteshire:

Bute County Library, Norman Stewart Institute, Rothesay, Bute. (Arran, Bute and Cumbrae Islands)

Clackmannanshire:

Clackmannan County Library, Church Street, Alloa.

Dumfriesshire:

Dumfriesshire Libraries, Ewart Library, Catherine St., Dumfries.

Dumbartonshire:

Public Library, Dumbarton Road, Clydebank.

Fifeshire:

Public Library, Central Library, Abbot Street, Dunfermline.
Fife County Library, East Fergus Place, Kirkcaldy.
Public Library, War Memorial Grounds, Kirkcaldy.

Galloway:

See Dumfries and Wigtown.

Glasgow:

George Outram & Co., Ltd., 65 Buchanan Street, Glasgow, C. 1. (Publishers of *Glasgow Herald.* Library contains works on local history on Scotland and particularly Glasgow.)

University of Glasgow Library, Glasgow W. 2. (Strong on Glasgow local history.)

Inverness:

Burgh and County Public Library, Castle Wynd, Inverness.

Kincardineshire:

Angus and Kincardineshire County Library, County Library Repository, High Street, Montrose, Angus.

Kinross-Shire:

Perth and Kinross County Library, Old Academy, 7 Rose Terrace, Perth, Perthshire.

Kirkcudbrightshire:

Broughton House, High Street, Kirkcudbright.

Lanarkshire:

Public Library, Wellwynd, Airdrie.

Lanark County Library, 4 Auchingramont Road, Hamilton.

Public Library, Central Library, Cadzow Street, Hamilton.

Morayshire:

Elgin and Morayshire Literary Association, Elgin Museum, High Street, Elgin.

Orkney:

Orkney County Library, Laing Street, Kirkwall.

Perth:

Perth and Kinross County Library, Old Academy, 7 Rose Terrace, Perth.

Renfrewshire:

Museum and Art Galleries, High Street, Paisley. (Paisley history.)

Ross and Cromarty:

Ross and Cromarty County Library, The Old Academy, Dingwall.

Roxburghshire:

Public Library, Bridge Street, Hawick.

Roxburgh County Library, County Offices, Newtown, St. Boswells.

Shetland Islands:

See Orkney and Zetland.

Stirlingshire:

Stirlingshire County Library, Education Offices, Spittal Street, Stirling.

Sutherlund:

Sutherland County Library, Education Offices, Brora.

Wigtownshire:

Wigtown County Library, Stranraer.

Zetland:

Zetland County Library, County Library Headquarters, St. Olaf Street, Lerwick, Shetland.

Northern Ireland

Vital statistics

Births, Marriages, and Deaths: Subsequent to 1922: General Register Office, Fermanagh House, Ormeau Avenue, Belfast. *Prior to 1922:* General Register Office, Custom House, Dublin.

Church Records: On April 1, 1845, registration of Protestant marriages commenced; baptisms, marriages, an[d] burials of Roman Catholics, on January 1, 1864. These original records are in the custody of the Superintendent Registrars and District Registrars of the districts in which these events took place. See: Report of the Record Office of Northern Ireland, 1924, and the Twenty-Eighth Report of the Deputy Keeper of the Records of Ireland, Appendix II, Dublin, 1896.

Land Records: Registry of Deeds, Dublin.

Wills, Probate Records: Public Record Office, Law Courts Building, May Street, Belfast.

h research ggestion

Falley, Margaret Dickson: *Irish and Scotch-Irish Ancestral Research.* A Guide to the Genealogical Records, Methods, and Sources in Ireland. 2 vols. 1962.

raries

Public Libraries, Central Library, Royal Avenue, Belfast.

Belfast Library and Society for Promoting Knowledge, 17 Donegall Square North, Belfast.

Tyrone County Library, Dublin Road, Omagn, County Tyrone.

Down County Library, Downpatrick, County Down.

Fermanagh County Library, Enniskillen, County Fermanagh.

Eire (Irish Republic)

al records

Births, Marriages, and Deaths: Registrar General's Office, Custom House, Dublin.

chives

Public Record Office, Four Courts, Dublin.

esearch ggestion

Falley, Margaret Dickson: *Irish and Scotch-Irish Ancestral Research.* A Guide to the Genealogical Records, Methods, and Sources in Ireland. 2 vols. 1962.

braries

Genealogical Office, Dublin Castle, Dublin, Eire.

Cork County Library, 18 Dyke Parade, Cork, County Cork.

Donegal County Libraries, Court House, Lifford, County Donegal.

Dublin County Library, The Courthouse, Kilmainham, Dublin.

Galway County Library, The Courthouse, Galway, County Galway.

Kerry County Library, Library Headquarters, Tralee, County Kerry.

Kilkenny County Library, Book Repository, John Street, Kilkenny Co., Kilkenny.

Laois County Library, Portlaoighise, County Leix.

Longford and Westmeath County Library, Dublin Road, Mullingar, County Westmeath.

Mayo County Library, Castlebar, County Mayo.

Meath County Library, Navan, County Meath.

Waterford County Library, County Library Headquarters, Lismore, County Waterford.

Wexford County Library, County Hall, Wexford, County Wexford.

Philippine Islands

Vital records

Custodians of Births, Marriages, and Deaths: There is a civil registrar for every municipality, and also a civil registrar for the city of Manila. All civil registrars are supervised by the Civil Registrar General, Director of the National Library, Manila. If necessary, write to the Civil Registrar General for information and assistance.

Libraries and archives of other countries

Argentina

Archivo General de la Nacion
Av L. N. Alem 250
Buenos Aires

Australia

Commonwealth National Library
Canberra, A.C.T.

Austria

Osterreichische Nationalbibliothek
(Austrian National Library)
Vienna

Vital Records: Standesamt (Civil Registry Office) of place where event occurred.

Belgium

Stadsarchief (Archives de la Ville)
Venusstraat 11,
Antwerp

a

Biblioteca del Congreso Nacional
Palacio Legislativo,
La Paz

Vital Records: Oficialia del Registro Civil of district where event occurred.

l

Instituto Genealógico Brasileiro
Rua Dr. Zuquim 1525
Sao Paulo

Arquivo Nacional
Praca de Republica
Rio de Janeiro

Vital Records: Registro Civil of district or city where event occurred.

aria

Vassil Kolarov (State Library)
Boulevard Tolbukhinll,
Sofia

a

National Library, Museum, and Art Gallery
Rangoon

da

(See section in this book on Canada.)

on

Colombo National Museum Library
Edinburgh Crescent
Colombo 7

Archive Nacional
Av. Bernardo O'Higgins y Maclver
Santiago

Vital Records: Oficina del Registro Civil of place where event occurred.

a (People's blic of a)

National Library
Peking 7

Nanking Library
Nanking

nbia

Biblioteca Nacional
Apartado 2525
Bogota

a Rica

Biblioteca Nacional
Calle 5, Avenidas 1/3
San Jose

Vital Records: Registro Central del Estado Civil, San José, for all records since January 1, 1888.

Archivo Nacional de Cuba
Havana

Vital Records: Oficina de Registro Civil or Juzgado Municipal of district or town where event occurred.

Czechoslovakia
Narodni Knihovna (National Library)
Prague

Denmark
Samfundet for Dansk Genealogi og Personalhistorie (The Danish Genealogical and Biographical Society)
SDR. Fasanvej 46,
Copenhagen 46, Copenhagen Valby

Dominican Republic
Biblioteca de la Universidad de Santo Domingo
Ciudad Universitaria
Ciudad Trujillo

Ecuador
Biblioteca Nacional
Quito

Vital Records: Dirección General del Registro Civil, Quito for records since 1901.

El Salvador
Biblioteca Nacional de El Salvador
8A Avenida Norte 16
San Salvador

Egypt
Alexandria Municipal Library
Alexandria

Finland
Suomen Sukututkimusseura-Genealogiska Samfundet i Finland (Genealogical Society of Finland)
Säatytalo, Snellmanik
Helsinki

France
Direction des Bibliotheques de France
55 rue St. Dominique
Paris VII

Guide to French Archives: Guide Des Recherches Généalogiques Aux Archives Nationales. Par Jacques Meurgey de Tupigny . . . Avant-Propos de Charles Braibant, Directeur de Archives de France. Paris, Imprimerie Nationale 1953.

Vital Records: Mairie (Office of the Mayor), place where the event occurred.

Germany
See: Wasmandorff, Erich Von: *Vd FF Verzeichnis der Familienforscher Und Familienverbande Familienstiftungen Und Familienkundlichen Vereinigungen Archive Und Bibliotheken.* Vierte Auflage. 1956. Glucksburglostsee, Starke. (List of Genealogists, Family Societies, Family Foundations, Genealogical Societies, Archives and Libraries.)

Taschenbuch fur Familiengeschichtsforschung Begruudet von Dr. Phil. Friedrich Wecken Neubearbeitet von

Dr. Phil. Johannes Krausse Schellenberg bei Berchtesgaden. Degener, 1951.

Vital Records: Standesamt (Civil Registry Office) of place where event occurred.

e National Library
Odos Venizelou
Greece

nala Biblioteca Nacional de Guatemala
10a Calle 9-31, Zona 1
Guatemala

Vital Records: Oficina de Registro Civil nearest to place where event occurred.

Bibliotheque Nationale d'Haiti
Rue Hammerton Killick,
Port-au-Prince

ras Biblioteca Nacional
Tegucigalpa

ry Magyar Országos Levéltár Könyvtára
(Library of the Hungarian National Archives)
Budapest, I, Bécsikaputér 4.

Landsbokasafn Islands
(National Library of Iceland)
Reykjavik

Delhi Public Library
Queen's Road
Delhi 6

National Library
Teheran

Baghdad Public Library
Baghdad

Municipal Library
8 Montefiore Street
Tel-Aviv-Saffa

Biblioteca Nazionale Centrale
Vittorio Emanuele
Via del Collegio Romano 27
Rome

Vital Records: Municipie (municipal town government) of place where event occurred.

National Diet Library
1-1 Akasaka, Minato-Ku-Tokyo
Tokyo

Jordan — Gulbenkian Library
P.O. Box 4001,
Jerusalem

Lebanon — Library of the American University
Beirut

Luxembourg — Bibliotheque Nationale
14A Boulevard Royal

Mexico — Biblioteca Nacional de Mexico
Republica del Salvador 70
Mexico City, D.F.

Vital Records: Oficina del Registro Civil of place where event occurred.

Morocco — Bibliotheque Municipale
Avenue General-d'Amade
Casablanca

Netherlands — Universiteitsbibliotheek
(University Library) Singel 421
Amsterdam

New Zealand — Auckland Public Library
Auckland

Nicaragua — Biblioteca Nacional
Managua

Vital Records: Oficina del Registrador del Estado Civil of place where event occurred.

Norway — Statsarkivet (State Archives)
Torvgaten 12
Hamar
Riksarkivet
(National Archives of Norway)
Bankplass 3, Oslo

Panama — Biblioteca Nacional
Apdo. 1633
Panama City

Paraguay — Biblioteca Nacional del Paraguay
Asuncion

Peru — Biblioteca Nacional
Apdo. 2335
Lima

Philippines — Bureau of Public Libraries
Manila

Poland — Biblioteka Narodowa
(National Library)
Warsaw

gal	Biblioteca Nacional Lisbon
nia	Biblioteca Academiei Republicii Populare Romine Calea Victoriei 125, Bucharest
Arabia	Library of the Education Dept. Mecca
	Biblioteca Nacional Madrid
	Library of the University of Khartoum Khartoum
en	Riksarkivet (Public Record Office) Arkivgatan 3, Stockholm
erland	Bibliotheque National Suisse 15 Hallwylstrasse Berne
	Al Maktabah Al Zahiriah (National Library) Damascus
nd	National Library Na Phra Thad Road Bangkok
a	Bibliotheque Nationale de Tunisie Tunis
y	Milli Kutuphane (National Library) Yenisehir Ankara
of South	South African Public Library Government Avenue Cape Town
of Soviet listic blics	State Public Historical Library Red Square Moscow
uay	Biblioteca Nacional del Uruguay Montevideo
zuela	Biblioteca Nacional Caracas
slavia	Narodna Biblioteka Belgrade

Heraldry

The use of coats-of-arms is generally misunderstood. What is generally not realized is that the similarity of a surname does not mean that the coat-of-arms granted to a person of the same name is a reason for adopting that coat-of-arms. For instance, a person whose surname is Richardson who finds a coat-of-arms of a Richardson fami has no justification for adopting that coat-of-arms as that c his family merely because of the similarity of surname. In order for a person to be entitled to claim arms, he must prc descent in the male line from the person to whom that coa of-arms was granted. The following bibliography will be helpful in research on this subject:

Jacobus, Donald Lines: Royal Ancestry, *The American Genealogist.* Vol. 9, p. 93.

Lancour, Harold: *Heraldry—A Guide to Reference Book* New York Public Library, 1938. Pamphlet.

Moriarty, G. Andrews: "English and American Heraldry, *The American Genealogist.* Vol. 9, p. 194.

Throckmorton, C. Wickliffe: "The Rules of Heraldry," *American Genealogist.* October 1937, p. 81.

Zieber, Eugene: *Heraldry in America.* Philadelphia, 190

Historical geography

United States

The importance of colonial expansion and changes in boundaries of political subdivisions such as towns, countie and states cannot be emphasized too much in the work of a researcher. The changes in the boundaries of these politica subdivisions become extremely important in the location of official records. The following is a brief bibliography of reference books and other material that will be helpful:

Adams, James Truslow, ed.: *Atlas of American History.* 1943.

Complete Pronouncing Gazetteer or Geographical Dictionary of the World. J.P. Lippincott, 1905.

Friis, Herman: *A Series of Population Maps of the Colonies of the United States, 1625-1790.* American Geographic Society.

Halverson, F. Douglas: *County Histories of the United States* Giving Present Name, Date Formed, Parent County, and County Seats. (n.d.)

Halverson, F. Douglas: *Origin of Cities of the United States,* Giving Dates of Settlement, Incorporation, and Some Historical Facts. (n.d.)

Jameson, J. Franklin: *Dictionary of United States History,* 1931. See particularly pages 571 to 591.

Lewis, Marcus W.: *The Development of Early Emigrant Trails East of the Mississippi River.* Pamphlet.

List of Post Offices in the United States, including all established before December 31, 1807, with the counties in which they are situated and their distances from Washington City. Westcott & Co., Washington, 1808.

Morse, Jedediah: *The American Gazetteer.* 1797.

Paulin, Charles O.: *Atlas of the Historical Geography of the United States.* 1932. See particularly page 22 and following pages and plates.

Pennsylvania: *Department of Internal Affairs: Genealogical Map of the Counties.* Compiled by the Land Office Bureau, 1833.

Rosenberry, Mrs. Lois (Kimball) Mathews: *The Expansion of New England; the Spread of New England Settlement and Institutions to the Mississippi River, 1620-1865.* 1909.

Smith, Philip M.: *Directories in the Library of Congress,* volume 13 (July 1936), page 46, contains a list of cities and towns, county residential directories, regional county and state business directories. This list covers the earliest directories beginning in 1785.

United States Department of Commerce, Bureau of the Census: *A century of Population growth from the First Census of the United States to the Twelfth, 1790-1900.* Washington, 1909. Pages 52, 53, and 61 to 70 show changes in boundary lines of the 13 colonies and also other territory.

United States Government Printing Office: *United States Official Postal Guide.*

In some cases help may be obtained from the *Board on Geographical Names,* Department of the Interior, Washington, D.C. This board has a card index of geographical sources.

ı Isles

Bartholomew, J. G.: *The Survey Gazetteer of the British Isles,* 1914. Very helpful in locating the counties in which parishes are located. In connection with this book, use *The Key to the Ancient Parishes of England and Wales.*

Brabner, J. H. F., ed.: *The Comprehensive Gazetteer o England and Wales.* 6 vols. London, n.d.

Burke, Arthur Meredyth: *Key to the Ancient Parish Registers of England and Wales.* London, 1908.

Smith, J. P.: *The Genealogists' Atlas of Lancashire.* Liverpool, 1930.

Paleography

The following references will be found helpful in the problem of deciphering ancient handwriting.

Bolton, Charles Knowles: "Colonial Handwriting," *The Essex Antiquarian.* Vol. 1 (1897), p. 175.

Byrne, Muriel St. Clare: "Elizabethan Handwriting for Beginners," in *The Review of English Studies.* Vol. 1 (Apri 1925), p. 198.

Haselden, R. B.: *Scientific Aids for the Study of Manuscripts.* Printed at the Oxford University Press for th Bibliographical Society, London, 1935.

McKerrow, R. B.: "The Capital Letters in Elizabethan Handwriting," in *The Review of English Studies.* Vol. 3, nc January 1927.

Tannenbaum, Samuel Aaron: *The Handwriting of the Renaissance,* "being the development and characteristics the script of Shakespeare's time." New York, 1930.

Wright, Andrew: *Court-Hand Restored* or, the *Student'. Assistant in Reading Old Deeds, Charters, Records, etc.* Tenth ed. London, 1912.

Names

Holman, Winifred Lovering, and Donald Lines Jacobus "Female Diminutives," *American Genealogist.* Vol. 34 (Ap 1958), pp. 96-98. This list of nicknames is a very valuable to the genealogist.

National Genealogical Society, Genealogical Inquiries Committee: *Family Name Register.* 1958. 40 pp. Useful fo research by correspondence.

lex